Counselling Survivors of Domestic Abuse

by the same author

Introduction to Counselling Survivors of Interpersonal Trauma
Christiane Sanderson
ISBN 978 1 84310 962 4

Counselling Adult Survivors of Child Sexual Abuse
3rd edition
Christiane Sanderson
ISBN 978 1 84310 335 6

The Seduction of Children
Empowering Parents and Teachers to Protect Children from Child Sexual Abuse
Christiane Sanderson
ISBN 978 1 84310 248 9

of related interest

Picking up the Pieces After Domestic Violence
A Practical Resource for Supporting Parenting Skills
Kate Iwi and Chris Newman
ISBN 978 1 84905 021 0

Rebuilding Lives after Domestic Violence
Understanding Long-Term Outcomes
Hilary Abrahams
ISBN 978 1 84310 961 7

Supporting Women after Domestic Violence
Loss, Trauma and Recovery
Hilary Abrahams
ISBN 978 1 84310 431 5

Talking About Domestic Abuse
A Photo Activity Workbook to Develop Communication Between Mothers and Young People
Cathy Humphreys, Ravi K Thiara, Agnes Skamballis and Audrey Mullender
ISBN 978 1 84310 423 0

Talking To My Mum
A Picture Workbook for Workers, Mothers and Children Affected by Domestic Abuse
Cathy Humphreys, Ravi K Thiara, Agnes Skamballis and Audrey Mullender
ISBN 978 1 84310 422 3

Vedi? . . . di morte l'angelo
Radiante a noi si appressa . . .

sweetly sing Radamès and Aïda, almost happy, though half dead of asphyxiation in their funeral cave; as though, within the darkness in which they are il-
luminated by love, these two lovers—of a kind, however, never thus far encountered outside novels and operas—imagined in the dazzling guise of a
single archangel the burn that Aïda was, at least, for Radamès and Radamès
for Aïda.

1948–1955

About the Author

Michel Leiris was born in 1901. While "vaguely" pursuing studies in chemistry, he associated with the nightowls of postwar Paris and became friends with Max Jacob and the painter André Masson. Passionate about poetry, he joined the surrealist group in 1924. From this initiation into the arcana of dream and language were born the poems in *Simulacre* (1925), later the games in *Glossaire, j'y serre mes gloses* (1939), and the novel *Aurora*, which was not to appear until 1946. Anguished by writing, by his marriage in 1926, by his break from the Surrealists, Leiris went into psychoanalysis in 1930. Out of a subsequent desire to measure himself against reality, he accompanied the 1931–33 "Mission Dakar-Djibouti," an ethnographic expedition of which he published a "personal chronicle," *L'Afrique fantôme*, in 1934. He worked as an ethnologist at the Musée de l'Homme until 1971 and, parallel to this study of other peoples, conducted an extensive study of himself. His first autobiographical essay, *L'Age d'homme* (1939), only revealed to him new games involving masks, the rules of which he proposed to discover in the four works that constituted *La règle du jeu* (*Biffures*, 1948; *Fourbis*, 1955; *Fibrilles*, 1966; and *Frêle bruit*, 1976). *Le ruban au cou d'Olympia* (1981), a collection of essays, similarly belongs in the vein of autobiographical texts dominated, although without complacency or vanity, by a concern to know himself—which necessarily brings with it, according to Leiris, knowledge of the other, knowledge of the world. Leiris died in 1990.

Counselling Survivors of Domestic Abuse

Christiane Sanderson

Jessica Kingsley *Publishers*
London and Philadelphia

First published in 2008
by Jessica Kingsley Publishers
116 Pentonville Road
London N1 9JB, UK
and
400 Market Street, Suite 400
Philadelphia, PA 19106, USA

www.jkp.com

Copyright © Christiane Sanderson 2008
Printed digitally since 2011

Library of Congress Cataloging in Publication Data
Sanderson, Christiane.
    Counselling survivors of domestic abuse / Christiane Sanderson.
        p. ; cm.
    Includes bibliographical references and index.
    ISBN 978-1-84310-606-7 (pb : alk. paper) 1. Victims of family violence--Mental health. 2. Victims of family violence--Counseling of. 3. Family violence--Psychological aspects. I. Title.
    [DNLM: 1. Counseling--methods. 2. Domestic Violence--psychology. WM 55 S216c 2008]
    RC569.5.F3S24 2008
    362.82'9286--dc22
                                                        2007051548

British Library Cataloguing in Publication Data
A CIP catalogue record for this book is available from the British Library

ISBN 978 1 84310 606 7

Dedication

For all those who risk connection despite repeated betrayal

Think of yourself as dead. You have lived your life.
Now take what is left and live it properly.

(Marcus Aurelius 2002, p.24)

CONTENTS

ACKNOWLEDGEMENTS

The seeds for this book were sown over a number of years through numerous training workshops and innumerable lectures on domestic abuse, but bore fruit only through the encouragement of the many students who highlighted the need for a book to accompany the training. I wish to thank them for their inspiration.

I also wish to thank my publisher Jessica Kingsley and commissioning editor Steve Jones for their support in writing the book and making it a reality. I am hugely indebted to Christine Firth, whose expertise, focus and professionalism ensured that the editing of the manuscript was a smooth, highly efficient and pleasurable process.

A special thank you goes to all those colleagues and friends who demonstrated an unwavering belief in me, in particular Didi Daftari, Breda Doyle, Martin Sixsmith, Andrew Smith and Kathy Warriner. Finally my illimitable thanks go to Paul Glynn for providing me with the necessary sustenance and constancy to remain connected, and James and Max for being present.

INTRODUCTION

There has been growing awareness in recent years of the impact and consequences of domestic abuse (DA), especially the relationship between DA and
mental health. To appreciate the causal link between mental health and DA, professionals need to understand the complex nature of DA, and the
psychobiological impact of repeated exposure to coercive control and terror. It is
with such understanding that effective intervention strategies can be implemented, including counselling and psychotherapy. *Counselling Survivors of Domestic Abuse* aims to examine the psychobiological impact of DA within a trauma
framework, and look at how counsellors can facilitate recovery from DA within a
secure, supportive therapeutic relationship.

Traditionally, mental health professionals, including counsellors, have
received minimal training in DA exposing them to the risk of misdiagnosis, or
pathologising survivors. Thorough training in DA allows professionals to rou-
tinely screen for DA, accurately assess impact, and implement appropriate treatment. However, counselling must not be reified. To provide a truly holistic
response to DA, counselling must be seen as complementary to the support
offered by existing services wherein all aspects of survivors' well-being are
addressed.

Mental health professionals can no longer ignore the effects of DA on mental
health as this negates survivors' experiences and deprives them of the appropriate
care and support. Equally they must guard against medicalising the effects of DA
and not lose sight of the wider social, political and cultural contexts within which
DA occurs. The aim of counselling is to empower survivors to make informed
choices in their relationships, either current or future, and to inoculate them
against further abuse, not pathologise them. As DA engenders a range of impacts,
counsellors need to be aware of a variety of effective interventions and tailor these
to each individual's experience. For some survivors this may entail supportive
counselling during, or when leaving, an abusive relationship, while others require
in-depth trauma therapy. Most crucially, accurate assessment and safety are paramount when working with survivors of DA.

For many survivors, DA can be a severely traumatising experience and counsellors need to be cognisant of the complex relationship between DA and trauma
symptoms. It is crucial that counsellors contextualise the manifest

psychobiological effects as *symptoms of abuse*, not personality disturbance, to prevent stigmatisation and pathologising the survivor. Symptoms such as anxiety, depression, self-harm, substance misuse and suicidality need to be seen primarily as responses to trauma. Counsellors need to be able to dissemble actual symptoms of abuse from perceived individual pathology, or personality disturbance, and link these to the traumatic effects of prolonged and repeated abuse.

Pathologising survivors of DA by applying spurious diagnostic labels serves only to further alienate them and promotes victim blaming. The ramifications of this encompass altering professionals' perceptions, and redirecting the focus away from the abuser's behaviour to that of the survivor. This not only replicates the abuse experience, but also has negative repercussions when making decisions around child protection issues, contact or residency orders, or when assessing culpability. A further pernicious effect is that it reinforces the abuser's accusation that the survivor is crazy, and it is mental instability that is at the root of nefarious allegation of DA.

Mental health professionals also need to be mindful of not hijacking the survivor's self-agency through medicalising the effects of DA. They need to be aware of the broad spectrum of effects of DA and to prioritise these accordingly to suit individual circumstances. Exploring all available options enables survivors to make informed choices about which services to access. Inviting survivors to take control of their recovery is the first step in rebuilding autonomy and self-efficacy to make personally meaningful choices.

To provide such support, practitioners need to create a safe therapeutic environment in which to explore the abuse experiences without further traumatising the survivor. The therapeutic space acts as a secure base in which to make sense of DA; creating narrative out of chaos. It is only when survivors are in a place of safety that the painstaking work of rebuilding their sense of self can take place. The therapeutic relationship can also offer an opportunity to re-establish trust in self, others and the world.

The primary goals when counselling survivors of DA are assessment, safety, working through trauma, grieving, and the restoration of self to make personally meaningful choices that minimise the risk of future abusive relationships. To accomplish this, counsellors need to contextualise the psychobiological effects and symptoms associated with DA as normal responses to trauma, not individual pathology or personality disturbance. Crucially, existing survival strategies and internal resources need to be validated by the counsellor and honed to strengthen the sense of self and restore self-agency.

Despite adopting a trauma framework, counsellors cannot afford to ignore the socio-political, cultural and economic factors that underpin and support DA. They need to appreciate that the prevailing socio-political macro-system is commonly reflected in the micro-system of personal relationships. For this reason, socially constructed meaning around gender, race, power and control, domination and submission, and the hierarchical structure of families all need to be understood within the context of DA. This is particularly salient when working with survivors from marginalised or ethnic minority groups whose access to external resources may be more limited.

Use of language

Different terms have been used to denote what is commonly referred to as 'domestic violence' (DV). However, the term DV is seen by many as not representative of the range of domestic abuse behaviours. Domestic violence implies the use of physical force and physical assault, not psychological, emotional, financial or sexual abuse. Individuals experiencing these types of abuses may feel excluded and fail to name their experience as DA. In line with an increasing number of DA agencies, local authorities and DA forums, this book will adopt the term 'domestic abuse'.

Although the experience of DA is one of victimisation, survivors are rarely passive victims. Invariably they are active survivors who have developed strategies to manage the DA. To emphasise these active responses, and to dispel the negative connotation associated with the term 'victim', the term survivor or victim/survivor will be used.

Although both genders experience DA, the female pronoun is used more frequently for the survivors throughout the book, to avoid confusion. The terms black and ethnic minority will be used to denote African, Caribbean and Asian individuals, unless specified. While the author acknowledges the differences and similarities between counsellor and therapist, these terms will be used synonymously.

About the book

The structure of *Counselling Survivors of Domestic Abuse* concentrates on increasing awareness of the complex nature of DA, to develop deeper insight into its relationship to mental health and how counsellors can work most efficaciously. Chapter 1 aims to increase knowledge of DA by examining the prevailing myths associated with DA, and evaluating these in relation to recent research. In order to understand what constitutes DA, current definitions, the range of abusive behaviours, and the complex nature of abusive relationships will be explored. This chapter will also look at both survivors and perpetrators of DA to provide a deeper understanding of the dynamics of DA relationships.

Chapter 2 explores the impact and long-term effects of DA within a complex trauma framework. It will assess the impact of prolonged coercive control and terror on the survivor, resident children and family functioning. The long-term effects of DA will be examined within the context of psychobiological responses to trauma rather than individual pathology. The aim is to highlight the range of impacts and long-term effects so that counsellors can ensure accurate assessment of the survivor's specific therapeutic needs, so that appropriate and effective treatment interventions can be implemented.

The focus of Chapter 3 is to increase understanding of survivors of DA, and to this effect, it examines the cycle of abuse which serves to intensify relational dynamics. This will enable counsellors to have a greater appreciation of traumatic bonding and the difficulties associated with ending abusive relationships. The chapter will also look at the range of survival and protection strategies that survivors use in response to abuse and trauma, and urges counsellors to validate these as constructive internal resources that can be built upon.

The effective treatment of trauma and abuse is predicated on a safe and secure therapeutic relationship. Chapter 4 explores how counsellors can support and work with survivors of DA in the most optimal way. It looks at treatment philosophy, range of therapeutic approaches, and highlights useful techniques, including the use of psychoeducation. Essential to effective treatment is an accurate assessment of therapeutic needs and a sensitively attuned therapeutic stance. This chapter will emphasise the importance of the therapeutic relationship, and the use of transference and counter-transference when working with survivors of DA. Issues around power and control, setting boundaries, and the pacing of the therapeutic process will be examined to understand their function and meaning in the therapeutic process.

Chapter 5 explores working with safety and protection strategies. Safety is the first and most crucial task, as healing and recovery cannot take place in the absence of safety (Herman 2002). This chapter will look at both external and internal safety to assess readiness to engage in the therapeutic process. Until safety is in place, the counsellor needs to provide emotional support and stabilisation through affect regulation to consolidate internal safety. For survivors in abusive relationships, safety strategies to manage the abuse may need to be honed, while those who intend to leave may need to plan safe exit strategies. Most crucially, counsellors need to provide emotional support irrespective of whether the survivor decides to leave or not. A good knowledge of the range of available external resources, and how these can be accessed is critical. Ideally counsellors need to establish links with other agencies so that the survivor can benefit from a truly holistic approach.

Once safety has been established counsellors can start to explore the traumatic impact of DA. Chapter 6 assesses how to work with the symptoms of trauma and complex post-traumatic stress responses. It will also examine the impact of trauma on neurobiology, somatic and cognitive functioning, as well as self-structures. A range of therapeutic techniques will be discussed to allow counsellors to choose which they consider to be most effective for each individual survivor.

Chapter 7 looks at working with disruptions to the self such as the erosion of self-esteem, and diminished self-efficacy. It will consider ways in which counsellors can help to rebuild these self aspects and restore self-agency. It highlights the importance of helping survivors to identify their needs and find ways of satisfying these. This can be accomplished through implementing strategies for self-care and self-nourishment, and setting appropriate boundaries. The therapeutic relationship is central in enabling the survivor to reconnect to self, and plays a pivotal role in the healing process.

Once reconnection to the self has occurred, survivors can begin to reconnect to others. Chapter 8 explores ways of working with relational aspects of DA. Initially it will look at interpersonal relationships, both inside and outside DA, and then focus on rebuilding or re-establishing these with a stronger sense of self and healthy boundaries. It will also look at relational dynamics with children, family and friends. An essential part of healing from the trauma of DA is to rebuild a support network and counsellors are encouraged to prioritise this so that survivors can begin to reconnect to others.

Chapter 9 looks at how to work with loss and the restoration of hope. It emphasises the importance of the grieving process to mourn the multiple losses inherent in DA. These losses cluster around emotional, intrapersonal, interpersonal, physical, cognitive, material and spiritual losses. The grieving process is a fluid one in which survivors oscillate between the various phases of grief. To appreciate the agony of managing multiple losses simultaneously, how overwhelming this can be, and the courage needed not to retreat into despair, counsellors need to be aware of how difficult the grieving process can be. Counsellors are encouraged to validate the strength of survivors who, despite their grief, still manage to function, and recognise the courage required to risk connection despite repeated betrayals without relinquishing hope.

Finally, Chapter 10 looks at professional issues such as counsellors' attitudes and beliefs around DA, as well as their own experiences of power and control. It examines the impact of working with DA, and the personal and professional impact of secondary traumatic stress. It highlights the importance of supervision, networking, specialist consultation and multiagency links. Most crucially it emphasises the importance of self-care for counsellors. It is only when counsellors are able to nurture and nourish themselves that they can work with survivors of trauma. Counsellors need to be emotionally present and not recoil or retreat from the horror of DA. In being present and sensitively attuned, they can provide survivors with the safe and secure base required to build trust, restore hope and rebuild their lives free from domestic abuse.

CHAPTER I

UNDERSTANDING DOMESTIC ABUSE

To appreciate the impact of domestic abuse (DA), and understand its relationship to mental health, counsellors need to be aware of the complex nature of DA. It is only with such understanding that effective intervention and treatment strategies can be implemented. Clinicians must ensure that they have considerable knowledge of prevailing myths surrounding DA, including their own stereotypes and biases. This needs to be supported with an understanding of precisely what constitutes DA. As there is no single, universally agreed definition of DA, both survivors and professionals may be hindered in identifying and naming such abuse experiences. Clinicians require a clearly specified definition of DA to guide their practice, and understand prevalence and incidence rates.

Survivors and perpetrators of DA are not a homogenous group and clinicians need to be aware of who are at risk of abuse or abusing. While the majority of DA appears to be directed at females by male perpetrators, current research shows that females also abuse males, and that DA is a feature in a number of same sex relationships. Clinicians need to have a good understanding of the range of perpetrators of DA, and the underlying factors that give rise to the need for coercive control and abuse. Such knowledge will enable the counsellor, and ultimately the survivor, to identify that DA is driven and fuelled by anxieties, insecurities and internal pressures emanating from the perpetrator, and not due to the survivor's putative inadequacies. This will enable the counsellor to separate survivor dynamics from abuser dynamics, and facilitate the rebuilding of self-structures that have been damaged during DA.

While it is critical for clinicians to understand the relationship between mental health and DA, counsellors cannot afford to ignore the socio-political, cultural and economic factors that support DA. An awareness of theories of DA which incorporate socially constructed meaning around gender, race, power and control, domination and submission, and the hierarchical structure of families will allow for a more comprehensive understanding of the many dynamics that give rise to DA, and which create obstacles to leaving abusive relationships.

This chapter aims to increase knowledge of DA by examining prevailing DA myths and evaluating these in relation to recent research. In order to understand what constitutes DA, current definitions, the range of abusive behaviours, and the complex nature of abusive relationships will be explored. This chapter will also look at survivors and perpetrators profiles and consider the range of theories thought to account for DA within a socio-political-cultural framework.

Myths associated with domestic abuse

There are a number of prevailing myths associated with DA and clinicians need to familiarise themselves with these and ensure that they have access to current research to challenge these myths, and identify their own biases and stereotypes.

MYTH

DA is just about physical violence.

REALITY

DA is any incident of threatening behaviour, violence or abuse (psychological, physical, sexual, financial or emotional) between adults who are or have been intimate partners or family members, regardless of gender or sexuality (Home Office 2006). Physical violence or threat of violence is used to control, intimidate and subjugate the partner and to induce fear and control. Many abusers need to use violence only intermittently to reinforce control and domination, rather than resorting to violence continuously.

MYTH

DA happens only to females and is perpetrated by males.

REALITY

Statistically, the majority of survivors of DA are female, but there is considerable evidence that males are abused by females (Cook 1997), and that DA occurs in same sex relationships (Kaschak 2001). It is likely that such DA is more hidden due to underreporting and fear of humiliation or stigmatisation.

MYTH

All domestic abusers are alike.

REALITY

Perpetrators of DA are not homogenous and can vary enormously in terms of motivation to abuse, and how the abuse is enacted (Dutton 2007; Jacobson and

Gottman 1998; Lachkar 2004). Understanding the range and type of abuser enables the counsellor, and survivor, to separate abuser dynamics from survivor dynamics and increase awareness of the impact of abuse.

MYTH

There is a singular reason why DA occurs.

REALITY

There is no singular reason to account for DA. It is the complex interaction of a range of historical, political, socioeconomic, cultural and psychobiological factors (Herman 1992a; Lockley 1999).

MYTH

Survivors in DA relationships have certain personality characteristics that predispose them to it.

REALITY

While there are vulnerability factors that elevate the risk of DA such as previous history of victimisation, or traumatisation in childhood, these are not personality defects or disturbances. In essence such vulnerability factors reflect damaged self-structures which prevent survivors from identifying their needs (Herman 2005). Counsellors must ensure they do not pathologise survivors, or collude in victim blaming (Dutton 1992).

MYTH

Victims of DA are helpless, passive and fragile.

REALITY

Survivors are often strong, and use a variety of coping strategies to manage. Any examples of passivity or helplessness may be symptomatic of trauma, not personality disturbance. Counsellors need to validate the survivor's courage and strength, identify existing coping strategies, and build upon these (Herman 1992a).

MYTH

If a survivor of DA doesn't leave the partner it must be because he/she enjoys it and is masochistic.

REALITY

This myth is associated with victim blaming and pathologising, and shows a profound lack of understanding. Professionals need to be aware that the greatest danger and risk is when the survivor leaves. In addition there are many psychobiological, social and practical factors that make it extremely difficult to leave an abusive relationship (Herman 1992a).

MYTH

Victims of DA come from low socioeconomic status (SES), have little or no education, no job skills, and have numerous kids.

REALITY

Research has shown that survivors can come from any SES group, educational or employment background. Survivors from higher SES groups may not come to the attention of agencies as they seek help privately and are not included in statutory statistical analysis.

MYTH

Battered women have done something to provoke it and therefore deserve it and are culpable.

REALITY

No one deserves DA and while many relationships have arguments and disagreements, this is not the same as DA. The only person who is responsible and accountable for DA is the perpetrator. Despite perceived difficulties, perpetrators of DA choose to use coercion, control and violence and must be held accountable for that choice.

MYTH

Perpetrators of DA are socially inept, socially inappropriate or violent in all their relationships, including friends and at work.

REALITY

There is no evidence for this. Most abusers are able to control their violence and abuse and enact it only at home. Many domestic abusers present as charming, high-functioning and socially very able individuals who perpetrate abuse only in intimate relationships (Dutton 2007; Horley 1988; Jacobson and Gottman 1998).

MYTH

Perpetrators of DA have anger management problems.

REALITY

This is not supported by research evidence, which indicates that many perpetrators exercise extraordinary control over their anger outside the domestic arena (Dutton 2007; Jacobson and Gottman 1998). Generally perpetrators of DA do not physically attack friends, colleagues or strangers because their anger is invariably contained and controlled, and is unleashed only on their intimate partner.

MYTH

Alcohol and drug use cause DA.

REALITY

While alcohol and drugs are associated with DA, they do not cause DA. Alcohol and drugs exercise a disinhibiting effect which permits DA but does not cause it (World Health Organisation (WHO) 2006).

MYTH

Abusive relationships will never change for the better.

REALITY

Some abusive relationships can recover and heal, providing both the survivor and perpetrator are committed to such change. Counsellors need to support survivors in whichever option they want to consider and support them in their decision. If the survivor chooses to stay, the abuser must give assurance to relinquish not only the violence but also the need to control.

MYTH

DA often stops on its own.

REALITY

There is considerable evidence that DA escalates over time and increases in frequency and severity (Walby 2004) and clinicians must monitor and assess the degree of danger and threat throughout the therapeutic process.

MYTH

Victims could stop DA by changing their own behaviour.

REALITY

The abuser is solely responsible for the abuse and needs to change abuse behaviour. Survivors frequently modulate their behaviour through compliance, mind reading, and acquiescing to abuser demands to minimise abuse, and yet find that this does not protect them from it.

MYTH

Survivors of DA grew up in abusive families.

REALITY

Some survivors may have experience of DA and abuse in childhood, but by no means all. Research shows that perpetrators of DA are more likely to have a family history of abuse, and impaired attachment (Dutton 2007).

MYTH

Clinical assessment of survivors DA will lead to pathologising them.

REALITY

While there have been many examples of this in the past, this is not necessarily the case. Clinicians need to ensure that any assessment is conducted in an ethical and sensitive manner with an awareness of the dangers of pathologising. Equally, to minimise the psychobiological impact of DA is to invalidate the survivor's experience, disavow its traumatic effects, and ultimately deny appropriate treatment intervention (Dutton 1992; Herman 1992a).

MYTH

Psychotherapy is more effective for abusers than punishment.

REALITY

This is not true for all. While psychotherapy can be helpful for some perpetrators of DA, some abusers will manipulate such interventions (Dutton 2007; Jacobson and Gottman 1998). The advantage of punishment and custodial sentences is that it provides a clear message that DA is unacceptable and will not be tolerated.

MYTH

Once the survivor has left the abusive relationship, they will be safe from future abuse or DA.

REALITY

Survivors are often at continued risk as many abusers will continue to exert control even after leaving the abuse relationship (Abrahams 2007). Survivors will be better equipped to manage such risks if they have a better understanding of the dynamics of DA, and if self-efficacy and self-agency have been restored (Herman 1992a). The counselling process can provide a safe therapeutic space in which to dissemble or unravel the complex factors in DA, restore damaged self-structures and restore internal and external safety, and rebuild life to minimise susceptibility to any future abuse experiences.

Defining domestic abuse

To challenge the myths surrounding DA, professionals need to understand precisely what DA is. Currently there is no single, universally agreed definition of DA, although it is generally accepted that DA is the use of coercive control within an intimate or family relationship. While statistically females appear to be more vulnerable to DA, one cannot ignore, invalidate or marginalise female DA towards males, or same sex DA. This may be due to reporting bias and greater fear of stigmatisation. It is essential that all professionals working with DA acknowledge female perpetrators of DA and the prevalence of DA in gay and lesbian relationships (Kaschak 2001).

The definition of domestic violence proposed by the Home Office (2006) is 'any incident of threatening behaviour, violence or abuse (psychological, physical, sexual, financial or emotional) between adults who are or have been intimate partners or family members, regardless of gender or sexuality'. While this definition acknowledges the range of DA behaviour, it does not reflect the use of coercive control in DA and the pattern of abusive or controlling behaviour perpetrated over time. DA rarely starts with act of violence or physical attack, but is characterised by controlling behaviours that escalates over time, which become a measure of the perpetrator's dominance and survivor's level of submission.

The British Medical Association (BMA 2007) uses the term domestic abuse, and asserts that DA can be passive or active. Passive DA is covert or suppressed anger often displayed in lack of concern for victim, poor care, emotional neglect or failure to protect, while active abuse manifests as overt anger directed at the victim resulting in assault, injury, intimidation and rape.

The Women's Aid Federation (2005) and Respect (2004) use the term domestic violence (DV) and define DV as

> a pattern of controlling behaviour against an intimate partner or ex-partner, that includes but is not limited to physical assaults, sexual assaults, emotional abuse, isolation, economic abuse, threats, stalking and intimidation. Although only some forms of domestic violence are illegal and attract criminal sanctions (physical and sexual assault, stalking, threats to

kill), other forms of violence can also have very serious and lasting effects on a person's sense of self, wellbeing and autonomy. Violent and abusive behaviour is used in an effort to control the partner based on the perpetrator's sense of entitlement. This behaviour may be directed at others – especially children – with the intention of controlling the intimate partner. Social and institutional power structures support some groups using abuse and violence in order to control other groups in our society, e.g. institutional racism, heterosexist, and parents' violence to children. The unequal power relations between men and women account for the fact that the vast majority of domestic violence is perpetrated by men against women rather than vice versa. (Women's Aid 2007)

The definition adopted in this book combines the Home Office (2006), Women's Aid Federation (2005) and Respect (2004) definitions with some changes to terminology.

Domestic abuse is any incident, or pattern of controlling or threatening behaviour, violence or abuse (psychological, physical, sexual, financial, emotional or spiritual) between adults who are or have been intimate partners or family members, regardless of gender or sexuality, disability, race or religion. Such abusive behaviour is used in an effort to control the partner based on the perpetrator's sense of entitlement and can have very serious and lasting effects on a person's sense of self, well-being and autonomy. Physical abuse is frequently used as coercive control and to inculcate fear which promotes domination by the abuser and ensures the submission of the victim and may also be directed at others – especially children – with the intention of controlling the intimate partner.

The range of domestic abuse

The Crown Prosecution Service (www.cps.gov.uk) identifies physical abuse, verbal and non-verbal abuse (which incorporates psychological abuse, mental abuse and emotional abuse), sexual abuse, stalking or cyberstalking, economic or financial abuse, and spiritual abuse as forms of DA. It is helpful to note that the boundaries between these abuses are not clear cut and that is unusual for one form of abuse to occur in isolation. For instance, physical abuse is frequently used to inculcate fear which facilitates the use of coercive control and domination by the abuser and ensures the submission of the victim.

Types of abuse

Domestic abuse includes acts of commission, such as assault, as well as acts of omission, such as neglect (Bifulco and Moran 1998), and can be overt or covert.

The different types of abuse used by perpetrators of DA will vary from individual to individual, and are often inextricably intertwined and difficult to disentangle. The range and type of abuses usually subsumed under domestic abuse are encapsulated in Table 1.1.

PHYSICAL ABUSE

Physical abuse can be either controlled or impulsive and commonly consists of physical assaults on the victim. These result in injuries ranging from bruising, scalding, burning or stabbing, to internal injuries or broken bones. Persistent blows to the head can cause serious head injuries, which are sometimes undetected and thus untreated. Some abusers are assiduous in controlling where to inflict physical injury by directing blows or injury to parts of body not normally seen, such as the torso, rather than leaving marks on the face or limbs.

Some abusers inflict injuries which leave no visible evidence such as inflicting ice-cold baths or asphyxiation, or incarcerating their victim by locking them up. Abusers may also employ physical neglect as part of their coercive control and subjugation, including failure to provide for basic needs such as food, elimination, sleep, rest, shelter, health care, or appropriate clothing. Female abusers often use weapons against their male partners, such as knives or sharp objects, or attack them while asleep. Ultimately, physical abuse can lead to death, in either male or female victims.

EMOTIONAL AND PSYCHOLOGICAL ABUSE

Emotional abuse can be both verbal and non-verbal, and is critical in establishing coercive control. It is persistent and corrosive in destroying self-esteem and self-worth. In emotional abuse, perpetrators of DA use antipathy and rejection in the form of criticism and disapproval to bind the victim to them. This is exacerbated by unpredictable and inconsistent behaviour that vacillates between punishment and reward (Dutton and Painter 1981). Abusers are rarely abusive all the time but oscillate between coldness and ignoring the survivor, and showering them with warmth and affection after episodes of abuse (Dutton 2007). A further form of coercive control is the enforcement of petty rules, which are severely punished when transgressed. These are usually employed by the abuser to justify and validate the violence.

Psychological abuse is invariably characterised by cruelty and humiliation designed to degrade and terrorise the survivor by manipulating deep-seated fears. Abusers often inflict extreme distress or discomfort by making the survivor do unpleasant things, using emotional blackmail or manipulation through threats of harm and violence to self or valued others, including children. To ensure total subjugation and surrender, some abusers corrupt the survivor by forcing her to

Table 1.1 Range of domestic abuse

Physical abuse	Emotional and psychological abuse
Throwing things	Coercive control
Bruising, broken bones, cuts, scratches	Terror, fear and intimidation
Kicking, slapping, hitting	Verbal abuse – unrelenting criticism
Pushing, shoving, grabbing	Threats – to survivor, children, family, pets, suicide
Choking, strangling, suffocating	
Using a weapon, knives, scissors, whips, firearms	Humiliation, degradation, derogation
	Isolation from family, friends, social network
Biting, burning, chemical burns, scalding, ice baths, left in cold	Denial of privacy
Head injuries – knocking unconscious, trauma to head	Emotional neglect – unresponsive, unavailable
Miscarriage, premature birth	Cognitive neglect – work
Physical neglect – deprivation of sleep, food, warmth	Interpersonal neglect – going out, use of telephone, hiding/burning clothes
Death	
Sexual abuse	**Financial abuse**
Rape	Denying access to cash, or credit
Sexual assault	Not consulting on decisions of how income is spent
Degrading and humiliating sexual acts	
Forced sex with others	Denying access to employment
Forced sex with children or animals	Not contributing to family income, expecting partner to fund everything
Unsafe sex	
Spiritual abuse	**Other forms of abuse**
Preventing observation of holy days	Damage to personal property
Preventing religious contemplation, rituals	Theft of property
Preventing worship	Threats and violence to pets
Ridiculing religious/spiritual views and beliefs	Stalking and cyberstalking, especially after relationship ended

engage in illegal or morally reprehensible acts or behaviours (Herman 1992a). Psychological abuse is often deliberate and calculating, rather than impulsively inflicted. Such premeditated cruelty is commonly experienced by survivors as more terrifying than impulsive violence (Abrahams 2007). Some abusers also deprive the survivor of valued and treasured objects, including children, to demonstrate their omnipotence and control.

At the extreme end of psychological abuse is malevolent intent and sadistic abuse (Fromm 1973; Goodwin 1993), in which terror is used for the express purpose of gaining absolute control over the victim. Millon (1996) proposes that there are different types of sadists: explosive sadists, tyrannical sadists, enforcing sadists and spineless sadists, all of which hold the survivor captive to coercion and absolute control. Counsellors need to be aware that psychological abuse puts survivors at risk of developing a range of difficulties such as shame, low self-esteem, depression, suicidal ideation, anxiety and dissociation. Research demonstrates that one-third of female survivors of psychological abuse suffer from post-traumatic stress (PTS) reactions, depression, anxiety, psychosomatic, eating problems and sexual dysfunction (WHO 2000), while one in ten males are at risk of depression, indicating that verbally abused survivors are as likely to develop PTS reactions as those who have been physically abused.

Psychological abuse also includes a range of omissions, or neglectful behaviours. In emotional neglect the abuser is emotionally unavailable and unresponsive to the survivor's emotional state and needs. This is most evident in ignoring distress signals, pleas for comfort, and appeals to stop the abuse. While such omissions appear to be subtle, they do have severe ramifications. Cognitive neglect is characterised by the abuser's failure to support the survivor's cognitive needs through access to information, media, newspapers or employment. A particularly crucial component of psychological abuse is interpersonal neglect in which the abuser deprives the survivor of social and interpersonal needs. Isolation from social sources cements traumatic attachment, as the individual becomes increasingly dependent on the abuser, and reduces the capacity to escape from captivity. It also deprives opportunities for experiencing relational worth.

SEXUAL ABUSE

Research indicates that 16 per cent of female and 2 per cent of male survivors of DA have experienced sexual assault by their partners, and suffered concomitant physical and mental injuries. WHO (2000) found that globally between 6 and 47 per cent of females report sexual assault by an intimate partner. Sexual abuse commonly consists of rape, sexual assault, sex with others, unsafe sex, or being forced to perform degrading and humiliating sexual acts. Sexual assault and rape put the survivor at risk of contracting sexually transmitted infections, including HIV. It may be that sexual abuse is underreported by survivors in committed relationships or marriage, as this is not perceived as rape.

FINANCIAL ABUSE

Financial abuse is usually characterised by the abuser denying the partner access to cash or credit, and exercising control over all financial decisions and major purchases, or holidays. Some abusers refuse to contribute to the family income and expect the partner to hand over the sum total of her income and fund everything, even if it entails crippling debt. To compromise moral integrity, some abusers force the survivor to engage in illegal activities including theft, and financial fraud such as claiming benefits that they are not entitled to. In some cases, abusers deny the survivor access to employment to maximise dependency and minimise social contact. Survivors with disabilities are most at risk of financial abuse, as are elderly people, which can lead to ongoing distress, as the survivor is left without money, medication or transport.

SPIRITUAL ABUSE

In spiritual abuse the perpetrator prevents the survivor from observing holy days, preventing religious contemplation and rituals, including worship, especially outside the home. This reinforces social isolation and impedes the survivor from seeking help or protection through links in the community. Some abusers accompany this with persistent ridicule of the survivor's religious or spiritual views and beliefs. This impacts on the survivor in removing a highly valued part of her identity and belief system, and reduces her ability to create meaning and maintain hope.

OTHER FORMS OF ABUSE

There are a number of other forms of abuse that perpetrators implement to control the survivor. These include damage to or theft of personal property, threats and violence to children or pets, and stalking or cyberstalking, especially after the relationship ended. This may include co-opting friends, family, neighbours and colleagues to monitor the survivor's movements and activities. It is also a way of reminding the survivor of the abuser's omnipotence and degree of control, even after separation or divorce. This means the survivor has to be hypervigilant at all times, can never relax, or escape the abuse.

The cycle of abuse

Domestic abuse is rarely continuous but cyclical. Walker (1979) found that DA is generally characterised by three phases known as the 'cycle of violence' (Walker 1979) with each phase lasting a different amount of time. The duration of each phase will vary among individual abusers, with the total cycle lasting anything from a few hours, months or even years to complete. In many cases the cycle speeds up over time with violence erupting much earlier on. As some of the phases can be quite subtle, and pivotal in traumatic bonding, many survivors do not identify the cyclical nature of DA, making it harder to seek help.

The first stage is referred to as *the tension-building phase*, in which there is a gradual incubation and escalation of internal pressure. This internal tension is usually expressed around minor incidents, but may represent primitive fears and insecurities in the abuser's self-structures. As the internal pressure mounts, the abuser needs to unleash the unbearable tension. This occurs in the second stage, *the abuse* or *crisis phase*, in which physical violence or verbal assault erupts. The catalyst for this tsunami-like eruption is commonly a minor external incident or event to which the abuser attaches his inner turmoil and tumultuous rage. It is during this phase that the survivor is most at risk and commonly seeks help.

Once the rage has been vented, it is replaced by contrition and remorse. It is this third stage, *the reconciliation* or *honeymoon phase*, that is critical in binding the survivor to the abuser in a folie à deux. This phase is characterised by pleas for forgiveness from the abuser, and is often accompanied with extremely attentive and loving behaviour. Many abusers lavish attention, gifts and special treats on the survivor along with promises and assurances that it will never happen again. The survivor, who is delighted at the restoration of loving behaviour, invariably forgives the abuser, until the cycle is activated again. It is this third stage that cements the relationship and acts as the superglue of traumatic attachment. It is the inconsistent and intermittent reward and punishment that acts as a potent reinforcer which paradoxically strengthens the attachment process rather than weakening it (Dutton and Painter 1981; Harlow and Harlow 1971).

Meloy (1992) proposes that during the tension-building phase, the abuser experiences a catathymic crisis that leads to the sudden eruption of violence. The inner pressure is the result of unbearable emotions that have a symbolic significance albeit unconscious at the time of violence. In many respects it is a form of 'deindividuated violence' (Zimbardo 1969) or 'deconstructed thinking' (Baumeister 1990) in which delusional thinking drives the abuser to violence in which the survivor is not seen 'as a person but as part of an overwhelming image' (Revitch and Schlesinger 1981). In essence, the abuser is overwhelmed by intense autonomic arousal and extreme anger, and perceives the survivor as an imminent threat to the ego structure. The eruption of violence is simply to reduce the threat and return to intrapsychic homeostasis.

The symbolic meaning fuelling the internal tension is centred on loss, or impending loss, including internal loss of control. This generates extreme rage, and agitation in which the abuser ruminates on the partner's perceived malevolence, which drives his rage even higher. When the rage is finally unleashed, it is uncontrollable in its desire to annihilate the survivor. Fuelling the rage is pathological jealousy and fear that the survivor will abandon the abuser. There is no conscious awareness that the rage is due to the perpetrator's insecurity, obsessive preoccupation, ambivalence and pathological jealousy (Crawford and Gartner 1992).

The prevalence and incidence of domestic abuse

It is notoriously difficult to measure prevalence and incidence rates of DA as it is such a hidden crime. To understand prevalence and incidence rates, counsellors must be able to distinguish between the two and how these are influenced by definitions of DA. Prevalence rates measure and estimate the proportion of the population that have been abused, while incidence rates measure and estimate the number of new cases occurring in a given time period. Clinicians need to remember that prevalence rates are always lower than incidence rates, because some survivors are victims more than once over time. While these rates provide a guide they are by no means conclusive, and professionals must be cautious in extrapolating from such data. Prevalence and incidence rates do not represent a cross-section as crime data, and clinical research is based on DA that has been reported, disclosed, or brought to the attention of professionals, and may not include the most severely abused. Clinicians must guard against generalising from these rates, as they do not include those who have not accessed resources or sought help (Carlson 1991; Henwood 2000).

The hidden nature and stigma associated with DA create barriers to reporting which in turn impacts on accurate statistical analysis. The fact that DA is conducted in the private and domestic sphere results in low public awareness, which impacts on priority thresholds, both nationally and locally. The lack of a universally agreed definition impacts on data collection and reporting, as many survivors of DA do not consider it to be a crime. The British Crime Survey 2005–06 found that 51 per cent of female survivors considered only the most extreme incident to be a crime, with 13 per cent normalising DA as part of life. Furthermore, the lack of agreed definition of DA results in major differences in prevalence rates, which obfuscates the data.

Walby and Allen (2004) found that 34 per cent of female and 62 per cent of male survivors have never disclosed their abuse because they believed it to be too trivial to disturb the police. Just under half of male survivors never sought help from police as they feared an unsympathetic response, or that they would not be believed. Of those who did involve the police, 89 per cent reported feeling that they were not taken seriously (Brown 1998). The accuracy of prevalence and incidence rates are further undermined by prevailing attitudes of professionals, and lack of knowledge and awareness of DA. This impacts on lack of detection, and lack of reporting due to doubt, or uncertainty around reporting procedures, or fear of offending the survivor. Mental health professionals who lack training in DA cannot identify DA, let alone name it, and therefore do not record or report it.

In addition, some clinicians may fear naming DA as this may compromise their therapeutic philosophy in being too directive.

Reporting rates are also influenced by the stigmatisation of DA, cultural norms, ethnicity, norms about family privacy and socioeconomic status. Rates of DA in lower socioeconomic groups may be inflated as these are more likely to come to professional attention in statutory agencies, than those from higher socioeconomic groups who may not access statutory services. Rural and inner city rates may also vary due to lack of service provision, and transport to access these. Survivors who dissociate and compartmentalise the DA present as extremely high functioning and would not necessarily fit the clinical picture of survivor of DA or trauma. There are also differences in reporting rates of violence between men and women (Szinovacz 1983).

Despite these difficulties, current prevalence and incidence rates do give a nominal picture of DA. The British Crime Survey 2005–06 found that 1 in 20 of all reported crimes in England and Wales were DA, with 29 per cent of females and 18 per cent males reporting DA (Coleman, Jansson and Kaisa 2007). According to Women's Aid (2007), two women are murdered every week in England and Wales by their partner or ex-partner. Walby and Allen (2004) found that in 80 per cent of cases the victim was female, which rose to 89 per cent in cases where four or more incidents were reported. Coleman *et al.* (2007) also found that in England and Wales, in 33 per cent of all female homicides the woman was killed by her partner, ex-partner or lover, while 23 per cent of all male homicides were killed by a partner, ex-partner or lover. In addition, of all crimes, DA has the highest revictimisation rate at 43 per cent of recurring abuse, and 23 per cent of being revictimised three or more times.

One-third of all crimes against women are DA, while one-third of all emergency medical care is administered to women experiencing DA (BMA 2007). According to the BCS the age group at highest risk is 20–24 year olds, with 16–19 year olds a close second. The Women's Aid Federation found that 26–35-year-old females are most at risk, necessitating refuge accommodation (Williamson 2006) and this decreases with age, possibly due to resignation and total surrender after years of abuse. Physical violence is seen in 23 per cent, or one in four females between the ages of 16 and 59, and in 17 per cent, or one in five males.

Vulnerable groups associated with domestic abuse

No individual or group is inoculated against DA as it occurs across gender, sexuality, ethnicity, culture, socioeconomic status, and individuals with disabilities, although some may be a higher risk. Counsellors need to be aware that DA occurs in a variety of relationship environments to fully dispel any pervasive stereotypes or myths.

FEMALES ABUSED BY MALES

Females abused by males are by far the most common, with 80 per cent of survivors of DA identified as female (BMA 2007), with an increased risk during pregnancy. Research has shown that 30 per cent of DA is initiated during pregnancy (Confidential Enquiry into Maternal Child Health for England and Wales (CEMACH) 2004) and that it is a more common risk factor to pregnancy than gestational diabetes and pre-eclampsia (BMA 2007). DA is also believed to be a contributory factor in maternal and foetal mortality, miscarriage, premature births and stillbirth. Women who are abused during pregnancy commonly present with multiple sites of injury including the breasts and abdomen, indicating that the foetus is a focus of rage as well as the woman (BMA 2007). Given the strong association between DA and pregnancy, the BMA recommends routine screening by all health professionals, particularly midwives and health visitors.

MALES ABUSED BY FEMALES

While the domestic abuse of males is less common than females, it is estimated that around one in five males experience DA (BMA 2007). The abuse of males by females is more complex as in some cases the violence may be self-defence, while others are unprovoked physical assaults. Females who physically abuse their male partners are more likely to use weapons, such as knives, sharp implements and firearms, or attack them while asleep, or in bed. Physical abuse of males is less common, as most female abusers resort to emotional humiliation. Female abusers tend to ridicule, shame, criticise, belittle or infantilise their partner, or emasculate him. This may not be perceived as DA in cultures, or subcultures, in which the stereotype of the 'henpecked' husband exists and is tolerated. Such attitudes fail to recognise the impact of humiliation and ridicule on the partner's sense of self and masculinity, and exacerbates fear of disclosure and reporting of DA. Generally males have difficulties in disclosing and reporting interpersonal violence, which is compounded by the lack of service provision for their specific needs.

While female violence is thought to be a response to frustration and stress, and male violence is associated with emotional control (James 1999), it must be acknowledged that some females do desire to control their partner. A common example is women who have been victimised in the past who choose partners whom they can control and dominate, to ensure they do not experience revictimisation (Welldon 2004). Whatever the motivation or type of abuse used, clinicians need to be clear that all abusers, whatever gender, are responsible and accountable for their actions and any DA must not be condoned, irrespective of degree of provocation, stress, frustration or distress.

SAME SEX RELATIONSHIPS (LGBT)

The research into DA in lesbian, gay, bisexual and transgendered (LGBT) relationships is severely limited. Research estimates that the rate of DA in LGBT relationships is similar to that seen in male to female abuse, with 29 per cent of gay men and 22 per cent of lesbians experiencing DA at some point in their lives (Broken Rainbow 2005; Henderson 2003). It is thought that DA in LGBT communities is grossly underreported, with 86.9 per cent of women and 81.2 per cent men failing to report DA (Secretary of State for the Home Department 2003). These data are far from conclusive, because DA rates in LGBT relationships have been largely ignored in crime surveys, with estimates often anecdotal. Vaughan (2000) and Island and Letellier (1991) suggest that rates are disproportionally double those found in heterosexual relationships due to homophobia and concomitant social isolation in which couples are more dependent on each other. A further factor is that some gay men do not name it as DA and thus do not take emotional or practical steps to seek help, or talk about the abuse. Some survivors may believe that they deserve abuse because they are gay and see themselves as defective, with low self-worth, dignity and self-esteem.

Silence around DA may also be a result of gay men internalising the oppression against men, which is acted out in horizontal hostility. Reporting is further hindered by shame and fear of not being believed, especially by the police. Wellard (2003) found that only 18.8 per cent of gay men and 13.1 per cent of lesbians who experienced DA reported it to the police, with only 5 per cent of men and 4 per cent of lesbians reporting incidents more than once. Some gay men experience 'homophobic control' by their abuser, who threatens to disclose their partner's sexuality, or HIV status, to family, friends or employer (Morgan 1998). Yet others face abuse from family members due to their sexuality, making it even harder to disclose. Disclosure is further compromised by limited service provision, inadequate protection and lack of institutional resources. Many gay and lesbian survivors fear that if they disclose they will have to reveal their sexuality and face homophobic reactions from service providers. Lack of safety for gay men is attested to by the lack of refuge provision, which in 2005 consisted of a mere 20 dedicated beds (Broken Rainbow 2005). Adequate responses to gay survivors are further hampered by lack of awareness and number of trained professionals.

DA is thought to occur less in lesbian relationships than in heterosexual relationships (Brand and Kidd 1986; Renzetti 1992) but this may be because it is more hidden due to homophobic attitudes, stigmatisation, limited access to social and professional support, lack of legal and public recognition, and minimal institutional resources. Renzetti (1992) argues that DA is more likely to occur in lesbian relationships in which there is a power imbalance, and in which one partner has greater access to resources such as financial, educational, or social opportunities. It is also elevated if the abuser feels entitled to control the partner, believes violence is permissible and morally acceptable, and if the survivor is obliged to acquiesce. This is compounded if the abuser also believes that violence will produce the desired effect, that there will be no negative costs attached to the abuser whether personal, legal, social or emotional.

DOMESTIC ABUSE AND MINORITY ETHNIC GROUPS

DA occurs across all cultures with between 20 per cent and 30 per cent of all women attacked by their partner at some point in their lives (Winchester 2002). To date there has been insufficient research of rates of DA in black and minority ethnic (BME) groups. This is in part due to resistance to speaking out, or seeking support, fear of racist responses from professionals, and fear of ostracism and reprisal from their community. It is argued that BME women are more likely to suffer DA for longer as there are fewer alternatives such as refuges available to them. A testament to this is that out of 3,700 refuges in England and Wales, only 25 are specifically for black or Asian women (Morgan 1998). In addition, many refuges are not able to cater for the specific needs of women from different cultures, such as religious worship and rituals. For instance, Orthodox Jewish women face difficulties in refuges due to their need to keep kosher, having to share the kitchen with non-Jewish females, and the observance of holy days.

The lack of service provision is exacerbated by fears of racism, language barriers, poor accessibility of refuges, legal and welfare services, stereotypical views of 'passive' women and judgement by professionals. There may also be fears of reporting to the police due to insecure immigration status and risk of deportation. The total lack of control and lack of protection may account for the high levels of self-harm and suicide among Asian survivors of DA (Bashir and Bashir 2001).

Family honour ('izzat') and shame ('sharam') constrain Asian women from contacting police or social services, or separating from the partner, as they face a real danger of 'honour killing' for bringing shame onto the family. Many Asian women believe they have no safe option, or support from family and community when leaving; they stay to prove that they are a dutiful wife. This is compounded by pressure from the extended family to conform to strong traditional roles. Alongside DA, many Asian women also commonly encounter abusive and oppressive practices in the family including forced marriage, abduction, imprisonment in the home, restrictive lifestyle, freedom of movement, strictly enforced dress codes, denial of education, limited career choices, controlling and belittling criticism, lack of independence and self-worth, and lack of social contact (Siddiqui 2003). A common form of domination and control used by Asian males is allegations of unfaithfulness, and punishment for lack of sexual cooperation, often directly or indirectly aided and abetted by fathers-in-law.

Young married Asian women may also be vulnerable to DA from their mothers-in-law or sisters-in-law, as they are subordinate not just to all adult males, but also to the oldest or senior female. Asian mothers-in-law who abuse do so either directly, and become the oppressor, or indirectly by colluding with males through goading, or instigating physical or verbal abuse. Indirect DA by mothers-in-law can include overworking the survivor, demeaning her, neglecting her, denying her basic necessities such as food, or criticising her for not bearing sons. The degree of DA is influenced by the survivor's stage in the life cycle, social class and caste (Miller 1992). Commonly, Asian women, who were victims of DA in their younger years, may become perpetrators when they are older and have power.

Many refugee women who experience DA suffer in silence as they fear losing their immigration status, or fear deportation if they leave their partner within the first year of entering the UK. As many refugees come from oppressive regimes, they have an inherent fear or lack of trust of the police and governmental agencies. Migrant domestic workers are also vulnerable to DA and may fear the ramifications of disclosure. In combination, such fears, language barriers, and patchy and inconsistent service provision make it much harder for survivors to disclose and seek support. Professionals and counsellors who work with survivors from BME groups must ensure they employ a good practice model in which they guard against misconceived commitment to antiracist practices. It is critical that counsellors are not paralysed by race anxiety to minimise DA under the auspices of 'respect' for cultural differences such as the disciplinarian behaviour of African Caribbean males, or the subservient role expected of Asian females (Pryke and Thomas 1998).

DOMESTIC ABUSE AND SURVIVORS WITH DISABILITIES

According to the British Crime Survey 2004–05 females with disabilities are three times more at risk of DA, while males with disabilities are two times more at risk. The types of abuse DA survivors with disabilities are vulnerable to are withholding of care, neglect, removal of mobility or sensory devices that are needed for independence, financial abuse through appropriating benefits, and ridiculing and denigrating the survivor's disabilities. The DA may be more prolonged as it is more hidden, and caring abusive partners are more able to fool professionals by presenting themselves as saintly carers. If mobility is an issue the survivor will feel more trapped as he or she is unable to avoid the abuse, seek refuge, or access specialist transport. In the case of communication impairments, these will prevent use of the telephone to ring helplines or make appointments, while cognitive impairments make it difficult to conceptualise their experiences as DA.

Survivors with disabilities face additional risks of DA due to isolation and increased dependency on the abuser, making it harder to leave. This is especially the case if the abuser is also the sole carer. Survivors with disabilities are less able to defend themselves, or to leave their partner for fear of being unable to cope on their own. They may also be reluctant to disclose or report DA, for fear of reprisal, or finding another intimate partner who is also willing to be their carer. In combination these increase the survivor's social isolation, making reporting difficult, as it is difficult to disclose without help, or the presence of the carer. Many refuges do not cater for survivors with disabilities due to lack of wheelchair access (48 per cent) or reporting (29.6 per cent) that they are unable to provide appropriate accommodation (Sale 2001). The specific needs of survivors with disabilities necessitates further research along with more clearly defined government policies and service provision. Professionals also need to be aware that some people with disabilities can also be perpetrators of DA.

SOCIOECONOMIC CLASS

DA is not the preserve of any one class, and occurs across all socioeconomic status (SES) groups. While the rates of DA appear to be elevated in lower SES groups, this may be due to reporting and recording bias. Survivors of DA from higher SES groups may be more able to hide the abuse from statutory agencies by seeking professional support privately, which is less likely to be recorded or subject to statistical analysis. In addition, these survivors may have more access to alternative resources of help such as legal representation, own income to find alternative housing, and social support network. Many middle-class or professional women present as high functioning (Lachkar 2004) and either do not report DA or access available resources for fear of stigmatisation and humiliation. More research is needed to increase level of awareness of incidence and prevalence of DA in higher SES groups.

INTERGENERATIONAL DOMESTIC ABUSE

Professionals need to be aware of intergenerational abuse in which male adolescents and young adult males commit DA towards their parents, especially their mothers. To date this has been most commonly associated with Asian communities in which there are strong sanctions around conforming to traditional gender roles, imbalanced power structures, and tolerance of violence within families. Disclosure of intergenerational DA is hampered by the same factors facing BME groups, which make it difficult to assess prevalence and incidence rates. More research needs to be conducted within and outside BME groups to ascertain the level of intergenerational abuse.

ELDER ABUSE

Elder abuse appears to be a growing problem, with over half a million elderly people suffering such abuse (Ogg and Bennet 1992). As there is a dearth of research into elder abuse, this figure may well be outdated, and represent only the tip of the iceberg. There are five main forms of elder abuse: physical, sexual, psychological, financial or material, and neglect or abandonment (National Center on Elder Abuse 1997; WHO 2002). There are a number of factors that contribute to elder abuse, not least the degree of dependency and the quality of the relationship over time. Elder abuse can be a continuation of DA that has been present in the relationship in earlier years, or turning tables where the victim becomes empowered through the frailty of the abuser and retaliates for years of abuse.

In the case of adult children abusing elderly parents, the abuse may be a consequence of strained family relationships, and extra stress due to caring for the elderly person, shared housing, increased dependency needs, socioeconomic factors and lack of support in caring for an aged relative. In some cases, if the adult child was abused in childhood they may seek revenge through the reversal of power dynamics. It is crucial that basic support networks for older people are developed, and that family carers are appropriately supported when caring for elderly relatives.

There are a number of other groups that experience additional oppressions and discrimination alongside DA. These groups may struggle with fears of stigmatisation, lack of appropriate support, or lack of understanding. Survivors of DA who also have mental health problems, or are older or very young, may present with complex issues that need specific attention. Included in this are people who are dependent on alcohol or drugs, those who work in the sex industry and people who belong to travelling communities.

Perpetrators of domestic abuse

Understanding the psychology of perpetrators of DA is critical for assessment and effective treatment. Clinicians need to be aware of the covert and subtle nature of coercive control to identify the behaviour and name it as DA. As DA consists of vacillation between overt displays of control, such as physical violence, and more covert or subtle forms of control, counsellors need to have an understanding of the cumulative effects of persistent coercive control. In addition, an understanding of the range of motivations underlying DA will aid the counsellor in exploring the abusers behaviour with the survivor. As the majority of survivors take responsibility for the DA, and blame themselves, it is useful for them to see that the abuser's behaviour commonly emanates from primitive fears and internal pressure rather than the survivor's behaviour. An understanding of such dynamics can minimise vulnerability to any future revictimisation.

Perpetrators of DA are not homogonous, and while they share some commonalities there are also considerable differences. As both males and females perpetrate DA, it is important to understand intimate abuse within a gender neutral framework (Merrill 1996). Underlying most DA is the desire to control the partner, and a belief that violence is acceptable to resolve conflict and release frustration. To some degree this is learnt behaviour as male and female perpetrators of DA are three times more likely to have experienced family violence in childhood, and have learnt to normalise such behaviour. However, such social learning interacts with individual motivation for which abusers must be held accountable. Clinicians must remember that abusers are not just passive learners, but seek and choose to abuse and control their partner.

Research has shown that perpetrators of DA share some common characteristics such as the need, and desire to control, lack of empathy, and considerable relational deficits (Dutton 2007). Perpetrators of DA often use their partners for their own convenience, have rigid beliefs about gender roles, and believe that their partner is not entitled to independence (Dutton 2007; Jacobson and Gottman 1998). A prominent feature is pathological jealousy, not just sexual jealousy but deep envy of the survivor's personality, vitality, popularity and attractiveness (Hirigoyen 2004; Jukes 1999). Some of these characteristics have led some researchers to understand perpetrators within a framework of abusive personality.

THE ABUSIVE PERSONALITY

Dutton (2007) proposes that the roots of the abusive personality can be traced to early attachment deficits, in particular insecure attachment, which incubates over years. While these attachment deficits may remain largely hidden during late childhood and adolescence, they can be unleashed when entering into adult intimate relationships. According to this model, intimacy and fear of abandonment generates abusiveness regardless of gender or sexuality, and is driven not by male dominance but intimate anger. The common characteristics of the abusive personality are chronic emptiness, jealousy due to fear of abandonment, a split between the public persona and private abusive personality, and a blaming attribution style. This is often accompanied by high levels of anxiety, anger and chronic irritability, which prevent negotiation in resolving intimate difficulties. It is this attribution of blame that 'is the midwife at the birth of misogyny' (Dutton 2007, p.116).

Early childhood trauma, excessive losses, separations and attachment disruption lead to hyperarousal and aggressive outbursts as unbearable and unmentalised internal tension threatens to engulf the abuser. Abusers have enormous difficulty in maintaining a strong, clearly defined self-image, and rely on their intimate partner to provide this. Partners are expected to ensure that the abuser's fragile sense of self is not undermined, to pacify pervasive anxiety, fear of abandonment and chronic aloneness, and prevent disintegration. In essence, the abuser unconsciously requires the partner to soothe bad feelings, make him feel better, and maintain his integrity. As this occurs outside conscious awareness, the abuser is unable to recognise or express these primitive needs. To defend against these unconscious needs and fears of abandonment or rejection, the abuser distances himself from the partner by denigrating and dehumanising her, until he can unleash the full force of inner rage during the abusive episode.

Fear of attachment and intimacy can also lead to borderline personality organisation (BPO) in which the individual oscillates between closeness and distance. While borderline personality disorder is most commonly diagnosed in females, several researchers argue that such personality organisation underlies the abusive personality (Dutton 2007; Henderson, Bartholomew and Dutton 1997; Millon and Grossman 2007), but traditionally abusive males have been excluded from such diagnosis, and seen as criminal. More research is needed to clarify the association between abusers and borderline personality disturbances, and how intimacy generates abusiveness regardless of sexuality or gender.

Commonly, perpetrators of DA mask their dependency as they are unable to communicate intimacy needs, fear of abandonment and deep-rooted anxiety, yet expect their partner to intuit these unexpressed needs. Consequently, the abusers poorly integrated sense of self, contradictory behaviour and tenuous ego integrity activates primitive defences such as splitting and projective identification (Freud 1936; Klein 1946). Through projective identification the abuser perceives in others those aspects that they are unable to tolerate in self such as dependency, neediness, or aggression. In effect the partner becomes the screen for the projection of unacceptable impulses, expectations, and primitive fears all of which existed prior to the relationship (Stosny 1995).

As the abuser cannot integrate positive and negative self-qualities, all the bad qualities are projected onto the partner in order to retain the good qualities (Mollon 2000). These defences are manifest in the cycle of abuse wherein during the tension-building phase the abuser defends against disintegration by inflating the sense of self, omnipotence, entitlement and infallibility. To achieve this, the abuser needs to vilify and devalue the partner, in order to justify the violence or abuse. In the contrition phase the abuser idealises the partner, and in the process begins to devalue self-aspects, which deflates positive attributes and replaces these with a sense of unworthiness, to begin the cycle again.

MALE PERPETRATORS OF DOMESTIC ABUSE

Dutton (2007) identifies four abusive personality types: *over-controlled, antisocial (sociopathic/psychopathic), impulsive/under-controlled,* and *instrumental/under-controlled*. While these refer primarily to male perpetrators of DA, they can equally apply to some females. The over-controlled personality type is characterised by avoidant personality traits, which manifests in avoidance of conflict and denial of anger. This unexpressed chronic rage demands periodic release, resulting in the eruption of violence. While over-controlled abusers execute violence less frequently, they nevertheless dominate their partner, and put them at risk of murder.

The over-controlled abuser masks high dependency needs, and chronic resentment through passive-aggressive tendencies by presenting a charming public persona to cover up. The antisocial type of perpetrator uses violence outside intimate relationships, and is frequently in conflict with the law. The motivation for the use of violence is instrumental in order to control, intimidate and dominate others, and is often manifest in early childhood and linked to conduct disorders, or hyperactivity-impulsivity-attention deficits. Such abusers frequently present with flattened affect, a cold and calculated stance, a lack of conscience or remorse, exaggerated control techniques, and premeditated violence. In some instances such responses are a result of chronic child abuse leading to what Porter (1996) refers to as 'secondary psychopathy', or if they are capable of empathic responses as 'pseudo-psychopathy' (Herve 2002).

The impulsive/under-controlled abuser is emotionally volatile and engages in cyclical use violence which is used to discharge accumulated tension. This abusive personality is associated with emotional/verbal/physical abuse and is highly correlated with borderline personality organisation (BPO) (Dutton 2007). The abuse is confined to intimate relationships as they evoke early attachment experiences. The abuser usually presents as extremely likeable in other relationships, which makes it harder to detect DA, and thus makes it more dangerous for the partner. In intimate relationships the abuser displays hyper-emotionality, high levels of morbid jealousy, 'conjugal paranoia', dysphoria, and anxiety-based rage. Such abusers have an insecure, fearful attachment style in which they fear abandonment and aloneness. This creates considerable ambivalence to the partner, chronic anger, and poor self-esteem and BPO traits. The instrumental/under-controlled abuser resembles the antisocial abuser in presenting an anti-social-narcissistic-aggressive profile. This type is associated with more physical violence, dismissive attachment style, and sadistic traits. Such abusers may have a history of antisocial behaviour, violence inside and outside the home, and lack of empathy.

In a similar vein, Jacobson and Gottman (1998) divide male perpetrators of DA into two main categories: the *cobras* and the *pit bulls*. Cobras are thought to account for 20 per cent of DA abusers and are commonly over-controlled, cold, calculating and ferocious. Their motivation to abuse is to get what they want. They are often very charismatic and captivating, which belies their underlying belligerence, contempt and psychopathic tendencies. They often taunt and provoke the partner into a frenzy while remaining calm and in control. This makes them emotionally more aggressive, vicious and sadistic as they strike swiftly and lethally. Cobras choose their partners very carefully and seek total control over them. They are incapable of forming truly intimate relationships, keep intimacy to a minimum, and make only superficial commitments that serve a specific purpose such as status, or access to resources such as sex. There are a subset of cobras who are more out of control, severely violent and explosive, who experience the discharge of rage and violence as cathartic, and a primary relief of tension.

In contrast, the anger and rage in pit bulls is born of fear. Pit bulls are deeply insecure and are consumed with fear of dependency, abandonment and betrayal. They are highly unstable, cannot tolerate intimacy and need to control and dominate their partner as their fear of abandonment is expressed as morbid jealousy. The pit bulls' insecurity and fear compels them to restrict their partner's independence and autonomy without acknowledging that they are in control, seeing themselves as victims instead. They are less intimidating than cobras, with a much slower fuse and longer incubation period before violence or rage erupts. While pit bulls display more remorse, they are harder to leave as they rationalise and justify the abuse, even after the relationship has ended. They frequently continue to control and abuse through stalking even after separation, and as such remain a continual danger. As their namesakes indicate, they sink their teeth in, and are tenacious in not letting go.

What emerges from these profiles of male abusers is anger and violence born of fear (Bowlby 1977) with insecure attachments, fear of abandonment, and highly controlling behaviour to prevent rejection. Many abusive males become involved in relationships extremely quickly in order to 'capture' the survivor and commence the process of coercive control and enslavement. Perpetrators of DA usually have unrealistic expectations of their partner, which are not expressed, and display a tendency to blame others for their problems, feelings and behaviours. They are often hypersensitive, lack conflict resolution skills and are unable to manage stress. Such abusers have great difficulty in self-regulation and containing feelings and expect their partners to soothe them. If the symptoms do not dissipate, then the partner is blamed. As abusers have poor insight into the cause of their difficulties, and cannot link these to disordered attachment, they avoid seeking help. If the survivor suggests this, they are ridiculed and punished. Given these tendencies, Mitchell and Gilchrist (2004) propose that DA may be better understood as panic, or anger attacks directed against intimate partners, or within the family.

FEMALE PERPETRATORS OF DOMESTIC ABUSE

Historically there has been a gender bias in relation to domestic abusers, with female abusers either ignored, or dismissed as resorting to abuse only as 'self-defence'. More recent research indicates that domestic abuse committed by females may be as prevalent as males, but that it is much more hidden and not as comprehensively researched (Dutton 2007). While there may be some differences in motivation to abuse, there may be some gender-equivalency as females also experience attachment deficits, affective dysregulation, exposure to shame, and abuse in childhood. Motz (2000) proposes that female violence, while less common, is due to unintegrated murderous feelings, and aggression projected onto their partner, who in turn enacts this. According to Browne (1987), women who kill do so only after years of unbearable humiliation, degradation, isolation and terror.

It is pertinent to note that female violence in the home is not commensurate with rates of female violence outside the home, and as such is seen as more abnormal, and associated with mental health problems and personality disturbances. The changing role of women, mutable power dynamics, and more females becoming primary breadwinners may to some extent account for changing patterns of violence and abuse towards male partners. In addition, some females who have suffered DA may reverse this by abusing their future partners as a defence against being controlled. Whatever the motivation of female abusers, they are just as responsible for the abuse as their male counterparts and must equally be held accountable.

Researchers have highlighted a number of characteristics that are associated with female abusers (Dutton 2007; Ehrensaft, Moffit and Caspi 2004; Magdol *et al.* 1997; Moffit *et al.* 2001) and note that these arise from the same need for power. In addition, the abuse is invariably controlled and deliberate rather than self-defence, or difficulties in anger management. As with male perpetrators of DA, many female abusers present with an insecure anxious attachment style, fear of abandonment and rejection, morbid jealousy, unbearable inner turmoil, tumultuous emotions and poor self-control. Many female abusers are commonly emotionally volatile, with rapidly fluctuating emotions, impulsive and a range of borderline features, and an inability to cope with stress (Dutton 2007).

Survivors of domestic abuse

Many of the characteristics and symptoms associated with survivors of DA are normal responses to extreme and prolonged coercive control and abuse (Dutton 1992; Herman 1992a). Traditionally survivors of DA were deemed to be masochistic, and suffering from psychological disturbances. This has resulted in pathologising survivors and victim blaming. Many of the presenting symptoms such as psychic numbing, resignation, erosion of self-identity, self-esteem and self-efficacy are the result of DA, not the cause and need to be understood within that context (see Chapter 3).

Invariably many survivors of DA are highly resilient to unrelenting coercive control and abuse, and far from being passive victims, they are active survivors who employ a number of survival strategies to manage the abuse. Many survivors of DA display considerable strength in the face of adversity, despite the power and control of the abuser, which endeavours to erode these strengths and destroy the survivor's hope and vitality. Abusers are extremely clever in manipulating the survivor's trust and credulity, as well as their benevolent feelings towards them.

Many survivors nourish the hope that the abuser will change and acknowledge the impact that DA has on the partner, not realising that this hope and the survivor's forgiveness is perceived by the abuser as a reproach which serves to increase his hatred and rage.

To manage the abuse, survivors have to repress their feelings, creativity and vitality and become impervious to the abuse by adopting a facade of invincibility in which there exists an illusion of control. The more severe the abuse, the greater the survivor's test of strength, and the greater the confirmation of invincibility. This activates a stubborn refusal to give up on the abuser as the survivor does not wish to believe or imagine that there is no solution or that change cannot occur. This is compounded by females' socialisation, which demands that they are responsible for the success or failure of their intimate relationships and are made to feel guilty or ashamed for abandoning their partner.

Impact of domestic abuse

COST OF DOMESTIC ABUSE

The cost of DA is not just on the victims and their children, but also ultimately to the state. While the physical, emotional and psychological costs are primarily to the victims and those close to them such as children, the financial cost is to the state.

FINANCIAL COST

It has been argued that there are a number of direct and indirect financial costs to the government, public and voluntary agencies. Walby (2004) estimates that the total annual cost in England and Wales is in the region of £5.8 billion. This is made up of £3.1 billion to public services such as health services, social services, housing, the criminal justice system, civil and legal services, and £2.7 billion loss to the economy. The cost to the National Health Service itself is thought to be £1.2 billion for physical injuries and £176 million for mental health resources, although this might be considerably higher as such problems as self-harm, alcohol/drug abuse, post-traumatic stress disorder (PTSD) and depression may not necessarily be linked to DA. One-quarter of the £1 billion annual criminal justice system budget for violent crime is on DA, with the average cost to the police for each individual person £2,700 (Secretary of State for the Home Department 2003). The annual additional human and emotional cost is estimated to be a further £17 billion (Walby 2004).

PHYSICAL COST

According to the BMA (2007), the long-term physical costs to the survivors of DA are chronic pain, fractures, arthritis, hearing and sight deficits, seizures, frequent headaches, stress, stomach ulcers, spastic colon, indigestion, diarrhoea, constipation, angina and hypertension. Those victims who are pregnant are at direct risk of miscarriage, premature birth, low birth weight, foetal injury and foetal death. The indirect health costs are to the health of the foetus due to the mother self-medicating with alcohol or drugs, or because the mother is prevented from seeking or receiving proper antenatal and postpartum medical care. Further costs are incurred through the impact of DA on children, half of whom are at risk of being beaten, hit or neglected as a result of DA.

MENTAL HEALTH

The mental health costs of DA on survivors is physiological alterations in the brain, limbic system, midbrain, frontal lobes, dissociative disorders, post-traumatic stress disorder, borderline personality disorder, depression, obsessive compulsive disorder, numbing, habituation, self-harm, suicide, withdrawal, increased vulnerability to reabuse, numbing and habituation due to successive violent episodes (BMA 2007; Golding 1999; Shepherd 1990) (see Chapter 2).

Theories of domestic abuse

Professionals working with survivors of DA need to have an understanding of the range of theories that have been proposed to contextualise DA in socio-political-cultural framework. As DA is so wide ranging and is seen in all educational, economic, religious and ethnic groups, though not necessarily equally, it is likely that no one single theory can account for DA, but that it is due to a combination of factors. To really understand DA, individual factors and socio-cultural factors need to be taken into account. The myriad individual factors include genetics, hormones, learning disability, and alcohol and drug misuse (WHO 2006). Other influential factors that increase the risk of DA are a previous history of abuse, especially witnessing DA in childhood, abusive parenting, and abusive expressions of power differentials, poor conflict resolution and communication skills, and lack of interpersonal respect. Male perpetrators of DA have additional risk factors such as attention deficit hyperactivity disorder, conduct disorder, anti-social, or offending behaviour, insecure childhood attachment, and personality disorders, including borderline personality disorder.

Social factors that are thought to account for DA include cultural and historical norms and inequalities between gender, age, race and sexuality. Economic inequalities, poverty, social deprivation and lack of educational and professional opportunities all contribute to stress and frustration which may be unleashed in

DA. Alcohol ⸱   DA, is
permitting ex   ce (BM

BIOLOGICA

The biological theory of DA emphaso   ale violence
evolutionary adaptation. In essence, it is argued that males have a
violence due to increased level of androgens, which is reinforced by cu.
social construction (Thornhill and Palmer 2000). Arguably, the only way to mi.
mise DA is through social education to lessen tolerance for the expression of violence, and find alternative forms of expression of inherited instincts such as anger
and aggression.

SYSTEMS THEORY

In systems theory the emphasis is on the intimate couples or family, and the
degree of imbalance in this system during times of stress. Within this model, couples or family therapy is the only way to restore equilibrium without either party
being to blame. In contrast, working with the male abuser separately is thought to
perpetuate the symmetrical, adversarial context between males and females. A
concern in this model is that it does not hold the abusers solely responsible for the
violence or the need to control and dominate their partner. Many clinicians
believe couples therapy is contraindicated in DA and that perpetrators must be
held accountable for their choices, which must be explored through their own
individual therapy (see Chapter 4).

PSYCHODYNAMIC

Psychodynamic theory proposes that the root causes of DA are to be found in
childhood, where early experiences of violence or aggression, are later replayed
in adult relationships. The emphasis is on the felt rage towards the parents which
is unleashed onto the adult intimate partner, while fears of abandonment and
rejection necessitate total control and domination over the partner (Jukes 1993,
1999; Stosny 1995). It is thought that males can end DA through acknowledging these primitive fears, gaining insight, and ventilating feelings through
psychotherapy.

SOCIAL LEARNING THEORY

Social learning theory emphasises that violence is learnt through observation and
modelling, and the concomitant rewards (Bandura 1979). If violence achieves
the desired goal, such as ending an argument, without any negative or punitive

the abuser, then it is more likely to be repeated and reinforced. Knowing there are few or no sanctions attached to violence leads to cognitive distortions such as minimising, rationalising and justifying the abuse. To create change, this model advocates the use of cognitive behavioural therapy.

COGNITIVE THEORY

Cognitive theory emphasises differences between males and females in terms of conflict resolution, in which females are more verbal and seek negotiation, whereas males are more likely to suffer from alexithymia, which impairs emotional expression (Krystal 1998). Anecdotally male abusers do report that they feel disempowered by the partner's verbal facility, and resort to physical expressions of stress, anguish and anger. Along with these differences, cognitive theory also focuses on cognitive schemas and distorted perceptions that support DA, which need to be restructured to make DA unacceptable, whatever the circumstances.

SOCIAL STRUCTURAL THEORY

Social structures define gender roles, with the male role defined as dominant, superior and entitled. When men cannot fulfil these roles because of disadvantages such as unemployment, poverty, housing and the changing roles of males and females, this leads to frustration and stress, which in turn leads to the eruption of violence. In order to prevent DA, males need to be offered opportunities for change through employment, better housing and re-education about gender roles. While social structures undoubtedly contribute to perceptions of gender role, professionals must remember that these impact on all males, but not all men perpetrate DA. Those that do have choices and they must be held accountable.

PRO-FEMINIST

Dobash and Dobash (1988) argue that male violence is rooted in patriarchy, which permits the structural and ideological subordination of women, and that DA merely reflects gender inequality, and how males seek to gain and maintain power and control. Change is thought to occur through re-education about gender roles, and use of power and control in relationships. While this model describes male violence, it does not fully account for female violence other than as self-defence. Advocates of this model reject the use of anger management as it promotes even more control in those who already use violence as a form of control.

SOCIO-CULTURAL SYSTEMS

The focus in socio-cultural systems theory is on socio-political, cultural, ethnic and economic factors. It combines social stress, poverty and social class with what it means to be female within specific cultures, the degree of control females have over their lives, expectations of how to behave, and female role models. It also considers cultural norms that legitimise violence in the family, religion, cultural tolerance and acceptance of male violence, sexual inequality and male domination. It is thought that families with high levels of conflict, which resemble a war zone rather than a place of safety, and in which children are exposed to violence, are breeding grounds for DA.

MULTIFACTORIAL MODELS

Dutton (1985) proposes an ecological nested theory of DA which consists of four nested layers. The first, the *ontogenic layer*, consists of core individual factors such as denial, hostility, shame, depression. The second, the *micro-system layer*, contains factors such as witnessing inter-parental violence, or experiencing neglect, abuse and abandonment. The third, the *exo-systemic layer*, is informed by alcohol or drug misuse, un/underemployment, rigid gender role organisation, and fundamentalist religious training. The fourth, the *macro-systemic layer*, consists of chronic poverty, disadvantage, socio-political gender inequalities, the degree of violence, especially male to female violence portrayed in the media, the privacy of the family, customs of marriage, and racial and ethnic prejudice customs.

In a similar vein, Roy (1988) proposes that psychiatric disorders are compounded by additional psychosocial factors such as poverty, financial dependence on female partner, sex role stereotyping, marriage on impulse or due to pregnancy, external stressors, isolation and social mobility. With regard to socio-political factors, Roy (1988) argues that DA is more likely to occur when females are perceived as the property of males, where males have the right to chastise women and children, and in the presence of sexual inequality.

Kahn (2000) considers the interaction of four factors linked to DA. Significant cultural factors include gender-specific socialisation, cultural definitions of appropriate sex roles, role expectations in relationships, belief in inherent superiority of males, and male property rights over females. DA is also more likely to occur under cultural beliefs in which the family is revered as a private domain under male control, alongside customs of marriage such as dowry or bride price, and in which violence is an acceptable form of conflict resolution. Relevant economic factors include female economic dependence, limited access to education, training and employment, or finance and credit. Legal factors that are associated with DA are the lowered legal status of females, either in written law or practice, and laws regarding divorce, child custody, maintenance, and inheritance and property rights. This is compounded by legal definitions of rape and DA, low level of legal knowledge among females, and insensitive treatment of females by police and the judiciary. Finally, Kahn, Ubaidur and Hossain (2001) propose that political factors such as under-representation of women in power, politics, media, legal and medical profession, and the limited organisation of women as a political force are also factors linked to DA.

Difficulties in leaving

The myriad psycho-social-cultural factors can paralyse the survivor of DA making it extremely difficult to leave. Counsellors need to ensure that they have an accurate understanding of these difficulties rather than misinterpreting survivors' motivations for staying as indicators of their pathology. Survivors of DA encounter both psychological and practical difficulties when leaving an abusive relationship. The trauma of prolonged coercive control and DA incapacitates survivors, leaving them paralysed, lacking in self-agency and self-efficacy. This prevents them from considering alternative options, let alone acting upon them. This is compounded by genuine fears of retaliation and increased danger. Research has shown that survivors of DA are most at risk of murder after they have left the abusive relationship (Women's Aid Federation 2005) and counsellors need to acknowledge this increased risk. Some survivors may also be at risk of murder through 'honour killings' as retribution from their family and community.

In addition, survivors will be further hindered by considerable practical difficulties in effecting separation. Survivors cannot just simply vanish and need access to support, money, housing and other resources. Most survivors do not know what resources are available, or how to access them. They invariably fear negative responses or lack of empathy from professionals or services, including loss of custody of children. Crucially, the social isolation experienced during DA means that they have reduced access to emotional and social support at a time when they most need it. The betrayal in DA impacts on the survivor's ability to trust others, and it may feel safer to stay with the known experience of DA than risk the unknown. The emotional attachment to the partner through traumatic bonding will make it extremely hard for the survivor to extricate herself from the abuser. Fear of revictimisation, low self-worth and low self-esteem will further bind the survivor to the abuser.

Counsellors need to be sensitively attuned to the survivor's difficulties and support her in whatever decision she takes. It is imperative to enable the survivor to explore all options available to her and encourage her to make the informed choice that seems most appropriate to her circumstances. To facilitate this, counsellors need to assess the survivor's needs and explore the access to social support and to the range of resources available. Counsellors need to enable the survivor to acknowledge personal strengths and inner resources that have helped her to survive, and to build upon these. This will restore internal safety and control, and build up depleted energy and vitality to manage the practical difficulties (see Chapter 5). Counsellors need to continually assess danger and risks, and develop safety and escape strategies to enable the survivor to leave.

A critical component of the therapeutic process to enable the survivor to leave is to explore the survivor's needs and find ways of fulfilling these. This must be combined with setting healthy boundaries, appropriate self-assertion and feeling comfortable in expressing feelings and needs in relationships. This enables the survivor to reclaim identity, power and control. Re-establishing social support is crucial in enabling the survivor to restore trust and belief in others. Safety is of prime importance, as is the pacing of the therapeutic work. The survivor may weave in between emotional needs and practicalities associated with leaving, and counsellors need to give the survivor control over the therapeutic process (see Chapter 5). At times deeper therapeutic work may be diverted and counsellors need to respond to this sensitively rather than interpret this as resistance. In those instances supportive counselling in which the focus is on listening and understanding needs to be implemented until deeper work can be resumed.

Summary

- To appreciate the impact and relationship between DA and mental health, counsellors need to understand the complex nature of DA. In order to identify DA, clinicians need to be aware of the prevailing myths surrounding DA, including their own stereotypes and biases. These myths and biases need to be challenged and replaced with more accurate understanding.

- This needs to be supported with an understanding of precisely what behaviours are subsumed under DA, so that DA can be identified and named. Clinicians require a clearly specified definition of DA to guide their practice, and to understand prevalence and incidence rates.

- Counsellors need to be aware of the range of individuals who experience DA, including male victims of female abuse, couples in same sex relationships, survivors with disabilities and those from BME groups, and how DA impacts on them.

- Perpetrators of DA are not a homogenous group and clinicians need to be aware of the range of perpetrators of DA, and the underlying factors that give rise to the need for coercive control and abuse. Such knowledge will enable the counsellor to identify underlying dynamics of DA that emanate from internal pressure in the abuser, not the survivor. Understanding that the abuser's anxieties, insecurities and inner turmoil are what fuels DA enables the survivor to relinquish the responsibility for the abuse, and make the abuser more accountable for his actions and choices.

- In addition to the abuser's internal pressures, counsellors also need to have an awareness of theories of DA which incorporate socially constructed meaning around gender, race, power and control, domination and submission, and the hierarchical structure of families. This allows for a more comprehensive understanding of the many dynamics that give rise to DA, and which create obstacles to leaving abusive relationships.

- Difficulties in leaving must be contextualised within socio-political-cultural context in which access to limited resources is a real problem, as well as acknowledging the real dangers and risks incurred when leaving. Counsellors must not pathologise such difficulties, or interpret these as resistance or masochism and continue to provide appropriate and sensitive supportive counselling in the face of what are real obstacles.

CHAPTER 2

UNDERSTANDING THE IMPACT AND LONG-TERM EFFECTS OF DOMESTIC ABUSE

Prolonged and repeated interpersonal abuse is a powerful traumatogen, especially when experienced in isolation and secrecy. Experiencing attachment trauma alters an individual's view of self, others and the world, and gives rise to a range of trauma symptoms. The characteristic symptoms and behaviours observed in survivors of domestic abuse (DA) must be seen by mental health professionals as survival behaviours and normal responses to trauma, not as individual pathology. It is critical that clinicians recognise these as survival strategies and indicative of the resilience of survivors rather than focusing on weaknesses, passivity or personality disturbance.

This chapter looks at the psychobiological impact of DA within an attachment trauma framework. It will examine the impact of trauma on a variety of dimensions and how this gives rise to long-term effects. The intention is not to provide a 'shopping list' approach, but to familiarise counsellors with the range of effects in order to have a clearer understanding of the range of effects. This will not only aid accurate assessment of survivors of DA, but also provide a focus on specific therapeutic needs for each individual. Most crucially, linking the long-term effects to survival strategies ensures that counsellors do not pathologise survivors of DA.

Impact of domestic abuse

The primary impact of DA is lack of external and internal safety. This generates terror and fear in which the survivor's very life and survival is subject to persistent and unpredictable threat. External threat activates internal responses to trauma which disrupt psychobiological synchrony and ruptures the stress response system. The vicious cycle of repeated and escalating arousal inherent in DA leads to structural changes and alterations in brain chemistry, locking the stress response system into overdrive. In addition repeated heightened arousal renders hippocampus and prefrontal cortex less functional giving rise to a number of trauma related symptoms including complex post-traumatic stress reactions. The hyperarousal in DA prevents mentalisation of the experiences and full range of feelings, which are blocked from awareness. As the survivor becomes more out of contact with feelings and needs, tolerance of the abuse is increased while capacity to problem solve is reduced.

In addition, repeated trauma induces psychological changes in the individual's perception of self, others and the world. Crucially, trauma limits the capacity to process and integrate horrific experiences into a coherent narrative making it impossible to derive meaning. The absence of meaning generates confusion, self-blame, erosion of self-esteem and self-efficacy. The betrayal of trust in DA fractures trust in others, leading to withdrawal and social isolation. This reduces capacity to challenge the perpetrator's behaviour, reinforcing his power and control, and increasing the survivor's enthrallment.

PHYSICAL IMPACT OF DOMESTIC ABUSE

The immediate impact of DA in which there has been physical violence is physical injury, which can range from contusions, cuts, burns, broken bones, strangulation and damage to internal organs. Repeated blows to the head can also cause considerable internal bruising and damage to the brain, which may not always be diagnosed. They may also have a number of old injuries that have failed to heal properly and continue cause pain. Survivors of DA are commonly physically exhausted due to hypervigilance, inability to relax and deprived sleep. To manage perpetual physical pain and tension, survivors numb somatic responses and lose contact with their body.

The cascade of stress hormones released can result in hypertension, elevated blood pressure and disruptions to appetite. Survivors of DA commonly report digestive disorders, reduced appetite, nausea and vomiting when consuming food, or chronic bowel problems. Elevated stress responses and agitation can also result in breathing difficulties, including asthma attacks. The unpredictability of DA results in heightened elevation of the alarm system, generalised anxiety, panic attacks and chronic stress responses. To manage overwhelming arousal, some survivors shut down and become numb and unresponsive to their environment, appearing almost catatonic. This constriction of activity and paralysis reflects not only the loss of energy and vitality, but also activation of primitive psychobiological defences to danger.

NEUROBIOLOGICAL IMPACT OF TRAUMA

Trauma activates the autonomic arousal system, releasing a cascade of physiological, biochemical and neurochemical changes to enable the organism to respond to danger (see Chapter 6). This consists of activation of two structurally distinct biological defence systems: the sympathetic and the parasympathetic nervous system (Engel and Schmale 1972). The sympathetic nervous system is implicated in the fight (aggressive) and flight (fear) responses as it mobilises high levels of energy, which enables the organism to be active in its environment. The parasympathetic nervous system is implicated in the freeze (defeat) response, which is most commonly seen in survivors of DA.

Activation of the parasympathetic nervous system leads to heart-rate deceleration, lowering of the metabolic rate, lowering of activity level, and passivity. The associated physical symptoms are lassitude, weakness, tiredness and fatigue, hypotonia and depressive-type symptoms. In this state the organism depresses sensory detection, ceases all sensory activities and becomes unresponsive and submissive. These physiological symptoms are commonly experienced as feelings of helplessness, emptiness, shame and hopelessness (see Chapter 6).

These activated biological defence responses disrupt hippocampal and prefrontal cortex function, fuelling overactivation of the stress response system. Such disruptions lead to disorganisation of mental states and memory impairment, which limits the survivor's capacity to problem solve or make decisions. The release of endogenous opioids induces bodily and emotional anaesthesia, inhibits the influence of cortisol, and produces a state of apparent calm allowing the survivor to disengage from current reality. Prolonged and frequent activation of the stress response system locks it into overdrive, creating a vicious cycle of escalating arousal and disruptions to psychobiological synchrony.

POST-TRAUMATIC STRESS REACTIONS

Complex post-traumatic stress (PTS) reactions are activated when an individual experiences psychologically stressing events characterised by intense fear, terror and helplessness (American Psychiatric Association 2000). The classic features of PTS reactions include hypervigilance, altered appraisal processes and lowered stress tolerance thresholds. These are displayed as hyperactivity, increased irritability, elevated startle response, insomnia, avoidance tendencies and an inability to modulate arousal and affect. This leads to the activation of post-traumatic stress disorder (PTSD) symptoms such as flashbacks, hypervigilance, nightmares, amnesia, dissociation, emotional 'frozenness', withdrawal, aloneness and being haunted by intrusive recollections of the trauma (see Chapter 6). PTSD is the most prevalent disorder associated with DA (Humphreys and Thiara 2003; Jones, Hughes and Unterstaller 2001; Krause *et al.* 2006; Stark and Flitcraft 1996). Research shows that between 31 per cent and 84.4 per cent of survivors present with PTSD, with a mean of 63.8 per cent compared to a mean of 3.47 per cent in the general population (Golding 1999). Traditionally clinicians have focused on depressive symptoms rather than more accurately diagnosing the impact of DA as features of PTSD. The majority of symptoms cluster around re-experiencing, avoidance, numbing and hyperarousal.

Repeated activation of stress response systems impairs self-regulation and affect modulation and ruptures the survivor's capacity to tolerate or contain feelings appropriately. Traumatised individuals tend to vacillate between extremes of dissociation, or psychic numbing in which no feelings are experienced, and hyperarousal in which they are so overwhelmed by turbulent emotions that they fear disintegration. Repeated trauma also fractures internal resources for resilience and mentalisation.

PSYCHOLOGICAL IMPACT OF DOMESTIC ABUSE

The complex dynamics of coercive control has considerable psychological impact on survivors. The terror inherent in DA enthrals the survivor and reinforces her captivity. The power and control of the abuser activates existential angst in which the survivor fears for her life and survival. The survivor also fears the consequences of challenging the abuser or disclosing the abuse. To manage this, the survivor must silence herself, become voiceless (Scarf 2005) and withdraw from social contact.

Invariably the perpetrator imposes an identity onto the partner which the survivor absorbs and has no choice but to adopt. The imposed identity reflects the perpetrator's negative appraisal of the survivor, which cannot be evaluated or reality tested due to the survivor's social isolation. The projective annihilation (Mollon 2002a) increases the survivor's psychological dependency on the abuser, which endorses traumatic bonding and acceptance of the abuser's controlling and abusive behaviour. Being stripped of any personal control and repeated projective annihilation prevents the survivor from seeing herself as separate from the abuser or being able to survive outside of the abuse relationship.

COGNITIVE IMPACT OF DOMESTIC ABUSE

The impact of DA generates shifts in cognitive schemas such as increased tolerance of cognitive inconsistency, diminished perception of alternatives, and development of a continuum of tolerance or 'survivability' (Blackman 1989; Dutton 1992). Distortions in perception of self lead to self-blame, adoption of full responsibility for failures in the relationship, and belief that she provoked the abuse. Perceptual distortion impacts on alterations in appraisal of reality, impaired judgement, self-doubt and inability to recognise the abuser's cruelty. The omnipresent feelings of insecurity lead to dread and anxiety. To manage these distortions the survivor employs survival strategies such as dissociation and compartmentalisation. These enable the survivor to block conscious knowledge of the abuse and remain oblivious to the terror and betrayal in order to tolerate and survive the abuse. It also allows the survivor to disconnect from self, denying the full range of feelings, needs, desires and personal goals.

Alongside cognitive distortions to schemas and self-structures, DA also shatters assumptions about self, others and the world as a safe and benign place. Such shattered assumptions impact on a sense of foreshortened future, loss of hope and loss of meaning. The loss of meaning prevents the creation of coherent narrative further amplifying 'learned voicelessness' (Scarf 2005). A common reaction to unspeakable trauma is alexithymia (Krystal 1988) which is a defence against articulating feelings. In alexithymia meagre energy is directed to operative thinking and practical survival strategies rather than the verbal expression of emotion.

The impact of trauma also disrupts mentalisation in which the survivor is unable to reflect on their experiences and feelings, or make sense of them. In survival mode, there is no space or energy for reflection, or permission to be in contact with needs, desires and hopes. Ultimately, lack of mentalisation fractures internal resources and resilience leading to resignation and feelings of being trapped. The impact of DA is exacerbated if the survivor has a history of attachment trauma in early childhood that has not been integrated or resolved.

Counsellors must also be cognisant of the considerable impact of DA on relational dynamics and children. The primary impact on relational dynamics is betrayal of trust and traumatic bonding (Dutton and Painter 1993) which binds the survivor to the perpetrator, increasing dependency and decreasing self-efficacy. Lack of trust also impacts on ability to trust others, leading to withdrawal and social isolation. The terror of DA impacts on relationships with children, and has the potential to reduce capacity for healthy parenting (Calder, Harold, and Howarth 2006; Hester, Pearson, and Harwin 2007).

Long-term effects of domestic abuse

There has been considerable research that links DA with long-term mental health difficulties, in particular post-traumatic stress disorder (Golding 1999; Humphreys and Thiara 2003; Jones *et al.* 2001; Krause *et al.* 2006; Stark and Flitcraft 1996), depression (Golding 1999), substance dependency (Batsleer *et al.* 2002; Ettore 1997; Stark and Flitcraft 1996), self-harm (Chantler *et al.* 2001; Newham Asian Women's Project 1998) and suicidality (Golding 1999). The longer-term effects of complex post-traumatic stress responses include disruptions to identity, boundary awareness and interpersonal relatedness, affect regulation and reduced awareness of needs (Allen 2001; Briere and Spinazzola 2005). Prolonged and repeated abuse also causes significant long-term impairment to physical health, neurobiological disruptions, intrapersonal, interpersonal and relational difficulties, along with behavioural and cognitive changes (see Table 2.1).

Table 2.1 Long-term effects of domestic abuse

Physical effects and health

Injuries, scars

Chronic pain

Inability to relax

Somatic and sleep disorders

Acute stress disorder

Exhaustion, chronic fatigue

Disembodied

Hypertension

Disruptions to immune system

Lung disease

Nervous system disorders

Circulatory disease

Digestive disorders

Endocrine disorders

Self-harm, self-injury

Suicidality

Eating disorders

Substance dependency

Sexual inhibition

Neurobiological effects

Impaired amygdala, frontal lobes

Overactivation of stress response system

Post-traumatic stress disorder (PTSD)

Complex PTS reactions

Hyperarousal, hypoarousal

Hypervigilance

Dissociation

Psychic numbing

Memory impairment

Disruption to mentalisation

Disruption to affect regulation

Impairment to self-preservation system

Intrapersonal effects

Loss of personal control, self-trust

Erosion of self-esteem

Loss of identity

Fear, anxiety

Anger (suppressed)

Morbid hatred

Depression

Sadness

Grief

Shame

Subjugation, defilement

Stigmatisation

Affect dysregulation

Interpersonal and relational effects

Traumatic bonding

Paradoxical gratitude

Loss of trust

Loss of affiliative functions

Isolation

Distortion of relational schemas

Impaired relational dynamics

Fear of intimacy and affectional ties

Sexual difficulties

Vulnerability to revictimisation, both personal and professional

Reduced parenting capacity

Intrapersonal effects *cont.*

Out of contact with bodily cues, needs

Disruption to self-preservation system and resilience

Loss of self-efficacy, self-agency

Diminished socioeconomic status

Behavioural effects	**Cognitive effects**
Withdrawal	Shifts in cognitive schemas
Social isolation	Shattered assumptions about self, others and world
Walking on eggshells	
Submission, compliance	Perceptual distortions
Learned helplessness	Self-perceptual distortions
Appeasement behaviour	Loss of concentration, focus
Change in dress, demeanour	Impaired decision making, problem solving
Phobias	
Obsessive-compulsive behaviour	Tolerance of cognitive inconsistency
Ritualistic 'busyness'	Diminished perception of alternatives
Addictive behaviours such as spending, shopping, gambling	Development of a continuum of tolerance ('survivability')
	Alienation
Impaired functioning occupational, social and parental	Hopelessness, futility, resignation
	Impaired mentalisation

LONG-TERM PHYSICAL AND HEALTH EFFECTS

Apart from obvious injuries and tissue damage, the long-term effects of DA include permanent damage to tissues, organs or bones due to scar tissue or repeated injury. Repeated blows to the head can lead to brain injury, while recurrent damage to internal organs can lead to organ failure. Counsellors need to be aware that some old injuries, especially head or internal organ damage, may not have been diagnosed at the time and may not have healed. Fractured and broken bones may fail to heal properly, while wounds may take longer to heal due to scar tissue. Major injuries to the spine or pelvis will result in persistent and chronic pain in those areas.

Overactivation of the stress response system results in hypertension, circulatory disease, nervous system and digestive system disorders, endocrine disorders, acute stress disorder, and chronic fatigue syndrome (Dobie *et al.* 2004; Frayne *et al.* 2004; Walker, Logan and Jordan 2004). Hypervigilance leads to inability to relax and disruptions to sleep, leading to chronic exhaustion, fatigue, disruptions to the immune system, and loss of vitality.

Prolonged trauma can also give rise to somatoform disorders such as pain disorder, body dysmorphic disorder, hypochondriasis, conversion disorder and somatisation disorder (Allen 2001; Sanderson 2006). Somatoform disorders are characterised by complaints of bodily symptoms in the absence of organic or physiological aetiology (Calof 1995) and represent symbolic communication about the abuse. Clinicians need to ensure that complete medical examinations are conducted before diagnosing somatoform disorders.

To manage the DA many survivors resort to self-harm (Chantler *et al.* 2001; Newham Asian Women's Project 1998) and self-medication (Stark and Flitcraft 1996). Self-harming can range from poor self-care in terms of diet, exercise and relaxation through to self-injury or self-mutilation and suicidality. For many survivors self-harm is the only area in which they have control or experience a sense of empowerment, making this a valued resource. Some researchers have found that self-harm is particularly prevalent among young Asian women, as is suicidality (Chantler *et al.* 2001; Newham Asian Women's Project 1998). Golding's (1999) meta-analysis found that the mean prevalence rate for females who experienced DA was 17.9 per cent compared to the general population mean of 3.55 per cent.

Some survivors may also use food as a way to exert control, making them vulnerable to eating disorders such as anorexia nervosa or bulimia nervosa. Alternatively, some survivor may resort to food as a form of self-medication leading to overeating and obesity, and concomitant health risks.

In the absence of affect regulation, survivors may become vulnerable to self-medication, especially excessive use of alcohol or drugs. Research on the link between DA and substance misuse demonstrates that survivors of DA are fifteen times more likely to self-medicate with alcohol, and six times more likely to use drugs than the general population (Stark and Flitcraft 1996) and that this is the case cross-culturally (Batsleer *et al.* 2002). Counsellors need to be aware that in most instances substances are initially used to dull the pain, or provide an escape from the abuse, and are not indicative of dependency prior to DA. Over time survivors will become vulnerable to substance dependency which will need specific therapeutic attention. Survivors with substance dependency can present particular difficulties due to a complex range of symptoms and clinicians must ensure that the multiple therapeutic needs are met.

Some survivors of DA report sexual inhibition and reduction in libido. While this is elevated in those survivors who are also being sexually abused, other survivors may also experience sexual difficulties. This is in part due to not being able to reconcile the abuser who degrade and defiles, and the loving sexual partner. It is extremely difficult to trust the loving and affectionate aspects that the abuser may demonstrate during sex as the survivor lives in anticipatory fear and apprehension of future abuse. Loss of libido is further exacerbated by depression and lack of embodiment and concomitant reduction in sexual interest or desire.

LONG-TERM NEUROBIOLOGICAL EFFECTS

A consequence of prolonged and frequent activation of the stress response system results in it being locked into overdrive, creating a vicious cycle of escalating arousal and disruptions to psychobiological synchrony. Over time, disruptions to hippocampal and frontal cortex functioning lead to increased memory impairment, dissociation and compartmentalisation. In the absence of affect regulation, and to manage unbearable, turbulent feelings, the survivor may resort to dissociation and psychic numbing. The more the survivor dissociates the more she is able to block the abuse experience from memory, and the less she is able to integrate the experience. Lack of integration of trauma experiences account for many of the observed PTSD symptoms (see Chapter 6). It also prevents accurate appraisal of environmental cues such as danger, and impairs problem-solving capacities. A further long-term effect is impaired appraisal of internal arousal states which reduces capacity for affect regulation. Research demonstrates that PTSD and concomitant symptoms are most prevalent in survivors of DA (Golding 1999; Humphreys and Thiara 2003) and must be accurately assessed in order to provide appropriate therapeutic intervention.

Repeated activation of dissociation and dissociative states disrupts integrated functions of consciousness, memory, identity or perception which can be sudden, gradual, transient or chronic (American Psychiatric Association 2000). The most common dissociative disorders associated with survivors of DA are dissociative amnesia, dissociative fugue and depersonalisation disorder, all of which impact on disruptions to self-structures, identity and detachment from reality. Clinicians need to be aware that dissociative disorders have a high co-morbidity with other trauma induced disorders such as PTSD, acute stress disorder, self-harm, eating disorders and substance abuse. Given the co-morbidity with other symptoms seen in survivors of DA, clinicians must ensure that dissociative features are carefully assessed and appropriately managed.

LONG-TERM INTRAPERSONAL EFFECTS

A consequence of disruptions to the integration of self-structures is loss of identity and erosion of self-esteem. This is exacerbated by the abuser's persistent annihilation of the survivor's core identity and self-worth. Perpetrators of DA invariably denigrate and derogate their partners and impute negative identity on them as worthless, pathetic, inadequate and inherently flawed. Due to isolation, and the absence of contrary evidence from friends and family, the survivor has no choice but to absorb the imposed identity. As a result, the self-structures become identified with abuse, subjugation and dehumanisation.

As survivors are unable to express anger towards the abuser, the anger becomes internalised and used to attack the self, eroding any vestiges of self-esteem. Some survivors displace their anger and rage on to others such as children, family, friends or professionals, for fear of retaliation from the abuser. Some survivors are able to express their anger towards the abuser covertly, such as when in the presence of others, while others are more overt in expressing it directly to the abuser, despite the negative consequences. For many survivors anger is never expressed or let into conscious awareness (Dutton 1992), giving the impression that the abuse is forgotten or forgiven. Despite being blocked from conscious awareness, suppressed anger will be symbolised in somatic complaints such as chronic muscle tension, persistent headaches or stomach pains, difficulties in sleeping and chronic depression.

In the absence of being able to express anger and rage, some survivors become preoccupied or obsessed with morbid hatred towards the abuser. Commonly this is manifested in wishing the abuser dead, injuring or humiliating him, rather than retaliatory fantasises. Survivors of DA often report hoping that the abuser has an accident or fatal illness as the only way to end the abuse. Some survivors do permit themselves retaliatory fantasies in which they harm or kill the abuser, but rarely act upon them. In extreme cases some survivors do kill their abusers either in self-defence or because it is the only way to end the abuse (Dutton 1992; Motz 2000).

Loss of self-agency and lack of permission to express feelings or needs lead to dysthymia and chronic depression. Research indicates that depression and DA are highly correlated, with a mean prevalence rate of 47.6 per cent (Golding 1999; Lewinsohn 1975; Stark and Flitcraft 1996) in female survivors. It is critical that clinicians distinguish between PTSD symptoms and depression to ensure that appropriate interventions are made. Associated with depression are profound feelings of sadness and loss, leading to chronic grief reactions which need to be worked through (see Chapter 9). For some survivors, the only option to end the interminable pain is suicide. Stark and Flitcraft (1988) found that DA was the catalyst for one in four of all female suicide attempts, and one in two attempts among black women.

Stripped of personal control and lack of self-efficacy further corrodes self-worth, sense of inadequacy, and lovability. Over time the survivor begins to blame herself for the abuse as the abuser refuses to take responsibility for his actions. To avoid cognitive dissonance, the survivor incorporates self-blame and self-loathing into the self-structure as this is safer than risking further abuse by challenging the abuser (see Chapter 7). In self-blame the survivor experiences exaggerated feelings of responsibility for the abuse, and guilt for not managing it. Self-blame and guilt evokes increasingly more submissive and compliant behaviour to appease the abuser. Commensurate with this is a lack of empathy and compassion for self, instilling a lack of entitlement, or deserving better treatment.

Interpersonal trauma is also closely linked to shame (Mollon 2002b; Sanderson 2006) and feelings of subjugation, dehumanisation, defilement, disgust, humiliation and mortification, which lead to self-loathing and self-hatred (Dutton 1992; Ochberg 1988). Shame gives rise to a number of coping strategies to manage the conflict between a desire to express and need to suppress. Shame is associated with fear of expressing feelings and needs, thereby being vulnerable to more humiliation and abuse, or withdrawing and having to internalise, or dissociate from such needs. The excruciating humiliation experienced in shame propels survivors to withdraw from others and to conceal their turbulent internal world. A large proportion of energy is diverted into concealing shame through the repudiation of needs and feelings, especially feelings of neediness, vulnerability, weakness or inadequacy (see Chapter 7). This leads to extreme self-reliance and adoption of a facade of strength and invincibility that they can manage the abuse. This can put survivors in further danger as they may fail to truly acknowledge the risks to themselves.

The oppression of needs allows the survivor to tolerate the abuse and fuels an illusion of invulnerability. Shame is exacerbated by fear of stigmatisation through exposing the abuse. This reinforces the need to withdraw from others, and thereby strengthening the traumatic bond with the abuser. The more the survivor detaches from feelings and needs, the more affect regulation is disrupted. A further consequence is the disruption to resilience and reduction in coping strategies, leading to resignation.

Diminished socioeconomic status when leaving an abusive relationship further induces shame. When leaving an abusive relationship, survivors encounter numerous psychosocial losses, not least reduced financial resources, loss of home and previous lifestyle. Survivors may find themselves in straitened financial circumstances or lose employment opportunities, having to move from their neighbourhood and downsizing their accommodation. They may lose access to credit, private healthcare or education, and holidays, and experience change in social circumstances. This can lead to embarrassment and shame, which further isolates the survivor from former friends and social networks.

LONG-TERM INTERPERSONAL AND RELATIONAL EFFECTS

The betrayal of trust in DA disrupts relational dynamics and affiliative functions, which lead to a loss of trust in others, a fear of intimacy, and social isolation. Underpinning distortions in relational schemas is the specific nature of traumatic bonding which acts as 'superglue' to bond the abuser and survivor. In the presence of danger the natural impulse is to run to the person most close for comfort and soothing. In the case of DA this is the very person who is causing the fear. This creates monumental contradiction in the survivors, and cognitive dissonance. In this confusion the survivor becomes increasingly anxious and dependent on the abuser, while the abuser becomes more powerful and exerts even more control.

Paradoxically traumatic bonding creates emotional attachments that are far stronger, more intense, and much more difficult to sever due to the high intensity and arousal during the abuse, and the 'love bombing' during reconciliation, or honeymoon phase (see Chapter 3). The intermittent reinforcement through alternating intervals of lovingness and warmth act as a reward, while psychological or physical abuse acts as punishment keeps the survivor in a state of anxious anticipation, hoping that it will be all right eventually. The power of the abuser to preserve life evokes paradoxical gratitude or pathological transference (Ochberg 1988), in which the survivor is enthralled by the abuser and suffused with positive feelings of love, compassion and empathy. Survivors who have a history of abuse may be more vulnerable to traumatic bonding as their previous experience of abuse may exert a priming effect. When combined with dissociation in which anger and outrage are suppressed, each repeated abuse episodes become more tolerable as survivors shut down emotionally.

The lack of safety in their interpersonal realm precludes survivors from seeking comfort from others, and to fear intimacy. In such cases, the survivor's only option is to invest energy in practical tasks and skills, and seek stability in the safety of objects and things rather than people. Some survivors may continue to reach out for affiliation but might withdraw for fear of exposure and shame. A consequence of this is the vacillation between closeness and withdrawal.

Survivors often report that they have difficulty contemplating close relationships in the future as they fear intimacy and revictimisation. They also fear sexual difficulties as they are afraid of getting involved and being violated again. Some survivors consciously curb their sexual desires to avoid becoming involved, while others may seek brief sexual encounters which do not demand intimacy, which they believe will minimise future hurt. Some sexual acting may be associated with a sense of empowerment and freedom after years of coercive control.

Lack of trust may also play a role in fear of revictimisation by others such as family, friends and professionals. Clinicians need to be aware that survivors do at times experience revictimisation by professionals in the criminal justice system, or through insensitive treatment in the range of services they are dependent on such as social housing, health and mental health services, benefit agencies, as well as children's services. To minimise revictimisation, counsellors need to monitor and implement good practice models that are based on respect for the client's needs, without judging or pathologising the survivor.

Survivors with children may experience reduced capacity for healthy parenting and adequate nurturing and protection. When in survival mode, survivors may not always be able to be emotionally available to children, or protect them from the abuse, or the abuser (Calder *et al.* 2006; Hester *et al.* 2007). Most survivors are highly conscientious in shielding their children from the abuse but this is not always possible, due to the survivor's own psychological distress, depleted energy resources or self-medication. It is critical that counsellors assess the risk to children and implement statutory procedures. Professionals must remember however that invariably reduced capacity for parenting is the result of DA, not deliberate harm, and that with appropriate support and understanding from relevant agencies parenting skills can be restored.

LONG-TERM BEHAVIOURAL EFFECTS

Shame, fear of exposure and stigmatisation leads the survivor to withdraw from family, friends and social contact, which further reinforces isolation and alienation. The more isolated the survivor becomes the less she is able to reality test the appropriateness of her partner's behaviour, thereby increasing his power and control over the survivor. Withdrawal may also be necessary to avoid exposure of bruising and injury. Over time the social isolation can lead to agoraphobia and social phobia, further reinforcing the survivor's captivity.

In order to manage the abuse episodes, the survivor severely compromises her behaviour, becoming submissive and compliant in her interactions with the abuser. Invariably the survivor modulates her mood and modifies behaviour to what is expected of her, or what she knows pleases the abuser. The survivor becomes hypervigilant to her partner's mood and needs, and anticipates his every desire. This results in walking on eggshells at all times and never being able to relax. This may extend to children, who are instructed to be on their best behaviour, not challenge the abuser, and comply with his demands, no matter how bizarre, without question. Survivors often report that they visibly change their whole demeanour and become unrecognisable. One survivor ended up with two entirely separate set of clothes, those approved by her partner and those that she wore when he was not present. In addition she would change her jewellery, make-up and body language to what would please her partner.

In order to experience a semblance of control, some survivors resort to obsessive compulsive behaviours, especially obsessive cleaning and tidying. This has the added benefit in proving to herself and her partner that she is capable of being able to function efficiently in at least one area of her life. Some survivors resort to compulsive 'busyness', constant distractions and workaholism (Dutton 1992). To numb feelings and avoid emotional pain, some survivors indulge in other ritualistic and addictive behaviours such as compulsive binge eating, shopping, spending or gambling.

A further long-term effect is impaired functioning in a number of other dimensions such as occupational, social and parental. This may lead to loss of employment, reduced social contact, and impoverished parenting. These in turn impact on the survivor's sense of self-esteem, self-confidence and self-agency. Over time the survivor feels increasingly trapped, with no means of escape. This induces learned helplessness (Seligman 1975; Walker 1984) not predicated on passivity as originally proposed by Seligman (1975) but rather a resignation in which the survivor develops a range of coping strategies to manage the abuse and protect herself and her children (Blackman 1989). These involve compliance, appeasement, anticipating the abuser's every whim and need, and keeping the children quiet. These are active strategies that aid survival and should not be misinterpreted by clinicians as passive victim-like behaviours, or traditional conceptualisations of learned helplessness. The learned helplessness is more about the futility in resisting the abuse, and as such represents a freezing response, because this may be the best form of protection during attack. It does not accurately encompass the consistent endeavours to minimise or avoid abuse episodes, and implement protective strategies.

LONG-TERM COGNITIVE EFFECTS

Prolonged coercive control leads to shifts in cognitive schemas especially in tolerance of cognitive inconsistency, diminished perception of alternatives, and the development of continuum of tolerance, or 'survivability' (Blackman 1989; Dutton 1992). A common long-term effect in DA is the shattering of assumptions, especially around positive self-perception. In addition assumptions around the world as a safe, meaningful place are shattered in DA, along with the belief in the beneficence of others (Blackman 1989; Goldberg 1982; Janoff-Bulman 1985, 1992; McCann and Pearlman 1990).

The perpetrator's coercive control and distorted beliefs around his behaviour serve to distort the survivor's perceptions of self and reality. This is not just around perceptions of self but also family and friends, because the abuser drives a wedge between any potentially supportive relationships to enhance his power over the survivor. In the absence of reality testing the survivor has no option but to accommodate the abuser's distortions into her own cognitive schemas.

Distorted cognitive schemas about self and distortion of reality activates attributional errors. Miller and Porter (1993) propose that negative beliefs about self lead to the attribution of self-blame on three levels: blame for causing the abuse, self-blame for not being able to stop the abuse or change the abuser's behaviour, and self-blame at not being able to tolerate or manage the violence. Distorted perceptions about self also reduce the capacity for the survivor to trust her own perception and judgement. In combination, self-blame and guilt result in lack of self-compassion and inability to comfort or nurture herself.

Intense arousal, anxiety and fear impairs concentration and impairs cognitive capacity to problem solve and make decisions. This is exacerbated by reduction in concentration and focus, further rendering the survivor into a sense of resignation and hopelessness. Reduced cognitive processing also disrupts reflective functioning, or mentalisation, so that feelings and experiences cannot be processed in a meaningful way (Fonagy *et al.* 2002). Unprocessed and chaotic feeling increase confusion and reinforce lack of internal control as they spiral into turbulent emotions that cannot be released. Over time the survivor begins to be become increasingly resigned to her circumstances and the abuse, with no means of escape. This evokes an extreme sense of futility about her circumstances and a sense of hopelessness about the future.

The counsellor's role

Counsellors require a good knowledge of the range of long-term effects and ensure that they are interpreted as symptoms of trauma and abuse rather than individual pathology. Traditional views of passivity, 'learned helplessness' and masochism are no longer creditable conceptualisations of survivors of DA. Counsellors must relinquish quests into diagnosing personality disturbances, or survivor pathology, and focus attention on understanding manifest symptoms as trauma responses, and address them appropriately. In respecting the survivor's endeavours to manage the abuse with whatever available survival strategies, the counsellor can provide a non-judgemental environment in which the survivor feels validated. This will enable the survivor to begin to validate herself and begin the process of rebuilding trust in self.

Summary

- The nature of DA is a powerful traumatogen which can result in permanent changes in an individual's view of self, other and world, and give rise to a range of trauma symptoms. The characteristic symptoms and behaviours observed in survivors of DA must be seen by mental health professionals as survival behaviours and normal responses to trauma, not as individual pathology.

- The psychobiological impact of DA disrupts functioning on a variety of dimensions. There is considerable evidence that a large percentage of survivors of DA experience PTSD and post-traumatic reactions which can severely impair physiological, neurobiological and cognitive functioning.

- The immediate impact of DA is lack of external and internal safety, and physical injury. Physical injuries may have been incurred in the most recent episode of abuse, or be the result of restimulation of accumulated injuries, scar tissue or recurring injuries that have not healed properly.

- Terror and fear elicit a range of somatic responses including muscle tension, headaches, stomach complaints, nausea and a range of stress-induced physiological symptoms.

- DA also impacts on the neurobiological mediated stress response system, which can lead to disruption in psychobiological synchrony and disorganisation to mental states, including dissociation and lack of integration. This elicits PTSD symptoms which induce hyperarousal, hyper-reactivity, intrusion symptoms, avoidance responses such as psychic numbing, which impact on affect regulation and disruption to self-structures. These disruptions to self-structures lead to disconnection from self and others, as well as changes in self-identity, self-esteem and self-efficacy.

- The impact of DA also affects cognitive schemas and processing, especially in the ability to tolerate cognitive inconsistency, diminished perception of alternatives, and development of continuum of tolerance. The abuser's persistent negative appraisal of the survivor leads to cognitive distortions about self and others. The confusion in DA leads to lack of meaning and understanding of the experience. This impairs memory and development of a coherent narrative. It also prevents focus, self-reflection and mentalisation, leading to alexithymia.

- The long-term effects are an amplification of the immediate impact of DA, which because they are not processed accumulate over time and become chronic. These effects can create deeply entrenched changes to physical health, including self-harm, substance dependency and suicidality, as well as structural changes in neurobiological functioning.

- There are considerable long-term effects on intrapersonal and interpersonal functioning, in which the survivor disconnects from self and others, and withdraws. Shame, lack of self-esteem and self-worth serve to fuel the oppression of feelings and repudiation of needs, which strengthens the survivor's bond to the partner.

- The distorted relational dynamics characteristic of traumatic bonding make the survivor more fearful of being in relationship to others, further entrenching avoidance and social withdrawal. This isolation prevents reality checking and activation of survival strategies that lead to submission, compliance and appeasement behaviour.

- Over time, long-term cognitive effects such as impaired problem solving and decision making lock survivors into hopelessness that they will ever escape the abuse. This loss of hope evokes resignation and total acceptance of the abuse.

- Counsellors need to interpret the impact and long-term effects as reactions and responses to trauma and not as indicative of psychological disturbance or individual pathology. They need to respect survivors' responses to trauma and validate their survival strategies, rather than judge them. This will restores self-esteem and self-efficacy to the survivor, from which he or she can rebuild trust in self and others.

CHAPTER 3

UNDERSTANDING SURVIVORS OF DOMESTIC ABUSE

The experience of domestic abuse (DA), and concomitant trauma, engenders a permanent change in an individual's sense of self, relationship with others, and sense of security in the world. Prolonged coercive control leads to the formation of powerful attachment bonds in which the survivor and abuser become completely enmeshed. The abuser's aim is to dominate and control all aspects of the survivor's life, including her perception of reality. In effect the abuser co-opts the survivor into a folie à deux in which the survivor's self-identity and capacity for autonomous thought or action are severely curtailed. As DA is conducted under conditions of isolation, the survivor has no opportunity to ratify or evaluate her experiences outside of the abuser's distortions.

The accompanying fear and terror in DA result in psychobiological changes which deplete inner resources and resilience to abuse. To restore self-identity, autonomy and inner resources, the counsellor needs a comprehensive understanding of the survivor's responses to DA. To facilitate this, the counsellor needs to be aware of the pernicious dynamics of coercive control and how these corrode the survivor's sense of self and self-efficacy. Understanding abuse dynamics enables the counsellor to recognise how this impacts on the survivor's functioning. Many of the observed dynamics are as a consequence of intermittent reinforcement of reward and punishment seen in the cycle of abuse, which leads to trauma bonds of such tensile strength that are highly resistant to challenge or change. Counsellors need to have an understanding of both the survivor's and abuser's dynamics in DA in order to assess the specific therapeutic needs of each individual survivor.

The aim of this chapter is to enhance the counsellor's understanding of the survivor's reactions and responses to DA. To facilitate this, counsellors need to recognise the dynamics of coercive control and abuse, and how this impacts on the survivor, so as to avoid pathologising the survivor. It is also helpful to have an awareness of the abuser's dynamics to enable the survivor to re-evaluate the abuser's motives and motivations rather than colluding with self-blame. A full understanding of the three-stage cycle of abuse and traumatic bonding will also help the counsellor and survivor to appreciate how the survivor comes to be in thrall to the abuser, and feels trapped in the relationship. With this knowledge, counsellors will gain a better understanding of both the internal and external obstacles to leaving. Finally, the chapter will consider the role of the counsellor in understanding the survivor through validation, respect and thorough knowledge of DA dynamics.

Dynamics of coercive control

DA rarely starts as an act of verbal or physical abuse. Before any abuse can take place the abuser has to target and capture his victim. To do this the abuser needs to entice, ensnare and entrap the victim, in order to enslave her. This is usually achieved through the use of charm and highly solicitous behaviour during the initial courtship. Abusers seduce their victims through seduction and 'love bombing' (Halperin 1983). 'Love bombing' is a technique used by cults to recruit members in which they lavish praise, love and understanding on individuals, to lure them into the cult.

Perpetrators of DA use 'love bombing' in a similar way by focusing their full and seemingly inexhaustible attention onto the survivor. The abuser lavishes the partner with praise, affection, grand declarations of love and demonstrations of devotion. Survivors commonly report that initially the abuser is highly solicitous with prescient awareness of inner needs and desires without the survivor needing to articulate them. Generally, the abuser goes to enormous lengths to satisfy these unexpressed needs, which the survivor finds extremely flattering and fulfilling. So much so that survivors often see the abuser as a knight in shining armour, or a rescuer.

'Love bombing' is an especially potent, seductive technique if the survivor has a history of abuse or previously unmet needs. Some perpetrators of DA seem to intuit when prospective partners are emotionally impoverished or malnourished, or who fear abandonment, and deliberately target them as it makes the enticement easier. This process is not dissimilar to paedophiles, who target and groom vulnerable children to minimise the risk of detection.

Another powerful dynamic in ensnaring the victim is the abuser's inordinate interest in every aspect of the survivor's life. This is interpreted by the survivor as a demonstration of loving attention rather than control. Accompanying this is pathological jealousy, which masquerades as love and devotion. In reality this represents the abuser's dependency needs, profound insecurity and terror of abandonment. Gradually the attentive interest is replaced by more and more control in which the abuser scrutinises every aspect of the survivor's life. The abuser needs to know her every action, feeling and thought, as well as what she eats, how she sleeps, what she reads and what she wears. By the time attentive interest transforms into control, the survivor is so enthralled and entranced, that it is virtually impossible to relinquish the attachment. This is especially the case with female survivors, who are socialised to be responsible for sustaining relationships and making them work.

Once the survivor has become entrapped, the abuser starts the process of enslavement. Below the masquerade of love and desire, the abuser displays jealousy of any period of time that the survivor spends away from him, and begins the process of isolation. Initially this isolation is misinterpreted by the survivor as the abuser wanting to spend every waking hour with her, and a clear message of his dependency on her. To please and placate her partner, the survivor begins to reduce contact with family and friends, not realising that this increases the abuser's power and omnipotence over her. Moreover, social isolation from others increases the survivor's dependency on the abuser, and makes her more susceptible to his distorted perceptions, and seeing the world through his eyes.

Once the survivor has submitted to this, the abuser will test her submission and compliance by striking out, either verbally or physically, to assess the survivor's reaction and response. After the first abuse episode, the abuser will express profound feelings of remorse and regret, claiming no knowledge of how this came about and making promises and heartfelt assurances that it will never happen again. While these assertions may be genuine, it is impossible for the abuser to enact and sustain such assurances. The survivor wants to believe him and gives him the benefit of the doubt, doesn't share the experience with anyone and relegates it to a one-off incident. Over time, these abuse episodes recur and the cycle of abuse is activated (see below), leading to the entanglement of love and abuse, and development of traumatic bonding. The abuse does not necessarily consist of physical violence as the abuser uses other methods of coercive control, in which threats of violence, rather than actual physical assault, serve to ensure the survivor's continued submission. Many of the coercive methods of control resemble techniques used with political prisoners such as sleep deprivation, control of food and bodily needs, thought control, isolation, terror and threat of torture. The abuser instils fear through subtle control and 'inconsistent, unpredictable outbursts of violence and by capricious enforcement of petty rules' (Herman 1992a, p.98). In the absence of brute force the abuser resorts to the use of sly, underhand and undermining behaviour, including indifference and dismissal. Accompanying this is the juxtaposition of unpredictable gestures of love and affection, and verbal assaults.

The intermittent reinforcement of reward and punishment characteristic of the abuse cycle serves to enforce the survivor's dependency on the abuser and ensures her subjugation and submission. The persistent intimidation ensures that the survivor is in a state of constant fear which minimises the use of violence, other than as intermittent reminders of the abuser's power. In contrast the loving behaviour restores hope and belief in the positive aspects of the abuser and the viability of the relationship. Paradoxically, being nice is a more potent reinforcer than unremitting abuse. If DA consisted of unrelenting abuse with no conciliation, the survivor would not experience confusion, ambivalence and uncertainty and would find it easier to identify the abuse. This is why refusal to accept rewards and loving behaviour is one way for the survivor to reassert power and control, and reduce ambivalence. It is precisely the vacillation between reward and punishment, love and abuse that strengthens the emotional attachment that underpins traumatic bonding and the dynamics of abuse.

Understanding the dynamics of abuse

Once coercive control is fully established, the abuser can master every aspect of the survivor's life, while obfuscating his dependency needs. The enmeshment between abuser and survivor leads to the moulding of the survivor's identity in which the abuser relinquishes all responsibility for the abuse by projecting this onto the survivor. As the survivor absorbs all the blame for the abuse, she fails to recognise how much the abuser needs the victim to feel powerful and omnipotent. Instead the denigration of her as weak, pathetic, evil or crazy is incorporated into survivor's self-image, permitting her to idealise the abuser.

The survivor cannot see herself as separate from the abuser, and adapts to the abuse environment from which she cannot escape and with which she is familiar. This may become so normal that the survivor believes she cannot survive without being abused or attached to the abuser. In order to manage the abuse, the survivor retreats into psychological and emotional escape through dissociation, which allows her to survive each episode of abuse. By dissociating, the survivor is unable to retain any feelings, including anger at the abuse and abuser, and appears to be unaffected because all emotions are suppressed. Dissociation numbs the individual and renders the abuse bearable, resulting in a splitting of emotions and cognition that allows some parts of the individual to be protected, commonly the vulnerable 'feeling' parts, but leaves some cognitive functioning in order that the survivor can get through the periods between episodes of DA. Trauma and dissociation lead to the development of a self-structure that is defined by abuse and an inability to resist coercive violations due to the lack of a safe system to resist. The lack of safety and betrayal of basic affinitive functions compels the survivor to rely on practical strategies in order to deal with and accept the abuse. By retreating into the safety of cognitive functions such as intellectualisation and rationalisation, and adopting behavioural strategies of compliance and appeasement, the survivor is able to ensure her survival.

Dissociation permits the survivor to suppress thoughts and feelings and acts as a powerful defence against two contradictory propositions. To manage this dissonance, the survivor has to engage in what Orwell (1990) called 'doublethink' in which the individual has to hold two opposing beliefs in mind simultaneously, while accepting both of them. This requires considerable cognitive shifts which have the capacity to distort reality. Emotional suppression also aids survival in reducing extreme anger towards the abuser, and turning this against the self.

A consequence of abuse dynamics is alterations in the survivor's identity, body image, internalised images of others, and erosion of values and ideals. Survivors often describe being 'broken' by the abuse. These consequences are often still manifest even after leaving, as survivors find it hard to assume their former identity. The memory of their enslaved self, betrayal by the abuser and loss of personal integrity can lead to self-loathing and dehumanisation. To complete the subjugation the survivor directs anger at the self, relinquishes hope, succumbs to depression and suicidal ideation. It is at this point that the betrayal by the abuser threatens to break the survivor's spirit. The more broken the survivor becomes, the more the abuser feels omnipotent. To sustain this illusion of omnipotence, in which the abuser's feelings of inadequacy and helplessness are temporarily assuaged, the defence of projective identification is evoked. In projective identification individuals attempt to rid themselves of unacceptable impulses or feelings by denying them in oneself and identifying them in another (Klein 1946). In this interactive process individuals evacuate unwanted parts of themselves onto the partner, and derives gratification in seeing these projections absorbed by the partner, so that they can be despised and condemned.

Projective identification is frequently used by individuals who cannot tolerate the coexistence of both good and bad aspects of the self. The recipient of projective identification becomes a sponge that absorbs the projection and experiences the bad aspects, rendering them helpless, vulnerable and weak, and feeling useless. As they soak up the abuser's feelings of inadequacy and self-contempt, self-esteem is eroded and any vestige of control is relinquished. The more the survivor absorbs the abuser's distorted perception, the more she loses contact with her own feelings, becoming increasingly depressed and submissive. The denial of her own feelings and rage permits the survivor to tolerate and normalise the abuser's violence, cruelty and intimidation. This gives rise to a complex interaction between the two partners where they oscillate between murderous rage or complete vulnerability and the risk of unbearable abandonment. The consequent polarisation allows both partners to deny feared aspect of themselves (Motz 2000).

Counsellors need to ensure that they fully understand these complex unconscious dynamics and understand these as a by-product of the abuse relationship, not the survivor's personality disturbance or pathology. To avoid victim blaming, counsellors need to sensitively explore the full range of the survivor's fears and feelings, including those that have been split off and projected onto the abuser, so that they can be integrated. This will enable the survivor to have greater awareness of how split-off feelings can be projected which will inoculate her to future projections and minimise her own projections. Exploring these unconscious dynamics increases understanding and restores control, which reduces vulnerability to revictimisation in the future. Counsellors often fear exploring the role of the survivor in the abuse dynamics, not realising that in doing so they reinforce the survivor's passivity. The purpose of sensitive exploration of how the survivor is drawn into these powerful dynamics, and how their unconscious fears are acted out, is not to denigrate her, but to provide explication. It is this knowledge that will truly empower her in future relationships rather than merely rendering her a passive victim. Counsellors need to enable survivors to re-evaluate their understanding of love, and to avoid misinterpreting profound attachment or strong intense emotion. High emotional intensity is not an indicator for intimacy, or love, but could be an indicator of fear and danger.

Understanding survivor dynamics

There are a number of vulnerability factors associated with survivors of DA which counsellors need to be aware of. However, counsellors must contextualise these rather than see them as personality disturbance, or pathology. Commonly these factors are nascent and fully emerge as a consequence of the abuse. Survivors who have a history of childhood abuse or attachment deficits may be more vulnerable in asserting themselves in an abuse relationship as primitive relational templates, or attachment style is activated. This is not to say that they choose to be abused, but rather they may have difficulties in asserting themselves, setting boundaries and are susceptible to defence mechanisms such as dissociation, psychic numbing, denial and emotional suppression which allow for the development of continuum of tolerance for abuse.

Survivors who have a history of abuse are often out of contact with their needs and unable to express, or ask for them to be met. This prevents them from making accurate appraisals of appropriate behaviour and allows them to normalise their partner's abuse. If they have poorly developed self-structures that are suffused with shame and guilt, they are more liable to absorb the negative projections from the abuser, leading to abuse identification. Unprocessed and unintegrated previous victimisation also makes survivors vulnerable to the cognitive distortions and distorted reality of the abuser. In effect such survivors may have self-preservation deficits which need to be restored through restoring or building self-esteem and self-worth. Counsellors need to assess the resilience of survivors, and to what degree this can be restored, or built from scratch as this will impact on the nature of the therapeutic focus (see Chapter 4).

Counsellors must also assess the nature of the survivor's attachment to the abuser. There has been considerable research on the association between adult attachment style and DA (Bartholomew 1990; Dutton 2007). This research indicates that both the survivor and the abuser are most likely to present with an anxious ambivalent style (Ainsworth *et al.* 1978; Shaver, Hazan and Bradshaw 1988). Female survivors are most likely to fall into the subcategory of fearful/ambivalent, while male abusers are most frequently represented in the subcategory of fearful/ambivalent, preoccupied/anxious and dismissive (Dutton 2007). One of the most powerful predictors of DA is a combined attachment style (Bond and Bond 2004) of fearful/ambivalent female survivors and dismissive male abusers. While clinicians need to be wary of interpreting these findings as the primary causal link for DA, rather than the consequence of abuse, it is helpful to have an indication of the survivor's attachment style, as this can manifest in the therapeutic relationship.

Counsellors need to recognise that the therapeutic relationship is influenced by both the attachment style of the client as well as the counsellor. Critically, clinicians need to have a degree of awareness of their own attachment style and how this will interact with the survivor. Pistole and Tarrant (1993, p.168) argue that when working with survivors of DA, counsellors need to adopt a 'care giving attachment conceptualisation of the therapeutic relationship' in which they provide two complementary bonding systems: attachment and care giving. The provision of these enhances the therapeutic relationship characterised by empathically and sensitively attuned responses, allows the survivor to connect to self and others.

Some survivors adopt a maternal role towards the abuser by indulging and excusing his behaviour, and becoming the longed-for ideal mother that the abuser yearns for. This has the advantage that in infantilising the abuser, the survivor can make him more manageable, and experience some semblance of power and control. Alternatively some survivors' attachment to their abuser is fuelled by anger, not necessarily love. This is most common in prolonged and protracted DA, in which love has been eroded and replaced by anger. Some survivors intuitively recognise how dependent the abuser is on them as a victim, and gain a semblance of control in the relationship by refusing to fully surrender, and seeing the abuser as weak and insecure. This shores up their self-esteem, along with a sense of pride that they can endure the abuse without capitulating. Survivors may derive a sense of satisfaction from this because it reinforces their sense of invulnerability and invincibility.

In the case of survivors who have a history of abuse, the DA experience may unleash uncontrollable behavioural re-enactments which replay developmental devastating experiences. These unconscious efforts at mastery, or repetition compulsions, are a way of working through early trauma that has not been integrated or resolved. Van der Kolk (1987) proposes that repetition compulsion takes a different form in males and females whereby 'Abused men and boys tend to identify with the aggressor and later victimise others, whereas abused women are prone to become attached to abusive men and allow them and their offspring to be victimised in the future' (Van der Kolk 1987, p.17). While acknowledging this proposition, counsellors must be scrupulous in not blaming the survivor for the abuse, but rather see it as a susceptibility to revictimisation that is more likely to engender traumatic bonding, and make it significantly harder to extricate themselves from the abusive relationship.

Perpetrators play on the survivor's previous history of abuse in the pernicious erosion of identity and meagre self-esteem by constantly reminding the survivor of past abuses. This prevents any acknowledgement of growth and change, and keeps the survivor locked into an abuse identity. It serves to reinforce shame and lack of self-worth, that despite the survivor's achievements in surviving the early abuse, she is still a victim and does not deserve better treatment. Previous abuse history and victimisation can also be used by the abuser to manipulate professionals by imputing putative mental health problems and doubts about parental fitness.

Domestic captivity depletes the survivor's sense of competency, initiative and autonomy which leads to guilt, inferiority and profound sense of failure. This is especially in female survivors who are socialised to take responsibility for the success of their relationships and to preserve their partner's emotional world. When the relationship fails to function or fragments, self-blame, guilt and shame ensues. This serves the pernicious erosion of self-identity and pride in valued roles such as being a good partner.

Understanding abuser dynamics

Along with exploration of the survivor's dynamics, an understanding of the abuser's dynamics can empower the survivor to make more accurate appraisals and attributions of responsibility and accountability. Research into adult attachment style of perpetrators indicates that they present with insecure ambivalent attachment style usually in the subcategory of fearful/ambivalent and preoccupied/anxious and dismissive (Dutton 2007). A characteristic of the preoccupied/anxious style is pathological jealousy which is highly associated with DA, regardless of gender of abuser (Henderson *et al.* 1997). Such insecure attachment style gives rise to overwhelming fear of abandonment and loss, and it is this fear that leads to anger and violence. Thus, the palpable 'anger is born of fear' (Bowlby 1973, pp.287–288) and the violence is a further defence against that fear. Dutton (2007) argues that the 'anger proneness' seen in the fearful/ambivalent style may necessitate a change in terminology in relation to domestic abusers from 'fearful attached' to an 'angrily attached'. The fear of abandonment that gives rise to anger and violence provides a plausible account for why survivors are most at risk from 'abandonment homicide' when leaving the relationship.

Fonagy *et al.* (2003) also found a connection between disorganised attachment style and borderline personality disorder (BPD) and borderline personality organisation (BPO) in male abusers. This has been supported by other researchers who have found a link between BPO and interpersonal abuse (Dutton 2007; Gunderson 1984; Millon 1977; Rothschild 2003). While BPD and BPO have historically been associated with females, researchers argue that it has been undetected and undiagnosed in males (Dutton 2007; Rothschild 2003) because females tend to end up in the clinical population whereas males tend to end up in the criminal justice system. In the light of this research it may be necessary to re-evaluate diagnosis of BPD and BPO across both genders.

There are a number of powerful factors found in male perpetrators of DA that could certainly indicate BPO. Commonly perpetrators of DA experience themselves as helpless and humiliated in relation to their partner, who they perceive as omnipotent and omniscient, rendering him highly dependent on his victim. In essence, the abuser sees himself through the survivor's eyes and his sense of manhood and power is derived from her devotion to and fear of him. Abusers may appear confident, self-assured and in charge of their life, but this is a facade which belies a deep-rooted, gnawing sense of inferiority and labile sense of self-worth, significance and status. Abusers commonly feel incomplete and unlovable, and are suffused with terror that a confident partner will abandon or reject them. To ensure circumventing this, the abuser needs to weaken and control the partner through intimidation, erosion of self-worth and curtailment of independent thinking. To effect this, the 'abusive partner sups grandly on his mate's feelings of self-esteem, competence and dignity in order to augment his own uncertain sense of efficacy, mastery and control' (Scarf 2005, p.70).

Research shows (Curran 1996; Dutton 2007; Stosny 1995) that the majority of male perpetrators of DA are narcissistically vulnerable and constantly struggle with acute feelings of weakness, dependency and negative self-image. Many are suffused with feelings of self-loathing, self-doubt, insecurity around perceived masculinity, and fears of further harm to already damaged and brittle ego. Curran (1996) proposes that 'pathologically dominant, abusive and dominant men are those who feel deeply unsure about whether they are good enough, strong enough, forceful enough, self-sufficient enough, independent enough – whether they are *real* men' (Scarf 2005, p.71). As these negative feelings threaten to engulf the abuser, rendering him even more vulnerable, primitive psychological defence mechanisms, especially denial and projection, are activated.

Denying all weakness, ineptitude, insecurity and vulnerability in self enables the abuser to project these intolerable aspects onto someone else, usually their intimate partner. In this projection, the abuser relinquishes ownership of these threatening feelings and thoughts, and comes to believe that they exist within the partner. In evacuating pervasive feelings of powerlessness, deficiency and suppressed self-loathing, the abuser cleanses himself, while the survivor becomes the psychic container for all the abuser's disavowed and unacceptable attributes and feelings. As the survivor is co-opted into holding and carrying these, she is forced to take ownership of them. This allows the abuser to see the survivor as weak, vulnerable and loathsome and permits him to attack her for flaws and inadequacies. The more the survivor absorbs the abuser's disowned attributes, the more she becomes an object of disdain and loathing. In the words of Stosny (1995, p.x): 'Attachment abusers…blame the mirror for its reflection'.

Primitive defences such as denial and projection prevent the abuser from any level of honest introspection, self-appraisal or objectivity, rendering his inner world incomprehensible and minimising any capacity for insight or understanding. In disavowing his vulnerability he cannot access feelings of compassion or empathy either for himself, or his partner. This permits the continued derogation and subjugation of the survivor until she surrenders. Repeated emotional or physical assaults serve to fragment and devitalise the survivor, increasing her sense of helplessness. Criticisms and denouncements become a way of taunting and inflaming the partner to strike out so that the abuser feels justified in unleashing and discharging noxious feelings to defuse his own internal pressure. The survivor, oblivious to the abuser's intense self-condemnation and intolerable internal pressure, cannot understand the antecedents of the assault and assumes responsibility for the assault.

For some male perpetrators of DA, the female partner represents a powerful persecutory mother figure, whose separateness is a constant reminder that she may abandon him at any time. The abuser perceives his partner as a mirror image of a withholding, uncaring or rejecting mother and projects this onto his partner, rendering him hypersensitive to any perceived rejection or abandonment. Any perceived loss replicates earlier experiences of abandonment unleashing primitive rage which is displaced onto the survivor. Male perpetrators of DA often describe their partner as the 'ideal woman' whom he 'worships'. In reality, they desperately fear her, and are terrified of losing her through abandonment or rejection. The sustained physical and emotional abuse and intimidation enables him to feel that he is in control, enhancing his self-esteem, while providing a temporary sense of self-efficacy and power.

The terror of abandonment and betrayal compels the abuser to bind the partner to him through coercive control, intimidation and fear. Some survivors intuit their partner's fear of abandonment and endeavour to compensate for this by being extraordinarily tolerant of the abusive behaviour to prove their devotion and commitment, and make up for any early deprivation. Yet, no matter how much loyalty and devotion the survivor bestows on the abuser, his fears cannot be assuaged. The persistent need for proof of lovability and commitment gives rise to pathological jealousy. While jealousy often masquerades as love, in reality it is a direct representation of insecurity and need to control.

A proportion of perpetrators of DA will have been exposed to domestic violence in childhood and have learned that it is acceptable for males to control, dominate and abuse females. Exposure to parental violence in childhood also transmits powerful messages around conflict resolution and the use of coercive control as a way of avoiding conflict and emotional involvement. Counsellors need to be aware that the palpable aggression in DA is not to destroy the survivor but to preserve her in order to control and hurt her, to ensure that she does not leave. The survivor needs to be kept alive to act as a vessel in which to evacuate his self-contempt, and intolerable feelings of vulnerability and helplessness. While the abuser needs a living recipient of his cruelty and torture, counsellors and survivor must be cognisant that in extreme rage, and when under threat, he is capable of killing her.

Understanding the three-stage cycle of violence

Although initially applied by Walker (1979) to physical assault and battered women, the three-stage cycle of violence can equally be applied to verbal assault and emotional abuse. Victims who have experienced physical, verbal and emotional abuse state unequivocally that the emotional and verbal abuse is most hurtful, and has the more damaging long-term effects (Abrahams 2007; Dutton 1992). Often this is due to the fact that it is more subtle, erratic and unpredictable. Abusers commonly intersperse verbal and emotional abuse with bouts of violence. Through coercive control, survivors are already terrified and violence may be used intermittently, whereas the emotional and verbal assaults are used more frequently. Critically, the length and duration of this cycle varies from couple to couple and a single progression can take place over a period of days, weeks, months, or even years.

STAGE 1: THE TENSION-BUILDING PHASE

This first stage is characterised by a slow, simmering increase in tension and resentment in the dominant partner. The abuser becomes more oppressive, rigid, authoritarian and controlling. As he cannot or will not communicate or talk about what is going on, he becomes edgy or defensive when asked. Invariably, any solicitous questions posed by the survivor are perceived by the abuser as provocation which can activate the cycle. The abuser cuts off and shuts the partner out in which the partner may feel abandoned, rejected, fearful and agitated, evoking internal distress. The survivor enters a state of hyperarousal and hypervigilance, while the abuser's simmering tumultuous feelings amplify to a point in which they can no longer be contained. A trivial precipitant such as a solicitous enquiry, comment, oversight or failure to read his mind, an external rebuff not related to the partner, or an upsurge of internal self-criticism ignites the smouldering fuse. The abuser interprets this as an attack or deliberate provocation by the survivor in failing to meet his insatiable yet unexpressed needs.

   This unleashes a projective interaction in which the abuser subtly cues, goads or pressures the partner into feeling and behaving in ways that are congruent with his fantasies about the partner being withholding, nagging, untrustworthy and by definition 'all bad'. This allows the abuser to remain 'all good', highly moral, dependable and honourable, who is always let down by the partner. Significantly, as assaults are rarely initiated by a real conflict in the couple's relationship, it is the abuser's intolerable internal state which predominates. The abuser is filled with self-directed negativity and self-loathing to which no coherent or intelligible thoughts are attached. As this subliminal self-condemnation is outside conscious awareness, the abuser is unable to deal with the torrent of noxious sensations. This escalating and ever-amplifying internal pressure bursts forth as onslaught onto partner who often has no idea what is happening. Finally the abuser explodes into a chaotic, out-of-control, enraged attack upon what he perceives as an uncaring, or insufficiently 'respectful' subservient partner.

STAGE 2: THE ASSAULT OR PHYSICAL ATTACK PHASE

During this phase the perpetrator expunges the tension through indiscriminate verbal or physical assault. In the case of verbal and emotional abuse, this usually consists of inane, frenzied and insoluble argument to siphon off the abuser's inner turmoil. Such arguments serve an unconscious purpose to divert attention away from the abuser's inner barrage of harsh, self-criticism and overwhelming anxieties. Eventually as the abuser's fury is spent, his inner turmoil subsides and he 'comes to his senses'. In stark contrast, the survivor is now overwhelmed, distressed and full of the inner turmoil that belonged to the abuser. Seeing his partner's distress serves to pacify the abuser, as she has absorbed all the torment. As the survivor is flooded with fear and terror, the need to protect herself emerges, and she begins to withdraw emotionally. This withdrawal evokes terror of abandonment in the abuser and becomes the cue for him to seduce the partner back again, and activate the third phase of the cycle.

STAGE 3: THE RECONCILIATION OR 'HONEYMOON' PHASE

During the reconciliation or 'honeymoon' phase, the abuser is filled with remorse, regret and repentance. To demonstrate this, the abuser becomes complimentary and conciliatory and tries to win back the partner, by courting and pursuing her. Commonly, abuser bombards partner with profuse apologies and heartfelt promises that it will never happen again. This may be accompanied with gifts of flowers, jewellery, special treats or holidays. Slowly an atmosphere of calm and relative tranquillity ensues. Gradually the survivor feels bodily and psychological relief which is rewarding in itself. As she begins to believe the *good* part of the relationship has returned, hope is restored.

Crucially antecedents to and the abuse are not discussed so as not to undermine the calm and tranquillity, or more relaxed atmosphere, and consequently nothing is ever confronted or resolved. As issues are not addressed but suppressed, they are reinvoked when the cycle begins again. As the relationship continues, the severity of the abuse escalates while the reconciliation phase diminishes, or in some cases it disappears completely.

Some clinicians have employed a vampyric metaphor to understand the dynamics of DA in which abusers suck all the life, energy and beauty out of those they say they love, leaving an empty husk (Hirigoyen 2004). Just as vampires need to feed regularly, the abuse cycle is constantly repeated. Survivors often restore life energy and vitality during the reconciliation phase through their hope and belief in the relationship, only for the vampire to feed again on the survivor's life blood (Hirigoyen 2004). In this ongoing cycle the survivor has to replenish inner resources only for the abuser to gorge and devour. Over time the survivor finds it harder and harder to replenish ever-decreasing inner resources and surrenders to the abuser's feeding frenzy. The less she has to feed on, the more frequently the abuser needs to gorge, which explains the escalating nature of the abuse and violence.

Understanding traumatic bonding

Traumatic bonding or domestic Stockholm syndrome (DSS) is 'an automatic, often unconscious, emotional response to the trauma of becoming a victim' (Dutton and Painter 1981). It is commonly activated during a very high level of life-threatening stress or terror which activates biologically mediated survival instincts of dependency. In the presence of extreme danger where a captor holds the power of life and death, the captive must deny any feelings of anger and outrage to avoid risk of death, and come to depend on the captor. This helplessness and powerlessness recapitulates the dependency of early infancy in which survival is solely dependent on the primary care giver. In DA, the abuser embodies both the threat to life as well as the bequeather of life. To ensure survival the captive must deny the negative attributes of the captor and focus on their positive attributes and behaviour. This promotes the development of a strong positive emotional bond between captive and captor, which is primed by unconscious processes beyond the survivor's control. Research has shown that the natural impulse when endangered is to seek comfort from the person most close to, even if that person is the source of fear (Harlow and Harlow 1971).

The dynamics in traumatic bonding is like emotional superglue (Allen 2006a) in that they evince extremely strong and intense emotional attachments that are difficult to sever due to the high levels of arousal during the abuse and the unpredictable and intermittent nature of the abuse. The two critical features in traumatic bonding are power imbalance and the presence of intermittent reinforcement, in which periodic abuse is followed by contrition, remorse and conciliation. The vacillation between intimidation, abuse and punishment, and loving, caring behaviours leads to powerful emotional, albeit insecure, attachment; in effect a traumatic bond.

A significant factor in intermittent reinforcement is that it keeps the survivor in thrall to the abuser and evokes a state of anxious anticipation and hope. To sustain hope, the survivor demands an incremental focus on the good aspects of the relationship, especially during the abuse phase, while yearning for the loving and caring behaviour associated with the reconciliation phase. This is compounded when there are numerous good or highly rewarding aspects to the relationship, and when there are long periods between the reconciliation and abuse phase. Some survivors may be more vulnerable to traumatic bonding if they have a past history of trauma bonds, as these will act as a priming effect. Counsellors will need to enable survivors to make a link between previous and current trauma bonds and explore these.

There are a number of other factors that promote traumatic bonding, which the counsellor may need to assess. The severity, cyclical nature and duration of the abuse all act as strengtheners to trauma bonds, as does the degree of denial. In addition the abuser and survivor may mistake high intensity for intimacy, and collude in a belief that what they share is unique. This leads to a distortion and confusion of love and abuse, which is difficult to reconcile. The degree of social isolation or condemnation of the survivor, from family or friends, further increases the development of traumatic bonding. If the survivor retaliates, or asserts herself, to preserve a rapidly dwindling sense of self, the couple may switch roles in which the survivor takes on the role of abuser. This invalidates the survivor's valued belief system, undermines her equanimity and compromises her moral integrity. The concomitant self-loathing becomes a confirmation of the abuser's projective identification, which further binds the survivor.

Traumatic bonding demands considerable changes to the survivor's cognitive schemas (Brown n.d.). The interlinking of abuse and love engenders denial and cognitive dissonance which the survivor needs to reconcile. One way is to humanise the abuser by evoking empathy and compassion for him. In addition, the survivor adopts the perpetrator's belief system, including his derogation of her, leading to a reduction in self-compassion and dehumanising the self. This permits the development of a continuum of tolerance of the abuse and normalising the abuser's behaviour, despite contrary evidence. This is fuelled by the introjections of self-blame in which the survivor denies the total power of abuser by adopting full responsibility for the abuse.

While traumatic bonding aids survival in making it easier to befriend and appease the abuser, it severely compromises the survivor's self-structures. Such cognitive distortions undermine accurate appraisal of danger and diminish perception of alternatives. In the absence of alternative solutions, the survivor becomes entrenched in the abusive relationship making it even more difficult to leave. Dutton and Painter (1993) liken this to

> an elastic band which stretches away from the abuser with time and subsequently 'snaps' the woman back. As the immediate trauma subsides,

the strength of traumatically-formed bond reveals itself through an incremental focus on the desirable aspects of the relationships, and a subsequent sudden and dramatic shift in the woman's 'belief gestalt' about the relationship...[so that she] alters her memory for the past abuse, and her perceived likelihood of future abuse. (Dutton and Painter 1993, p.109)

UNDERSTANDING THE COGNITIVE BOND

It is clear that the cognitive changes in traumatic bonding act as a protective bond to the survivor's psychological integrity. Some researchers propose that to extend understanding of traumatic bonding, clinicians need to be aware of the induction of 'a mental model' or cognitive bond that accompanies DA (Brown n.d.). Brown argues that there are four stages in the development of the cognitive bond, each of which creates shifts in cognitive schemas and belief. In the first stage, the trigger phase, the abuse erodes any vestige of security in the relationship activating acute stress reactions and dissociation. This is followed by a phase of reorientation in which the survivor has to reduce the cognitive dissonance between abuse and continuation of the relationship. This is achieved through considerable cognitive restructuring in which the survivor attributes the abuse to her inadequacies, and adopts self-blaming beliefs designed to reduce the cognitive dissonance.

The third stage, or coping phase, is characterised by a number of cognitive strategies to manage the abuse, including psychic numbing, continued denial and dissociation. Dissociated states allow the survivor to focus on the positive aspects of the relationship, and compartmentalise the abusive aspects. The final stage, or adaption phase, is when the survivor surrenders to the abuser by incorporating all the abuser's cognitive distortions and projections. During this stage psychological integrity is compromised and characterised by depression, low self-esteem, loss of sense of self, and belief that she cannot survive without her partner. Moreover, the survivor begins to see the world through the abuser's eyes, introjects his belief system, which in turn is projected on those who try to challenge elements of the abuse, including the counsellor.

Counsellors need to be aware that these cognitive distortions are commonly deeply entrenched and highly resistant to change. Survivors will not be able to make cognitive changes until they feel safe, and are no longer in survival mode. This may take many months, or sometimes years, after they have left the abuse relationship. Recovery can be achieved only when physical and psychological distance from the abuser has been established and when the survivor can see herself as separate from the abuser. With this in place the survivor can reclaim her identity, personal power and control, and autonomy.

Counsellors need to focus on the survivor's anticipatory fear and anxiety, and find strategies to avoid mind games and manipulation, even after the relationship has ended. Some survivors may continue to protect the abuser in order to protect others from being harmed, especially children. Attention also needs to be paid to restoring destroyed dreams, hopes, aspirations, ideals and shattered belief systems. Critically, counsellors need to work with the survivor's inversion of reality, compromised integrity and eroded self-esteem and self-efficacy to dispel the impact of the web of abuse. Much of this can be facilitated through the therapeutic relationship in which the survivor can experience a healthy bond with the clinician that is appropriately bounded, in which the survivor is subject not object (see Chapter 4).

Mediating and vulnerability factors in domestic abuse

There are a number of mediating factors that ameliorate the severity of impact and long-term effects of DA, and which accounts for observed differences among survivors. A critical factor is access to tangible resources and social support. Pivotal to this are appropriate institutional responses in terms of respect and non-judgemental approach to survivor's needs, devoid of victim blaming.

Paradoxically, some personal strengths and inner resources can either enable the survivor to escape an abusive relationship or entrap them. Resilience and endurance can trap the survivor as she is able to bounce back faster and tolerate higher levels of distress and abuse. This apparent strength can also interfere with the ability to permit feelings of terror, vulnerability and grief, which need to be accessed to aid recovery from DA. This is particularly manifest in high-functioning survivors who are highly skilled at activating dissociative strategies such as compartmentalisation, emotional suppression, containment and intellectualisation. These skills all serve to increase levels of tolerance and acceptance, which unwittingly ensnare the survivor. Commonly, it takes much longer to dissemble these defensive strategies through therapy especially as the survivor derives a semblance of power and control from them which shore up feelings of invulnerability and invincibility.

Vulnerability factors not only exacerbate DA but also can complicate and prolong the therapeutic process. A powerful factor is the degree of positive and negative aspects of the abuse relationship, and how this links to traumatic bonding. Other current stressors may exacerbate the impact of DA, in particular pregnancy, very young children, unemployment, serious illness or disability, or if the survivor is disenfranchised, belongs to an ethnic minority, or suffers other forms of stigmatisation such as that caused by their gender or sexual orientation.

Understanding obstacles to leaving

There are numerous obstacles to leaving, both internal and external (Brown 1987; Dutton 1992; Herman 1992a). Internal obstacles cluster around terror and fear of retaliation. This fear is entirely realistic as survivors of DA are most at risk of losing their life when leaving or after leaving the abuser. Through traumatic bonding, the survivor cannot contemplate existing as separate from the abuser and fear that they cannot survive outside the relationship. In addition, many survivors accumulate considerable corrosive psychological effects of prolonged and repetitive abuse. The debilitating effects of DA may prevent the survivor from leaving due to chronic physical, emotional and mental exhaustion. Some survivors lack the physical strength to leave, while others lack the emotional and cognitive capacities to conceive alternative options other than to tolerate, or manage, the abuse. Depleted inner resources, and lack of vitality, combine to narrow self-efficacy and autonomy.

External obstacles to leaving are characterised by lack of knowledge and access to practical resources such as social support, access to adequate protection and safety, such as a refuge, access to housing, economic resources, medical aid, legal advice and childcare. The survivor may not know her legal rights in relation to the abuser in asking him to leave, taking out injunctions, or rights to shared property. The survivor may also lack information about refuges, temporary housing or accommodation, or benefit entitlements for her or her dependent children. Such lack of knowledge and realistic practical difficulties impact on the ease of separation, and can prevent survivors from leaving. Counsellors must acknowledge and validate these obstacles, rather than construe them as excuses. Some survivors can leave only by going into hiding, and counsellors need to understand how difficult this is for survivors to be cut off from family, friends and their familiar environment, when they most need support. Counsellors can help survivors access the range of external resources by providing emergency telephone numbers, or contact details of relevant resources, agencies and advice centres that provide help to survivors of DA.

The counsellor's role in understanding survivors of domestic abuse

Counsellors must ensure that they have a good understanding of abuse dynamics and the impact and long-term effects these have on the survivor. It is critical that they understand the more subtle forms of coercive control rather than the overt, dramatic behaviour or acts of abuse. It is the cumulative effect of small, subtle gestures of control that can have an equally detrimental effect. The survivor's responses to coercive control and abuse need to be contextualised as coping strategies rather than seen as indicators of personality disturbance or pathology. This will ensure that the counsellor does not engage in victim blaming or revictimisation.

To work most effectively, counsellors need to have in-depth knowledge of DA but most crucially, a thorough understanding of abuse dynamics and the impact on self-structures and relational functioning. This is especially the case as power and control dynamics are commonly enacted in the therapeutic relationship. Rather than recoil from these, or become defensive, counsellors need to explore and contextualise power and control issues. When working with survivors of DA, counsellors must be able to be more flexible in understanding the difficulties that survivors face in scheduling and attending appointments, rather than interpret these simply as resistance.

As knowledge is power, counsellors need to incorporate a psychoeducative component into the therapeutic process, not only in relation to resources, but also in understanding the dynamics of abuse and how abusers manipulate and control every aspect of the survivor. This will help the survivor to be more aware in future relationships not to be seduced into abuse dynamics and to set more appropriate boundaries. In addition to this, counsellors must not lose sight of the socioeconomic, cultural and political factors that underpin DA and reactions to survivors in the wider community.

Counsellors must also have a high level of self-awareness about their own experiences and fears around power, control, violence and aggression as well as feelings of helplessness and hopelessness. This is crucial in terms of developing the therapeutic relationship and counter-transference. Clinicians need to be comfortable in relating to their client and to be emotionally available and sensitively attuned to the survivor. They need to be aware of their own experiences of power, control and domination as well as relational experiences around abandonment, loss and rejection. It is with such knowledge that they can develop a more sensitive understanding how individuals can become vulnerable to coercive control and abuse in close intimate relationships. In addition, counsellors need to explore their own attachment style and how this impacts on fears around intimacy and closeness, both in their personal and professional relationships. This is especially critical as the counsellor's and client's attachment style can impact on the therapeutic relationship.

Survivors generally see counsellors as powerful authority figures that have the potential to betray, or abuse them, as their partner did. To defend against anticipated betrayal, survivors may perceive counsellors as dangerous, inadequate, rejecting or helpless in the face of DA. In addition, they may expect the counsellor to respond to them in the same way as the abuser did. In essence they fear the same critical, uncaring, hostile, and ultimately abusive dynamics to corrupt the therapeutic relationship (Pearlman and Courtois 2005). It is for this reason that counsellors need to have a good understanding of the dynamics of abuse and how this has specifically impacted on each individual client. Equipped with this knowledge the counsellor can understand their particular schemas about self and others, and work with them accordingly.

Counsellors must not personalise negative transference and monitor and control their counter-transference reactions as this can result in deleterious dynamics in the therapeutic relationship. Counsellors need to be aware when working with survivors of interpersonal trauma that they might be vulnerable to defence mechanisms such as denial, defensiveness, emotional avoidance, detachment and feelings of helplessness and hopelessness. These can severely disrupt the therapeutic process whereby the clinician avoids exploring the more traumatic aspects of the client's experiences, or withdraws from the therapeutic relationship (Herman 2001; Pearlman and Courtois 2005; Sanderson 2006). This evokes the survivor's abandonment fears and concomitant anxieties and defences.

Counsellors must ensure that any nascent or emerging counter-transference reactions are explored in supervision, and in some circumstances, a return to personal therapy may be indicated (see Chapter 10). To minimise secondary traumatic stress, counsellors must ensure that they balance the amount of DA and trauma clients in their caseload, and ensure they have a supportive personal and professional network. To avoid burnout counsellors must prioritise self-care and self-nourishment outside their professional work. It is only with this in place that counsellors can work effectively with survivors of DA and remain sensitively attuned to their therapeutic needs.

Summary

- To fully understand survivors of DA, counsellors need to have a clear understanding of the complex nature and pattern of DA, its impact and long-term effects. To facilitate such understanding demands a high level of awareness of the dynamics of abuse and the use of coercive control.

- DA rarely starts with an act of violence, as abusers need to gain the survivor's trust in the relationships. To achieve this abusers initially present as charming, loving and attentive individuals. Once they have the survivor entranced, the abusers begin the process of coercive control by scrutinising the survivor's every action, thought or feeling.

- Once the survivor is in thrall to the abuser, the perpetrator begins to enslave the survivor through petty rules, monitoring the survivor's somatic, emotional and mental experiences, and pathological jealousy. The abuser begins to juxtapose loving behaviour and abusive verbal or physical onslaughts. These serve to confuse the survivor leading to potent conditioning processes that impact on the survivor's self-structures and cognitive schemas.

- The enmeshment between abuser and survivor in DA leads to moulding of the survivor's identity in which the abuser relinquishes all responsibility for the abuse by projecting this onto the survivor. Over time, the denigration and negative projections become incorporated into the survivor's self-image.

- Counsellors need to understand the dynamics of the abuse and how these impact on the survivor's responses and reactions. It is critical that clinicians also understand the survivor's dynamics as well as those of the abuser, in order to recognise the unconscious processes underlying the abuser's need to control and dominate, and the survivor's vulnerability to coercion.

- Coercive control is best established through inconsistency and unpredictability, and the fusion of intimidation and fear. This is achieved not just through physical violence, but also in enforcing petty rules, subtle humiliation and denigration. As survivors are in a constant state of fear, physical violence can be intermittent, to serve as reminders of the abuser's power and omnipotence.

- The intermittent reinforcement of reward and punishment, characteristic of the three-stage cycle of abuse, creates powerful emotional bonds between survivor and abuser, which are highly resistant to change, even after the relationship has ended. The underlying dynamics of traumatic bonding need to be understood by survivors so that they can extricate themselves from their dependence on the abuser, and to relinquish responsibility and self-blame.

- Counsellors also need to be aware of mediating and vulnerability factors that increase or decrease the survivor's enslavement by the abuser. Knowledge of these, along with an understanding of the abuse dynamics, will provide valuable illumination of the internal and external obstacles to leaving.

- Counsellors need to be aware of their own experiences of power and control, fear of abandonment, sense of helplessness and hopelessness to avoid negative counter-transference reactions. They also need to be cognisant of their attachment style and how this interacts with the survivor's attachment style to ensure that the therapeutic relationship is preserved.

- Professionals who work with survivors of DA and trauma need to recognise the potential for secondary traumatic stress and take appropriate action such as supervision and self-care to ensure that they remain emotionally engaged and sensitively attuned to the survivor's specific therapeutic needs.

CHAPTER 4

WORKING WITH SURVIVORS OF DOMESTIC ABUSE

The complex nature of domestic abuse (DA) and its relationship to trauma and betrayal necessitate a safe therapeutic environment in which survivors can explore the full range of ambivalent feelings, create narrative out of chaos, and make sense of their experiences. Counsellors need to provide a safe haven to restore safety, mentalise feelings, and rebuild trust in self and others. To work with survivors of DA in a supportive way, counsellors need to have a thorough understanding of the complex nature of DA to avoid pathologising. Counsellors will also require knowledge of multiagency resources available in the community, and preferably form links with both statutory and voluntary agencies in order to provide a comprehensive and holistic supportive network for survivors of DA.

A sensitive, holistic approach is the most effective way for survivors to heal from DA and prevent further victimisation. Working with survivors also entails a more flexible approach and the adoption of a range of counselling skills and interventions. Most crucially the therapeutic relationship is central to enable the survivor to reconnect to self, reclaim control, and develop self-efficacy and agency.

This chapter will look at the therapeutic aims and treatment modalities required when working with survivors of DA, and the importance of accurate assessment. The cardinal principle when working with survivors of DA is safety, because no therapeutic work can proceed until internal and external safety is established (Herman 2001). To engender safety, counsellors need to provide a safe therapeutic setting and healthy relational stance. Factors that facilitate these will be examined along with the importance of pacing, power and control issues, transference and counter-transference, and potential difficulties when working with this client group.

Therapeutic aims

As the experience of DA is unique to each survivor, counsellors will need to tailor their approach to the individual needs of each survivor. However, there are some overarching principles that need to be incorporated. Before any therapeutic work can begin, counsellors need to carry out meticulous risk assessment in relation to internal and external safety, risk of self-harm, suicidal ideation and risk to others, including children. Assessment allows counsellors to identify the potential dangers and enable the survivor to establish safety. This is paramount, as in the absence of safety no therapeutic work can succeed (Dutton 1992; Herman 2001). To facilitate safety, counsellors must create psychological, emotional and environmental safety, including clearly stated boundaries. This can take considerable time and cannot be rushed, especially as safety can be threatened by external forces such as pressing practical tasks that need to be prioritised, or when in contact with the abuser.

Once a reasonable level of safety has been secured, and internal safety has been established through mastering affect regulation, the DA experience can be explored. Survivors need to create narrative out of chaos, express the full range of ambivalent feelings, and make sense out of their experiences in order to integrate them. An important aim of therapy is to provide a space for the survivor to grieve actual and symbolic losses. Survivors need to mourn the multiple losses associated with DA so as to restore vitality and reconnect to self and life (see Chapter 9). Through the grief process survivors can begin to take control of self-definition, build trust, and rebuild their lives outside the shadow of abuse.

Cognitive restructuring facilitates the reattribution of responsibility for the DA and reduces shame and guilt. Through the therapeutic relationship, the survivor will be able to explore relational dynamics, which will facilitate healthy boundaries with others. Trusting others and rebuilding a healthy support network enhances the survivor's interpersonal and psychosocial functioning, and restores trust in others. This allows the survivor to move from isolation to social connection. Through this the survivor is able to reclaim power and control, and reconnect to life in a more meaningful way.

Herman (1992a) proposes that in trauma there are three stages: safety, remembering and mourning, and reconnection to life. Similarly Dutton (1992) highlights three main goals: increasing safety, re-empowering through decision making, and healing psychological trauma of abuse. Most importantly these stages are not linear but a way in which to understand the complex nature of recovery. Invariably survivors vacillate between stages, revisiting earlier concerns with new understanding, and working towards a higher level of integration. As practical tasks compete with emotional needs, survivors are compelled to shift the focus of the therapeutic work resulting in detours and diversions. Counsellors need to be able to tolerate this constantly shifting focus and not impose a simplistic framework of neat consecutive stages.

The objective in working with survivors is to facilitate movement from unpredictability to control, and isolation to connection. Restoring internal safety promotes stabilisation which facilitates more in-depth therapeutic work. Given the prominence of power and control in DA, counsellors need to ensure that they adopt a collaborative approach in making informed decisions such as use of medication, pacing and duration of therapy through developing a strong therapeutic alliance. It is only when survivors are able to take control over their recovery that self-efficacy and self-agency can be assured.

In a secure therapeutic relationship, counsellors can focus on building emotional and social resources, and identify individual needs. This process allows survivors to acquire self-regulation and containment skills that allow them to take control of their somatic and psychological responses. When physiological and emotional responses become more manageable, survivors can begin to bear the full range of feelings, both positive and negative, associated with DA. Exploring and expressing turbulent emotions that no longer threaten to engulf survivors, allows them to work through all aspects of the DA experience. This will restore a reconstructed coherent narrative and meaning which encompasses and integrates DA.

During this process, counsellors need to devote attention to restoring severely damaged self-structures, specifically self-esteem, self-worth and self respect (see Chapter 7). Survivors can also begin to make sense of the complex dynamics of DA and develop greater understanding of relationship patterns. The more survivors understand, the more they will experience a sense of controllability. This allows them to change relational dynamics and establish agency (see Chapter 8). This permits the setting of boundaries and articulation of needs without fear of reprisals. Gradually the survivor is able to shift the emotional investment from the abuser, transform losses, and commit to present and future relationships.

The multiple losses incurred in DA resemble a massive bereavement, and mourning these is pivotal in restoring hope. The grieving process can be further complicated as previous unprocessed losses are revived, with survivors oscillating between current and past losses, and fears of future losses (see Chapter 9). The grieving process is often postponed until external safety is assured and survivors can give themselves permission to grieve. Counsellors need to appreciate the nature of delayed grief and tolerate detours into past losses to allow emotional completion. It is only through transforming these losses that survivors can restore hope and vitality, and rebuild their lives.

The complex nature and impact of DA necessitates a flexible therapeutic approach that demands knowledge of a range of therapeutic modalities. To offer a truly holistic treatment approach requires knowledge of trauma, the importance of stabilisation and self-regulation skills, and a balance between emotionally supportive and cognitive behavioural therapy (CBT) techniques. A central aspect of working with DA is the therapeutic relationship and it is critical that counsellors are emotionally engaged and sensitively attuned to the survivor. Counsellors may also need to employ a number of other skills not usually associated with their therapeutic philosophy or practice. These include psychoeducation, writing reports and a more proactive stance in forming links with other DA agencies to offer a comprehensive level of support.

Range of treatment modalities

DA experiences vary enormously and are unique to each individual. Its impact is on a number of dimensions, not least on intrapersonal and interpersonal functioning, behaviour, cognition and physical functioning. Effective therapeutic intervention must incorporate a focus on all these dimensions. A number of therapeutic modalities can be implemented when working with survivors of DA, and should be considered by counsellors for each individual survivor. These can be seen as useful adjuncts to the counsellors' therapeutic philosophical stance.

TRAUMATIC STRESS MODELS

A number of researchers and clinicians ground DA in a trauma framework (Department of Health 2005; Herman 2001; Humphreys and Thiara 2003; Pearlman and Courtois 2005). The impact of pervasive cumulative interpersonal violence and coercive control leads to complex trauma and concomitant psychobiological symptoms and complicated relational problems. Counsellors need to accurately assess the impact of DA on psychobiological functioning and identify specific symptoms. Traumatic stress models conceptualise symptoms of trauma as adaptive responses to abnormal events (Wilson and Lindy 1994), and do not pathologise the survivor. The treatment focus of traumatic stress models is predicated on the need for safety and stabilisation prior to any therapeutic work. A number of techniques are implemented to facilitate stabilisation of the survivor, including body awareness, biofeedback, desensitisation, affect modulation, cognitive restructuring and meaning attribution. Such treatment approaches are particularly effective with survivors of DA to restore internal safety and self-regulation.

When employing this model, counsellors need to facilitate rebuilding of self-regulation, affect modulation, restoring control and the expression of needs. Given the distorted relational dynamics in DA, emphasis is also placed on exploring attachment and relational style to promote development of healthier relationships. As trauma work can revive past traumatic experiences, counsellors need to feel competent to explore these along with the current trauma. Fundamental to the success of traumatic stress models is a safe and secure therapeutic relationship.

THE PSYCHODYNAMIC TRADITION

The aim of psychodynamic models is to facilitate access to repressed emotions and to examine psychic and somatic defences. The cathartic release of these allows them to be integrated. The therapeutic focus in the psychodynamic tradition is the role of transference in which the client unconsciously transfers ways of relating to a significant other, onto the therapist. While transference is a rich source of information that facilitates a deeper understanding of the client, counsellors need to be aware of their counter-transference, and how this is interpreted. To work successfully within this tradition, counsellors need to avoid the more traditional 'formal, distant, and emotionally abstinent stance' (Dale 1999, p.11).

Ideally when working with survivors of DA, counsellors need to work within an attachment framework in which relational processes along with actual abuse, attachment and loss are explored within a reparative relationship. This requires greater flexibility in ways of relating and setting boundaries, thereby humanising the therapeutic relationship in which transference and counter-transference dynamics are interpreted within the context of the actual therapeutic relationship (Cashdan 1988; Lomas 1987, 1994; Mair 1989). For the survivor of DA to risk connection and restore trust, counsellors need to be emotionally present, sensitively attuned and engaged in building the therapeutic alliance.

THE COGNITIVE BEHAVIOURAL TRADITION

A significant advantage of the cognitive behavioural therapy approach is that it enables survivors to reframe their DA experiences, allowing for more accurate evaluations and to create meaning. Many of the observed cognitive distortions and misattributions of blame have been constructed by the abuser and absorbed by the survivor. Survivors need to identify these imposed distortions, challenge and evaluate them. Identifying patterns of thinking and schemas allows survivors to link these with negative views of self, and their impact on mood and behaviour. Cognitive restructuring (Beck 1976) allows survivors to change negative and distorted perceptions about themselves and the abuse, and transform meaning. It also promotes more accurate problem solving and informed decision making.

The behavioural component of CBT focuses on developing a broader range of protective behaviours and strategies. Behavioural techniques also allow for the acquisition of new skills to help regulate intensity of emotion, grounding and relaxation techniques, setting boundaries, and relational skills. In combination the CBT approach allows counsellors to implement a range of techniques such as recognising and naming abuse, identifying needs, recording symptoms and recovery process, setting realistic goals and boundaries, and practising numerous exercises outside the session. These all enable survivors to take an active stance in their recovery and engender control and self-efficacy. As CBT is usually conducted in a time-limited framework, it is not always sufficient to integrate the more complex interplay of traumatic effects, which take considerably longer to resolve. However, they are at their most effective at the beginning of the therapeutic process when safety is the prime focus, and serve as an efficacious adjunct to the counsellor's core theoretical orientation.

PSYCHOEDUCATION

Traditional models of therapy have tended to minimise, if not restrict, the provision of psychoeducative material to clients. Psychoeducation is crucial when working with trauma and abuse. During chronic abuse, individuals are prevented from accessing information so that the abuser can execute total control. To restore control to survivors they need access to information, from which to make informed choices. Counsellors need to be transparent in stating their therapeutic orientation, how they work and what clients can expect from the therapeutic process. This needs to be accompanied with clear, up-to-date information on the range of resources available to survivors of DA. Such information needs to include both practical and social resources, along with emotional support through self-help groups.

THE HUMANISTIC TRADITION

Underpinning the diverse range of humanistic models is the belief that humans strive for growth to reach their full potential and self-determination. These approaches are based on non-authoritarian relationships between therapist and client, in which the therapist is 'real' and 'present', aiming for authentic contact in what is known as an 'I–thou' relationship (Buber 1987). Humanistic approaches emphasise the uniqueness of the individual and as such minimise diagnostic and classificatory systems and rigid therapeutic expectations and goals. This allows for flexibility in terms of the scheduling and duration of sessions, outside-of-session contact, and greater personal involvement of the therapist, including self-disclosure.

Many humanistic approaches are adaptable and incorporate a range of creative techniques, such as art therapies, and the use of 'action techniques' to facilitate communication, most notably psychodrama, role play, dance, movement and music. Many of the approaches also encourage journal writing, creative writing, play therapy, sand play and bodywork. In valuing the uniqueness of each client, there is no rigid prescribed approach but there is room for developing a tailor-made therapeutic space and techniques that are personally meaningful for the client. The therapeutic atmosphere of warmth, genuineness, unconditional positive regard, empathy and congruence allows the survivor to develop trust and build connection. The role of the therapist is to be non-judgemental and to enter the phenomenological world of the client and see the world through the client's eyes. Although humanistic approaches are more flexible than other modalities, some survivors find the lack of structure and unpredictability anxiety-provoking (Sanderson 2006). Initially survivors may need more guidance until their self-structures are restored and they can develop greater self-determination and agency.

THE EXISTENTIAL TRADITION

Existential psychotherapy has its roots in the psychoanalytic and humanistic traditions, in which the core emphasis is on the individual's search for personal meaning in life and the acceptance of responsibility for choices made (Frankl 1946; Laing 1967). Inherent in existential approaches is the importance of providing clients with a safe environment in which to facilitate their search for personal meanings (Spinelli 1994; Van Deurzen-Smith 1988) without imposing any specified ways to gain that meaning. An advantage of this model for survivors of DA is that it allows them to search for their own meaning in relation to their experience of DA. Many of the themes emphasised in existential psychotherapy include loss, death, isolation, loneliness, fate, and the absurdity of living; these have a poignant resonance for survivors of DA.

THE INTEGRATIVE PARADIGM

The complex nature of DA and its impact demands greater flexibility and a broader range of therapeutic techniques. Integrative models aim to reduce the rigidity of traditional models, in terms of both theoretical orientation and therapeutic techniques (Bergin and Garfield 1994; Clarkson 1993). The integrative approach allows for far greater flexibility, by employing therapeutic techniques from a variety of treatment modalities in order to work with specific difficulties. When using an integrative approach, clinicians are more able to address the diverse effects of DA and presenting symptoms.

FEMINIST MODELS

Feminist models emphasise the socio-political, cultural and economic factors that underpin and support DA. Rather than medicalising the effects of DA, attention is directed at understanding how the prevailing socio-political macro-system is reflected in the micro-system of personal relationships. The focus is how socially constructed meaning around gender, race, power and control, domination and submission, and the hierarchical structure of families are embodied in DA. These models have traditionally de-emphasised psychiatric and psychological approaches to DA due to the propensity for pathologising survivors of DA. Since pathologising survivors not only alienates them but also has serious ramifications that replicate the abuse experience, counsellors are urged to refrain from applying diagnostic labels. However, there is a comparable danger in not acknowledging the myriad psychobiological effects of DA in minimising the traumatic effects of DA. To provide a truly comprehensive approach to recovery of DA counsellors need to incorporate psychosocial as well as psychobiological factors when working with survivors of DA, and balance these appropriately.

An advantage of this model is its emphasis on the beneficial effects of emotional support through self-help groups to reduce social isolation and increase social support. The self-help model is pioneering, in giving survivors a voice and permission to take control of their recoveries. However, the model has received some criticism with regard to basic theoretical assumptions, such as not being able to explain female perpetrators of DA, abuse in same sex relationships, or the diverse range of DA experiences.

GROUP WORK

Self-help groups or group psychotherapy can be of enormous benefit to survivors of DA and can be a powerful adjunct to individual counselling. Group work facilitates safety, mutuality, commonality, learning from peers, and validation and support. The trauma of DA is compounded by social isolation and alienation, which are commonly enforced by the perpetrator. One way of triumphing over such estrangement and disconnection from others is to re-establish social relationships. Many clinicians have found that social support can ameliorate the traumatic experiences inherent in DA (Dutton 1992; Herman 1992a; Humphreys and Thiara 2003; Pearlman and Courtois 2005). Groups are also a valuable source for sharing experiences of DA, grieving the multiple losses, and empowering survivors to take control over their recovery. Counsellors are urged to consider this additional source of support and actively encourage survivors to avail themselves of such opportunity.

SYSTEMIC AND RELATIONSHIP COUNSELLING

In contrast, systemic models and couple counselling are contraindicated when working with survivors of DA. Such work renders the therapeutic space unsafe as survivors fear open and honest expression due to reprisals from the abuser. Many abusers present themselves as charming and benign individuals publicly, only to exercise tyranny privately. Cessation of physical violence is not sufficient to ensure safety, as abusers often demand submission from their partner in return. Perpetrators of DA must relinquish the need and desire to exercise coercion and control before the relationship is truly safe. This necessitates specialist interven-

tion, and abusers must enter an appropriate perpetrator programme or seek their
own counsellor.

The role of the counsellor

Many clinicians working with survivors of complex trauma and interpersonal
violence emphasise the centrality of the therapeutic relationship (Dutton 1992;
Herman 1992a; Pearlman and Courtois 2005). The coercive control and betrayal
of trust inherent in DA makes it very difficult for survivors to trust others. Many
fear revictimisation and further abuse and are terrified of connecting to others.
Counsellors need to understand the difficulties that survivors of DA have around
intimacy and autonomy, and should validate their courage to risk connection in
the therapeutic relationship.

When working with survivors of DA, counsellors need to possess in-depth
understanding of the impact of DA on relational dynamics, and how this may be
manifest in the therapeutic relationship. Care should be taken not to interpret
relational difficulties as pathology but to see these within the context of DA. Providing a therapeutic environment based on respect for the survivor's needs and
striving for self-agency in which the survivor is not judged is crucial to establish
safety and restore trust. Counsellors need to validate not only the survivor's experiences and survival, but also the survivor's courage in seeking help despite
repeated betrayals. It is only in a genuinely caring and accepting environment,
free of revictimisation, that survivors of DA can feel safe to explore the full range
of their feelings.

Counsellors need to conceptualise survivor's coping strategies as strengths
not pathology. Survivors are not passive victims, but active survivors, by adopting
a range of survival strategies which need to be identified and validated. It is crucial that defences such as denial, emotional blunting, disavowal, dissociation and
avoidance are understood as ways of managing the abuse rather than
psychopathological personality traits. Counsellors are exhorted to make links
between alteration in personality and erosion of self-structures and prolonged
abuse. Perpetrators of DA demand the annihilation of the individual's personality
so as to replace it with submissiveness and compliance. Survivors have no choice
but to adopt the identity imposed by the abuser. Similarly counsellors need to
explore survivors' previous abuse history and guard against using this to
pathologise the survivor, or to dilute the abuser's responsibility. Many perpetrators of DA exploit this by shifting responsibility for the abuse on the survivor, and
counsellors need to avoid colluding with this.

As DA also impacts on relational functioning, counsellors need to
contextualise these and incorporate any necessary therapeutic work. Consideration must be given to the survivor's attachment and relational styles in order to
facilitate more healthy ways of relating. Particular attention needs to be focused

on issues around power and control and how these are enacted in therapeutic setting. Counsellors need to understand these within the context of DA and explore these sensitively. Counsellors must not misinterpret such dynamics or become enmeshed with them. Much of this work can be achieved through the therapeutic relationship in which healthy boundaries coexist with intimacy and autonomy. Pearlman and Courtois (2005) propose a relational therapeutic framework in which respect, information, connection and hope (RICH) are emphasised to promote a healthy therapeutic relationship. Within this, counsellors are urged to be cognisant of their own way of relating as this will have considerable impact on the development of the therapeutic relationship (see Chapter 8).

There is no certitude when working with survivors of DA, and counsellors will be challenged in their search for certainty. A crucial component in therapy is to tolerate uncertainty, and manage and contain concomitant anxieties. Counsellors will also need to be more flexible in their therapeutic approach in tolerating diversion and detours. Working with survivors of DA is not a linear process with survivor's needs fluctuating between working on practical tasks and emotional support. Detours and diversions must be appropriately managed without the counsellor succumbing to frustration.

Flexibility will also be required around attendance and out-of-session contact. There are myriad genuine reasons for erratic attendance, not least potential danger, lack of childcare, and attending meetings to access social resources. Counsellors are urged to understand these rather than assume they are indices of resistance. It is imperative that counsellors explore how they intend to manage this and set clear boundaries. Out-of-hours contact will also have to be negotiated and explicitly stated so that survivors are clear about counsellor availability.

While the primary role of the counsellor is emotional support and psychotherapeutic change, they nevertheless need to recognise social, political and economic contexts of DA (Dutton 1992; Herman 1992a). Focus on survivors needs to be combined with understanding of the importance of personal and social networks, and the socio-cultural environment in which DA and healing occurs. Isolation supports coercive control whereas connection fosters growth. This also applies to counsellors, who will find considerable benefit when working within a multidisciplinary framework.

Counsellors need to have awareness of their own values and perceptions which underpin and inform practice (see Chapter 10). It is only with an examination and monitoring of their own assumptions that counsellors can provide a therapeutic environment based on respect and collaboration. Counsellors need to validate and reinforce the survivor's positive actions and achievements. It is essential that counsellors encourage autonomy by allowing survivors to take control of their healing by pacing the therapeutic work at a manageable pace, and setting personally meaningful goals. They also need to address the realities of power in social structures and in the therapeutic setting, to ensure a collaborative stance.

It is only when survivors experience autonomy that they can make requisite changes and take charge of rebuilding their lives.

To counteract some of these concerns, counsellors could consider contracting sessions into more manageable blocks of sessions, in which the client takes more control. For example, sessions might involve establishing specific therapeutic goals collaboratively, along with regular review sessions in which the counsellor and survivor can evaluate progress, discuss those therapeutic factors that have been most efficacious or unhelpful, and highlight outstanding difficulties. This enables the survivor to feel more focused and in control of the therapeutic process, rather than feeling it is imposed upon him. In addition, some survivors benefit from taking short breaks reducing their dependency on the counsellor, and enabling the survivor to acknowledge his progress, sense of self-efficacy and autonomy.

As language defines experience, counsellors need to be sentient of how language impacts on the construction of meaning. To this effect, counsellors need to pay close attention to use of language and terminology. To avoid pathologising the survivor, counsellors need to use appropriate terms and avoid applying diagnostic labels.

Therapeutic stance

When working with survivors of DA, counsellors must be able to detect and accurately translate multiple signals from the client. To achieve this, the counsellor must be authentic, emotionally present, visible and engaged. According to Salter (1995, p.262) '[the client] cannot heal in the absence of emotional visibility'. However, the counsellor must guard against being too charismatic as this can be perceived as controlling and overpowering, much like the abuser. In contrast, a distant, non-responsive therapeutic stance, with prolonged silences, can be experienced as rejecting in mirroring DA experiences.

The counsellor must be reliable and consistent in providing a secure and containing therapeutic space predicated on empathic attunement and resonance. Empathic attunement incorporates sensitive and empathic listening, whereby the counsellor tracks the client's feelings, consciously, subconsciously and somatically, and reflects these back to the survivor. In addition, the counsellor must also engage in sensing, by making full use of the therapist's 'self' (Figley 2004). The counsellor needs to be able to absorb what the client cannot allow herself to feel, including unconscious projections, and contain these.

The reactive style of the counsellor is crucial in determining the ease with which the survivor of DA will be able to engage in the therapeutic process and the development of the therapeutic alliance. As survivors experience relational difficulties around trust, intimacy and attachment, these need to be closely attended to. Counsellors may need to be more flexible in how they relate to clients.

Research has demonstrated that a distant clinical stance reinforces abuse dynamics and serves only to alienate the survivor (Wilson 2003, 2004; Wilson and Lindy 1994; Wilson, Friedman and Lindy 2001). In the light of research, clinicians may need to evaluate the effectiveness of their therapeutic stance and empathic attunement when working with survivors of DA and adopt a more engaged relational style in which the client can feel safe enough to reconnect to self, others and life. Counsellors need to ensure empathy and empathic attunement which allows them to connect, resonate and calibrate with the survivors whole being. In the absence of empathic attunement, counsellors may experience empathic strain or empathic rupture (Wilson 2003), which can lead to collapse of the therapeutic alliance. Counsellors need to monitor and calibrate empathic attunement in order to stay connected to the survivor and to relate to the survivor's whole being, not just verbal content.

Wilson (2002) argues further that there is a continuum of empathic functioning, which ranges from minimal empathic attunement, characterised by detachment and disengagement, to more optimal levels, in which empathic attunement and engagement are present, along with a dimension ranging from empathic separation or detachment to empathic connection. In optimal empathic attunement, the counsellor is receptive and able to track and match the client's internal and psychological state accurately with resonance and minimal distortion. In separation or detachment, counsellors block receptivity and are less adequate at matching, inaccurate in their resonance and vulnerable to distortion and interference.

It is worth noting that clinicians vary in terms of empathic capacity, empathic resistance, empathic tolerance and empathic endurance (Wilson 2002). Such variations are primarily determined by genetic predisposition, temperament, and resistance to stress, sensitivity, containment, resilience, stamina and personality of the counsellor. These can be exacerbated by level of experience, knowledge of trauma work, psychological well-being and access to resources, as well as type of trauma and personal characteristics of the client, such as age, gender and ethnicity (Wilson 2002). Examining these can empower the client to no longer feel enslaved by old or unconscious ways of relating, enabling them to feel, think and act in different ways through making positive choices and informed decisions.

Therapeutic setting

When working with survivors of DA, the counsellor will need to establish and maintain clear and consistent boundaries. The counsellor may need to adopt a more creative, non-rigid therapeutic model in which stereotypical treatment responses are not applied indiscriminately. Counsellors must respect the uniqueness of each client's experience of DA and work with each survivor in the most effective way. This may require the counsellor to challenge preconceived beliefs about DA and to evaluate their practice. Awareness of power and control, attachment style, and difficulties around intimacy and autonomy all need to be understood within the context of DA, not personality disturbance.

THE THERAPEUTIC SPACE

The therapeutic room should provide a calm, quiet environment that minimises distractions such as traffic noise, conversations, laughter and telephone calls. The therapy room should be pleasant and temperate, so that the survivor feels physically comfortable. Bathroom facilities should be provided and identified, as heightened anxiety can prompt a need to use these. The seats in the room should all be at the same height, in order to minimise power differentials. Seating should not be overbearingly close, as physical and psychological closeness can feel dangerous to the client; however, a huge distance between the therapist and client can feel cold and rejecting to the client. A large physical distance also makes it difficult for the client to track the counsellor's non-verbal reactions. This can be frightening for survivors who have a highly acute, attuned sensory alertness to changes in body language.

Ideally counsellors need to give the survivor some choice over where to sit, as clients may fear being trapped in a confined space with no escape. Survivors often prefer sitting close to an exit or facing the door, and may wish to align their chair accordingly. Counsellors must acknowledge the client's fears as valid and provide a choice such as offering the chair nearest to the door or within easy sight of and access to the door.

BOUNDARIES

Given the nature of DA, counsellors are required to pay particular attention to boundaries in the therapeutic setting. The counsellor needs to give a clear, explicit statement of boundaries before the working alliance with the client can begin. Boundaries of time, place, session frequency, location of sessions and duration of therapy must be clearly articulated. The counsellor must make clear statements of confidentiality and explain the circumstances under which information about the survivor will be shared, such as in supervision or if the client is at risk of hurting herself or others, or psychological reports. Any dilemmas of confidentiality such as how to proceed if the perpetrator is the next of kin must be confronted and discussed, including any reporting of child protection concerns. Counsellors should explain their system of keeping files, including ownership, storage and access issues. The counsellor may consider giving the survivor the option of how she wishes records to be kept, whether through audio- or videotape, note-taking during sessions or writing up notes after sessions.

Counsellors in private practice must provide clear information about the payment of fees. Some survivors are uncomfortable with bills being sent to a home address, and may prefer to pay per session or in advance. Counsellors must state explicitly their terms concerning cancellation fees and payment in the absence of the client attending. This is an important consideration as survivors may be prevented from attending and counsellors need to assess how that impacts on terms and conditions. Counsellors must state clearly their availability by telephone between sessions and the procedures that are in place in emergency and crisis situations. Other factors such as the client's and counsellor's holiday schedules should be discussed, along with the availability of therapeutic cover during the counsellor's absence.

Counsellors must make a clear statement about the therapeutic process, including what they can and cannot offer and what the client can expect. Counsellors also need to clarify how they work including survivor autonomy in directing the content and pace of the therapeutic process. For example, the client may wish to talk at times and at other times not, sometimes to work and other times to play, sometimes to revisit the trauma and other times just to be grounded in the present.

Counsellors also need to specify to what extent they can provide practical, social or legal support, prepare and write reports, or attendance at court. It is critical that counsellors are clear about what they can provide and set appropriate limits rather than make assurances that cannot be supported. Boundaries of safety may require implementation of safety contracts around self-destructive behaviours or suicidality. The role of medication, hospitalisation or residential treatment needs to be explored and survivors encouraged to make informed choices. Counsellors also need to assess internal and external safety and enable survivors to develop appropriate boundaries (see Chapter 5).

PACING THE THERAPEUTIC PROCESS

Counsellors ideally should give the survivor autonomy in the timing of focus, content, intensity and pace of the therapeutic encounter. Survivor control must be restored to direct and pace the therapeutic work. This requires counsellors to relinquish their own need to pace the therapeutic work or to rush the client. Counsellors must encourage clients to take back their own power and control over pacing, including allowing survivors to talk or not to talk in their own time. This can be beneficial in restoring control and autonomy.

USE OF SILENCE

Although silence can have therapeutic value, for survivors of DA long silences can be frightening and counterproductive. Silence can be the loneliest place on earth and can replicate the imposed silence surrounding DA. Counsellors need to recognise that silence can generate feelings of oppression reminiscent of the DA.

Silence can feel like a re-enactment of DA dynamics and be experienced as threatening and punitive. Counsellors must always acknowledge the client's difficulty in speaking and must not use it as a weapon to force the client to speak. Tracking the client's pace and coming back to the difficulty at a later point are more helpful than forcing the client to continue. Speaking the unspeakable provokes anxiety and fear, and counsellors are urged to understand this. Creating narrative out of chaos is a painstaking task and counsellors must avoid imposing a prematurely inauthentic order on the chaos.

For some survivors of DA, becoming silent is the only way they could exercise control, and this may be acted out in the therapeutic setting. Counsellors need to understand this as a coping strategy and not interpret this as resistance and punitive. Silence can become a threat to the client's very existence, especially if the abuser used silence to coerce and control the survivor. In any silence in therapy, the counsellor must hold the therapeutic space sufficiently so that the client does not experience it as hostile, angry or retaliatory and or an indicator of withdrawal or rejection. The balance between holding the silence to a tolerable level and breaking it can be difficult, and requires sensitive attunement from the counsellor in communicating that the client does not have to talk but that she can when she wants to, or is ready to.

TRANSFERENCE

Lack of autonomy compels some survivors of DA to abrogate responsibility for healing and recovery to the counsellor, hoping that they will be rescued. Survivors may fantasise that the counsellor will make up for past hurts and attempt to elicit the counsellor's 'helper script'. If the counsellor does not respond to these fantasised needs, the survivor may project her resentment on to the counsellor, who is then perceived as persecutor. The survivor may manifest a profound yearning for love, acceptance or nourishing and consistent love in order to make up for deficits in her partner. In a replay of the abuse experience, the survivor may become overly compliant and deny her needs, rather than access suppressed rage.

Fear that the counsellor will see the survivor as bad or disgusting may symbolise the survivor's issues around shame and self-blame. Some survivors have a compelling need to protect the counsellor from any disclosure or the full traumatic details, believing that the counsellor will not be able to cope with such information. This may be the result of unconscious transmission of unease from the counsellor or a response to explicit statements of unease. Protection of the counsellor may represent the client's own need to protect herself from the DA. Other survivors may displace their anger onto the counsellor as a test to see whether they will be punished. The counsellor needs to understand these within the context of transference.

Powerful transference dynamics can have a profound effect on the counsellor. They strike to the very core of the therapist's self-concept as someone who cares and wants to help or empower the survivor. Such dynamics can elicit 'the three most common narcissistic snares in therapists...the aspirations to heal, know all and love all' (Maltsberg and Buie 1974, p.627).

COUNTER-TRANSFERENCE

When working with counter-transference, counsellors need to ensure a high level of self-awareness of their own experiences of power and control, how these intrude consciously and unconsciously in the therapeutic space, and their narcissistic needs for omnipotence and omniscience. Traumatic counter-transference from working with traumatised clients can evoke helplessness, rage, grief, identification with the perpetrator, witness guilt and dissociative responses (Herman 1992a). Working with trauma can impact on the counsellor's sensory and somatic system and undermine self-structures and safety in the world, which can lead to uncertainty and self-doubt. This can evoke psychological needs such as safety, trust, esteem, intimacy and control.

Working with survivors of complex trauma can lead to emotional and cognitive counter-transference reactions (CTR). Emotional CTR include anger at the source of victimisation, anger at the survivor due to the intensity of affect, and anger at society for its failure to help victims of DA. Such intense feelings may threaten to engulf counsellors as they access their vulnerability, risk of abuse, and anxieties about their professional abilities. Alternatively, counsellors may feel guilt because they have been exempt from such experiences and have not suffered.

Many counsellors working with survivors of DA experience empathic sadness and grief reactions, such as dread, horror, shame, disgust or revulsion. This taps into the therapist's own sense of vulnerability, anxieties and fears, which can result in avoidance of the DA narrative. To manage this, the counsellor may employ cognitive strategies such as distancing and therapeutic blankness as a protective screen. Alternatively, the counsellor may over-identify with the survivor and become overcommitted to helping or rescuing the client. The counsellor thus adopts the role of a saviour, developing an excessive belief in personal responsibility in order to shoulder the burden of therapy. The counsellor may demonstrate narcissistic dynamics of grandiosity by forming an image of the survivor as a weak victim who is not capable of resolving the DA without the counsellor's help. In contrast, some counsellors retreat into inappropriate pathologising or medicalising to alleviate affective intensity as a way to restore therapist control. Counsellors may fail to see the link between trauma symptoms and DA and deny the impact of DA.

It is important to acknowledge counter-transference reactions and identify whether these are a result of transference, or derived from counsellors' own subjective experience, biases and attitudes. Whatever the source, counsellors must evaluate the extent to which they are responding to the client's transference and the degree to which emergent CTR represent the counsellor's own feelings.

Wilson and Lindy (1994) identified two types of CTR: avoidance or over-identification with the client. In avoidance, clinicians take an avoidant stance, in which they withdraw from the survivor and deny, disbelieve and distort the survivor's experiences by intellectualising the trauma and isolating themselves from the material by taking a rigid stance. This can lead to feelings of loathing, condemnation, blame and disgust for the survivor, which may mask the counsellor's own feelings of dread, horror, helplessness, hopelessness and grief. In over-identification, the counsellor tends to over-identify with the survivor and, eventually, to idealise and be in awe of the survivor, which elicits feelings of rage and vengeance. Alternatively, the counsellor identifies with the perpetrator, eliciting sadistic feelings. Whichever CTR are evinced, the result is the collapse of professional boundaries.

Ultimately, rescue responses lead to the therapist becoming enmeshed or merged with the client and overly involved with the client's process, rather than empowering the survivor to do so herself. Counsellors who adopt the persecutor role become impatient or irritated with the survivor's helplessness and become punitive. This can lead to becoming overly directive, asking too many questions and making too many suggestions because the counsellor's own fears have been stimulated. This may lead to feelings of guilt, resulting in generally unhelpful responses that reflect both the client's and the therapist's helplessness and anguish. Some counsellors oscillate between persecutor and rescuer, which destabilises both the survivor and the counsellor and is reminiscent of the DA experience, in which the abuser alternately punishes and then praises the survivor.

Herman (1992a) identified the presence of 'witness guilt' whereby the survivor doubts that the therapist can manage or understand the traumatic material because the counsellor did not suffer in the way the client did. This can trigger witness guilt in counsellors, who feel that they have not experienced enough trauma to work effectively with survivors. In contrast, some wounded healers who have had DA experiences become locked into comparing their own trauma with that of clients, and become enmeshed.

Counsellors may idealise the survivor by imbuing the latter with strength, value, resourcefulness, self-esteem or coping abilities, providing the client with an inflated sense of hope. In essence, this is a powerful avoidance strategy of the survivor's reality and rendering her invisible as it does not reflect accurately how the client sees herself. It is akin to saying 'You're fine! Things aren't that bad.' Counsellors need to balance encouragement and hope with allowing the survivor self-definition. The rescuer dynamic can lead to intense feelings of helplessness and becoming deskilled, which can result in a failure to support the survivor. Some counsellors may feel contaminated or violated by the survivor and her material. Counsellors must monitor feelings in the CTR, especially inappropriate anger on behalf of the survivor in order to allow the survivor to access such feelings in her own time.

Somatic counter-transference is a rich source of understanding the therapeutic relationships. Somatic counter-transference or embodied counter-transference (Field 1989; Samuels 1985) refers to bodily reactions or feelings experienced by clinicians when working with survivors of DA. Somatic counter-transference may represent somatic resonance of the client's feelings or lack of embodiment, or the counsellor's own somatic reactions. According to Shaw (2004), somatic reactions can give clinicians some idea about the client's bodily state, but clinicians cannot know this state fully, and must balance this with owning their own bodily reactions. Clinicians working with traumatised clients may experience dissociative responses such as lapses of consciousness, numbing or escape imagery.

Phases of the therapeutic process

When working with survivors of DA, the therapeutic process is generally agreed to consist of three main phases (Dutton 1992; Herman 1992a; Humphreys and Thiara 2003). These phases are not linear or sequential, with survivors vacillating between phases as earlier material is revisited and integrated with new knowledge. Before the therapeutic process can begin, counsellors need to conduct a thorough assessment of the survivor's therapeutic needs.

ASSESSMENT

The prime focus of the assessment is to assess risk to the survivor's life. Counsellors need to be able to assess potential danger, whether the survivor is still in the relationship, is intending to leave, or has recently left. Counsellors must never underestimate potential danger and always err on the side of caution. Part of the risk assessment must appraise the level of entanglement with the abuser and how this impacts on the survivor. In addition, counsellors need to assess risk of self-harm and suicidal ideation and institute a safety contract. Part of this process is also to assess risk of harm to others, including the abuser and children. If counsellors believe children to be at risk this must be discussed and appropriate agencies informed. If pharmacological intervention, hospitalisation or residential treatment is indicated, this will also demand discussion with an explanation of how such interventions can work synergistically to facilitate stabilisation and safety. If symptoms are severe and out of control, therapeutic work will be impeded, and medication can act as a container to manage arousal.

Counsellors need to assess level of trauma exposure and responses. This may be uncomfortable for the survivor as it will revive intense feelings of shame, embarrassment, anger and potent responses. If the survivor is overwhelmed it may be necessary to suspend assessment and return to it at a later point. Counsellors are advised to adopt a more informal stance in the assessment process and not push the survivor unnecessarily. Counsellors should endeavour not to enforce a full assessment in one session as the survivor may become overwhelmed or hostile in response to questions. Given these difficulties, a full assessment is best conducted over several sessions.

Counsellors also need to evaluate the impact and effects of trauma, and concomitant symptoms, such as complex post-traumatic stress disorder (PTSD). Counsellors need to recognise and identify symptoms, and see them explicitly as related to exposure to trauma of DA rather than locating such symptoms within personality disorders or pre-morbid psychopathology to avoid pathologising the survivor. While it is crucial to name trauma responses, counsellors must guard against applying damaging diagnostic labels (Dutton 1992; Herman 1992a).

When assessing impact of trauma, counsellors also need to determine prior history of trauma or victimisation, such as childhood abuse, and assess to what extent these may be interlinked. Commonly it is extremely difficult to separate cumulative effects of earlier trauma from the effects of current or recent DA, especially if earlier traumas have not been processed. This can impact the therapeutic process in directing focus to previous abuse, and how this is linked to current DA. In cases of prior traumatic experiences, counsellors need to incorporate this into therapeutic process as it will compound PTSD and trauma symptoms, and reduce survivors' ability to respond effectively to trauma of DA and impede recovery. If necessary, survivors of multiple trauma may need to be referred to a specialist in complex trauma.

Counsellors need to be attuned to somatic, emotional and verbal responses to trauma cues and distinguish between activation and avoidance responses. Activation responses trigger sensory re-experiencing, emotional arousal, cognitions and memories, while avoidance responses consist of emotional numbing, dissociation, disengagement, and denial that trigger avoidance. Counsellors must also monitor level of self-medication, and consider whether the survivor is attending sessions having self-medicated without obvious intoxication.

Counsellors also need to assess stress tolerance and distinguish between avoidance and resilience to stress. In prolonged DA, survivors are conditioned to tolerate inordinate levels of stress to manage and survive DA, which may take considerable time to dissemble. Existing survival strategies need to be assessed and validated so that they can be honed. Counsellors also need to assess the level of social support, such as family, friends and professional support, as these can ameliorate the effects of DA and aid recovery. If the survivor has children, counsellors need to assess access to childcare, because lack of support with children can impede attendance at sessions. Most importantly counsellors need to assess and identify the individual therapeutic needs of the survivor in order to provide efficacious intervention.

THE INITIAL PHASE

The focus during the initial phase of the therapeutic process needs to be on establishing safety within a safe and secure therapeutic relationship. This entails acknowledging and validating the DA and establishing treatment parameters. This may necessitate an element of psychoeducation about the nature of the therapeutic work and the client's expectations of therapy. Internal and external safety is paramount as the therapeutic process cannot proceed without a reasonable level of safety. As this is so pivotal, Chapter 5 will examine in depth how safety can be established, along with the importance of safety planning.

Until safety has been established, counsellors will need to provide crisis intervention and emotional support rather than psychotherapy. This is a time to develop a good working alliance based on a mutual, collaborative relationship. For a strong therapeutic relationship to develop, it is crucial to establish trust, in order to facilitate containment, affect management, self-care and symptom control (Dutton 1992; Herman 1992a). This is often necessary before survivors can begin to name their DA experiences, understand their meaning and restore a sense of autonomy and control.

Premature exploration of DA must be contained until boundaries of trust have been established as this can prompt difficulties in therapeutic engagement. Trust is the key to respectful relationships, and must be prioritised with survivors of DA whose trust has been repeatedly betrayed. Lack of trust may be unformulated and unexpressed, but it is nevertheless omnipresent and frequently tested. The building of trust is not always smooth and may be beset with acting out, testing and challenging. The building of trust should be seen not as an event but a process with fluctuating levels in engagement. Counsellors need to stay constant throughout and not be inconsistent in their reactions to being tested. In contrast, some survivors entrust themselves too quickly, only to feel let down.

To build trust, counsellors must demonstrate clearly to the survivor that whatever is brought to the therapeutic process, including ambivalent feelings and uncertainty, will be explored and can be managed. Counsellors also need to show that they can stay in the survivor's frame of reference and have the patience to let the client control the timing and pacing of sessions. Counsellors must be reliable, on time and consistent in their responses, give as much notice as possible of planned breaks, and handle unplanned breaks due to illness sensitively. Clear and safe boundaries need to be established and adhered to in a consistent manner.

In addition, survivors need to be affirmed and validated in their experiences and assured of confidentiality. Counsellors must be resilient and robust in relating to the survivor. For many survivors, closeness is associated with danger rather than nurturing or caring. Closeness is commonly associated with invasion, lack of autonomy, power and control, and abuse, and as such can trigger feelings of shame and humiliation. Some clients yearn for closeness and yet at the same time perceive it to be the main ingredient of dangerous relationships in which they may be exploited and abused; thus, they flee any perceived intimacy.

Interventions need to be timely, sensitive and not overwhelming in content, style or duration to the survivor. When highly aroused, survivors are not able to engage with the counsellor, especially if interventions move out of the client's frame of reference, or the counsellor is disengaged from the client's emotional state. Short interventions that mirror the survivor's emotional state, with a glimpse of cognitive understanding, are more helpful than trying to reframe the experience into a rational, cognitively driven interpretation.

In the initial phase, attention should also focus on affect modulation and regulation and developing containment strategies (see Chapter 5). It is during this phase that survivors begin to recognise and accept needs and discover ways of having them met. Trust facilitates work on relational dynamics such as intimacy and attachment. Traumatic bonding promotes insecure attachment in which fear of attachment and yearning for closeness oscillate. While some survivors are relieved to enter counselling, others feel ashamed by asking for help. Some survivors fear that this will be perceived as a moral victory to the abuser, or confirmation that they are crazy, compounding a sense of defeat. Counsellors need to reframe accepting help as an act of courage and strength not weakness, restoring power and control.

Existing survival strategies can be identified in this phase so that they can be honed. Psychoeducation plays a prominent role during this phase in normalising responses, and recognising the harmful nature of abuse and explanation of survivors' persistent difficulties. This will lay the foundations of more in-depth therapeutic work in the middle phase.

THE MIDDLE PHASE

In the middle phase the focus is on metabolising trauma and remembering the range of DA experiences, and developing a coherent narrative. It is a time for creating meaning and self-understanding, and permitting self-compassion. Central to this phase is mourning the multiple losses incurred in DA, which allows for integration and transformation of the trauma. Chapter 9 explores in depth the stage of the grieving process, the range of multiple losses and useful techniques that can facilitate healing from DA.

This middle phase is characterised by exploring the nature and pattern of abuse, the psychological effect and survival strategies. This should be done gradually using deconditioning principles of controlled exposure to traumatic material. An important ritual in recovery is to reconstruct the narrative so that the DA is no longer defined by 'shame and humiliation' but 'dignity and virtue' (Mollica 1988). When exploring the abuse, the counsellor needs to understand the nature and complexity of DA and reassure the survivor that she can talk about the full range of experiences, including both positive and negative feelings towards the abuser. Most crucially, both counsellors and survivors need to tolerate ambivalent feelings and uncertainty.

During this stage counsellors need to enable survivors to mentalise their emotions to enhance self-awareness, understanding and control. A number of clinicians have argued that making emotions more intelligible generates more awareness of self and others which facilitates more positive relational dynamics (Allen 2006a; Allen and Fonagy 2006; Fonagy *et al.* 2002). In essence mentalising allows an individual to be attentive and self-aware during an emotional episode in order to derive meaning. It allows the person to feel and think about emotions at the same time, rather than at a later point. To facilitate mentalisation counsellors must enable survivors to identify, or become aware of emotion, modulate the intensity and duration of the emotion, and express the emotion in an appropriate way.

Such mentalising also allows for identifying and expressing needs, desires, motives, intentions, hopes, goals, fears, thoughts, beliefs, attitudes, fantasies and dreams. During trauma, mentalisation is blocked or diverted to 'mind reading' the abuser. This impedes space for reflection, especially self-reflection. When in survival mode, survivors are unable to mentalise unmet needs, emotions and thoughts; these get blocked and pushed out of awareness permitting increased tolerance of abuse.

Mentalising emotions highlights the massive bereavement and multiple losses associated with DA which need to be grieved (see Chapter 9). Mourning is pivotal in accepting the reality and full extent of trauma and abuse. Grieving allows for reconsolidation and restructuring (Herman 1992a). Transforming loss allows the survivor to reclaim power and control. When this is restored the survivor can begin to reconnect to self and others, to consolidate gains and develop healthy interactions with the outside world, which is the focus of the late phase.

THE LATE PHASE

The focus in the late phase is on reconnection. This involves reconnecting to self, other and the world. Much of the reconnection to self will have been facilitated through the therapeutic relationship. This needs to be consolidated and built upon, which is further explored in Chapter 7. Survivors need to rebuild self-esteem, self-confidence and self-efficacy. These skills gradually unfold throughout the therapeutic process and need to be monitored, consolidated and honed.

Reconnection to others is also a gradual process in which survivors begin to trust others and reduce social isolation. Initially this is developed through the therapeutic alliance, and reinforced through the survivor's social support network. Reconnecting to others necessitates relinquishing defences and establishing healthy boundaries in which survivors can safely express needs and a full range of feelings, and say no without fear of punishment. Counsellors need to continue to work on relational dynamics in order for survivors to feel comfortable about intimacy without losing autonomy (see Chapter 8).

Reconnection to self and others allows survivors to restore hope and reconnect to life. The restoration of hope allows survivors to direct their life in which they can risk intimacy and begin to love again. In appreciating being alive, survivors will regain meaning and spirituality to rebuild their lives. Survivors can begin to making personally meaningful choices and set new life goals. The quality of life is now under their control to develop new life philosophy and direction. Restoring hope allows survivors to express their appreciation of life and being alive rather living in fear. This will restore vitality and restore capacity for pleasure, laughter and joy, in which survivors can cherish and enjoy being alive.

ENDING

Ending is implicit from the moment the therapeutic process begins. In time-limited counselling this is explicitly stated whereas in open-ended counselling this may not be articulated. Endings can create anxieties for both survivors and counsellors which need to be examined and expressed. Endings need to be planned and specifically worked towards either through goal setting or by reducing frequency of sessions. Endings can be staggered by reducing from weekly to fortnightly to monthly, or by using a mutually agreed timeframe, in which survivors can prepare fully for the ending. Top-up sessions should be considered if it is thought that they will make survivors feel more empowered and able to manage their life in a more satisfying way. It can be empowering for survivors to assess progress in the absence of regular sessions. Survivors experience a greater sense of autonomy and empowerment in discovering that they can manage outside of the therapeutic setting by putting into practice newly learned skills and changed perceptions. These can then be brought back into sessions to consolidate and develop further if necessary.

Personal growth is a dynamic process and continues after counselling. Subsequent experiences and life events may revive painful feelings or residual difficulties and counsellors need be clear about their position on returning to counselling to work on specific issues or to provide emotional support. Survivors often prefer to see the same counsellor in order to avoid having to start the whole therapeutic process again. In such instances, counsellors could consider brief solution-focused contracts that focus on the specific difficulty.

Factors that indicate ending counselling depend on what has been contracted around duration, or aims and objectives. These commonly include increased safety, improved self-esteem, and self-efficacy. Other indicators include restoration of cohesive self-structures and relational dynamics. The survivor will have attained a greater understanding of the impact of DA, restored meaning and hope, and accessed a desire to reconnect to life. During the ending phase survivors will be able to take their place in the world and feel they have a right to be in that world. The survivor will have integrated the abuse and transformed losses, and be open to continued growth. In addition, survivors will be equipped with the ability to embrace life, feel alive and be present in their world.

Summary

- The trauma and betrayal of trust associated with DA demands a safe therapeutic environment in which survivors can explore the full range of ambivalent feelings, create narrative out of chaos, and make sense of their experiences.

- Counsellors need to provide a safe haven to restore safety, mentalise feelings, and rebuild trust in self and others. To provide a sensitive and holistic approach, counsellors need to have a thorough understanding of the complex nature of DA to avoid pathologising, along with knowledge of multiagency resources available in the community.

- Working with survivors of DA entails a more flexible approach and the adoption of a range of counselling skills and interventions, and knowledge of other treatment modalities and techniques that can be incorporated into the counsellor's practice.

- Prior to embarking on therapeutic process, counsellors need to identify the aims of therapeutic work, and conduct a comprehensive assessment of client safety and therapeutic needs. Internal and external safety must be assessed and, if necessary, safety contracts instituted.

- The therapeutic setting plays a pivotal role in healing from trauma and counsellors need to prioritise building trust in the therapeutic relationship. Particular attention needs to be focused on the therapeutic stance and counsellor's reactive style to ensure sensitive and empathic attunement. It is imperative that counsellors adopt a warm, engaged style within which they are emotionally present if survivors are to connect.

- The therapeutic setting is of considerable importance and counsellors need to be explicit in what they can and cannot provide, and articulate the therapeutic parameters especially in relation to confidentiality, boundaries, pacing and autonomy.

- When working with trauma and abuse, counsellors also need to pay close attention to transference and counter-transference reactions. While these provide rich material with which to understand the survivor, counsellors need to be careful of how these are interpreted. It is imperative that counsellors distinguish between counter-transference reactions to client transference and those that reflect counsellors' own subjective experience.

- There are three main phases of the therapeutic process when working with trauma and abuse. The focus in the initial phase is on establishing internal and external safety as in the absence of this, no therapeutic work can succeed. This stage must be coupled with a degree of psychoeducation in which to understand symptoms as normal responses to extreme circumstances.

- The middle phase is characterised by exploring the full range of feeling and experiences associated with DA. Once a degree of safety has been established and survivors are no longer in survival mode, they can begin to mentalise emotions and experiences. This enhances awareness and understanding, and allows survivors to reconnect to their needs. Pivotal to this phase is mourning in which survivors can transform the multiple losses associated with DA, and begin to restore hope.

- The focus in the final phase is on reconnecting to self, others and life. Increased self-esteem, self-efficacy and restored vitality allow survivors to rebuild their lives, set new personally meaningful goals and embrace feeling alive rather than live in fear.

CHAPTER 5

WORKING WITH SAFETY AND PROTECTION STRATEGIES

The cardinal task when working with a survivor of domestic abuse (DA) is to establish safety. This is of paramount importance at the very start of the therapeutic process, and needs to be constantly monitored and assessed throughout by both counsellor and survivor. This is especially so in the case of DA, where external safety is threatened if the survivor is still in the relationship, and can also continue to be compromised after leaving.

Herman (2001) proposes that no healing or recovery can take place in the absence of safety. The therapeutic relationship is pivotal in restoring safety, both external and internal. It provides a secure base in which to build emotional and social resources. Counsellors can provide a safe haven in which to explore past and current turbulent feelings and make sense of their experiences. The therapeutic setting allows the survivor to think about feelings, or to mentalise them (Fonagy *et al.* 2002) with a trusted witness, who can provide support, encouragement, empathy and guidance. This allows the survivor to develop a deeper understanding of the impact of DA and restore safety.

The therapeutic relationship facilitates emotional awareness, or mindfulness, in which feelings can be felt and understood. Knowing and understanding feelings allows for greater control and regulation of emotions. A secure base can foster the development of self-confidence, autonomy, initiative, problem solving and self-efficacy. This is in stark contrast to DA, where the home and relationship resemble a war zone, characterised by unpredictability, inconsistency and traumatic bonding. Such chaos impairs psychobiological synchrony and disrupts healthy attachment, and a range of concomitant symptoms. When attachment is derailed, psychobiological growth is stunted as all energy is diverted to survival.

This chapter looks at the principal role of safety in healing and recovery from DA. It will look at the importance of assessing levels of danger and strategies to ensure safety. Identifying and validating existing survival strategies will empower survivors to acknowledge inner resources that have afforded protection in the past. These can be consolidated, honed and built upon to increase both internal and external safety. For those survivors still in an abusive relationship, additional protection strategies are evaluated including the role of safety planning in the event of emergency, or if planning to leave. Emphasis is placed on instituting and implementing safety plans during, and after leaving the abusive relationship.

As safety is the first task in the therapeutic process it is during this time that the therapeutic alliance is established. The importance of the therapeutic relationship is examined, along with the role of the counsellor in providing a secure base. Attention will also be focused on useful therapeutic techniques that support safety. It is only when safety is in place that survivors can begin to heal and recover from DA, and live outside the shadow of abuse.

Safety

Security promotes psychobiological synchrony in which somatic, behavioural and psychological systems are attuned to each other, and congruent. In the safety of the therapeutic relationship, the survivor can begin to heal and grow. As safety takes precedence over everything else, counsellors need to ensure meticulous assessment of danger. It is critical that they do not minimise the level of danger but conduct specific assessment of the nature and pattern of the DA. Counsellors need to know the level of physical violence, the potential for escalation, and the threat to life.

While risk assessment is imperative, it is not foolproof. It is impossible to predict the course of any abuse relationship and counsellors are advised to err on the side of caution. Due to the unpredictable nature of DA, counsellors are urged not to assume safety, despite survivors' reassurances, and closely monitor safety concerns. As it is impossible to control either the abuser or the environmental factors, it will be impossible to guarantee absolute safety, even after leaving the DA. This requires the counsellor to balance close monitoring alongside tolerating a level of uncertainty and fear. This will mirror the doubts and fears faced by the survivor, and counsellors must be conscientious in containing both their own and the survivor's anxieties.

As it can take months, even years, to guarantee external safety, the initial focus needs to be on establishing the basics of external safety, from which to proceed to developing internal safety. During this time the therapeutic focus may vacillate between crisis intervention and supportive psychotherapy until a reasonable degree of safety is in place. From this survivors can begin to explore and build internal safety. Developing an understanding of incomprehensible physiological arousal, tumultuous emotions and disrupted thought processes can enable the survivor to gain a level of control over somatic responses.

This not only restores bodily integrity, but also demonstrates to survivors that they can take control in what feels like an uncontrollable world. This allows survivors to build on taking control in other areas of their life and foster increased autonomy and self-efficacy.

INTERNAL SAFETY

To restore bodily integrity, survivors need to have some understanding of the impact of DA on psychobiological functioning. This can be achieved through psychoeducation, in which survivors come to recognise that their symptoms are normal responses to abnormal circumstances. Making the link between trauma and disruptions to physiological functioning clarifies their origins and normalises the survivors' responses.

To begin building internal safety, counsellors need to assess capacity for self-protection as it is potentially dangerous to rely on the partner's declarations of cessation of abusive behaviour. Relying on external assurances can compromise survivors' safety and is too hazardous. Survivors need to mobilise inner sources for self-protection, not only to minimise danger but also to develop control, self-efficacy and autonomy. Reclaiming control is instrumental in restoring self-worth, self-respect and self-agency.

Counsellors need to assess inner resources for self-protection by evaluating existing safety strategies. Survivors invariably acquire and implement a number of survival strategies during DA. These need to be identified and validated to reinforce the survivor's capabilities. Survivors often do not acknowledge existing survival strategies as indicators of their inner strength, and making them more conscious of them facilitates a more positive view of self rather than as a passive victim. These survival strategies can be honed and built upon to increase the survivor's sense of potency.

Counsellors also need to assess presence of self-destructive behaviours such as self-harm, substance misuse and suicidality. In such instances counsellors will need to institute safety contracts and consider medication. These will need to be explicitly discussed with survivors and executed with their full collaboration. In the case of severe substance misuse and dependency, alcohol or drug treatment programmes or rehabilitation may need to be considered. If suicidal ideation and suicidality cannot be contained within the therapeutic process, hospitalisation may be necessary. These need to be implemented within the context of stabilisation, not as pathologising the survivor. Counsellors need to be aware of the deleterious effects and repercussions of labelling the survivor, and such decisions must not be taken lightly, or without the survivor's full consent. Such interventions should not be forced on the survivor but be a collaborative decision, based on informed consent. They must be seen as a way to facilitate the therapeutic work, and enhance sense of self-efficacy and control.

Assessment also needs to incorporate level of physical injuries that need medical attention. This may include previous injuries that have not healed or been fully investigated. In addition, counsellors need to assess the survivor's ability for self-care, such as sleeping, healthy eating, capacity for rest and relaxation. These are usually not possible in DA due to hypervigilance, but are crucial to replenish already meagre energy resources. Consideration must also be given to assessing the survivor's vulnerability to engage in impulsive risk-taking behaviour such as fleeing into potentially destructive relationships. One survivor, who was helped by a male friend to escape her abusive husband, found herself subjected to the same abuse once the new relationship was formalised.

Once physical injuries are treated, focus can be directed on basic health needs. The struggle for survival in DA can undermine general physical health due to lack of sleep and opportunities for recuperation. In order to restore bodily integrity, counsellors need to enable survivors to restore disrupted biological rhythms such as sleeping, eating and exercise. This helps to regulate bodily functions and restore severely depleted energy levels. It also allows for the restoration of more adaptive self-regulation, and the development of self-soothing behaviours which were demolished during the DA.

Attention must also be directed at reducing any manifest trauma symptoms such as post-traumatic stress disorder (PTSD), hyperarousal and emotional reactivity (see Chapter 6). Psychoeducation can help survivors to recognise and label their symptoms within a trauma context. This needs to be combined with techniques to restore adaptive affect regulation so that they can learn to modulate their emotional states. Through body awareness, survivors can learn to regulate turbulent emotions and hyperarousal. Rather than being overwhelmed by seemingly uncontrollable physiological states, survivors can learn to decelerate and bring them under their control (see Chapter 6). The use of biofeedback in which they tune into their body, combined with calming images and accessing safe places, allows survivors to lower high levels of arousal and restore a state of equilibrium. When physiological arousal is under the survivor's control it permits greater understanding and mentalisation. Somatic control can also strengthen survivors' resolve to reclaim control in other areas of their life.

The prolonged coercive control inherent in DA can complicate establishing internal safety and bodily integrity. In DA survivors come to perceive their body as belonging to others and find it alien to take control. Furthermore, the unpredictability associated with DA undermines survivors' ability to plan and take initiative, which will be necessary to restore when taking care of self. As survivors have been prevented from taking control, it might be difficult for them to take charge of their own recovery, believing this to be the counsellor's role. Yet taking control enhances self-esteem and sense of competence, which are crucial to restore sense of trust in one's self, not just in the therapist.

When survivors are a danger to themselves through self-harm, suicidality, eating disorders, drug or alcohol misuse or impulsive risk-taking behaviour, establishing internal safety can be compromised and recovery becomes protracted. Such difficulties will interrupt the therapeutic process, and may represent symbolic re-enactments of abuse (Herman 2001). In the absence of adaptive internal safety strategies, survivors frequently resort to self-medicating to regulate intolerable feelings. Furthermore, they may be reluctant to relinquish what they see as trusted, albeit unhealthy, self-soothing strategies. It is crucial that counsellors and survivors persevere with healthy internal safety strategies to restore capacity for self-care and self-soothing.

The nature of prolonged coercive control instils dependency on the abuser, with survivors believing that they are incapable of independent judgement or taking initiative. This will complicate developing internal safety as survivors believe they cannot take charge of themselves or implement self-care strategies. Some survivors will cling to fantasies that eventually the abuser will show remorse, apologise and make reparation. Counsellors may need to disabuse survivors of such fantasies and enable them to face the stark reality that only one person can restore the damage, and that is the survivor. This may appear to be such an insurmountable task that some survivors will project rescue fantasies on to the counsellor. Counsellors need to guard against this to ensure that they do not become embroiled in a struggle over who is responsible for the survivor's recovery, and become more committed to the client's safety than the client.

The therapeutic relationship must balance emotional support with encouraging survivors to reclaim control by relinquishing their need to rely on others. Commonly survivors have become accustomed to automatically relinquishing control to others without considering that they have a choice. In addition, survivors often fear that their attempts to take initiative or control will result in being patronised and demeaned. Counsellors need to remind survivors that new skills entail practising to attain competence, and the pivotal role that reclaiming control has in their healing. Each positive action, however small, needs to be reinforced including keeping a concrete record of each achievement.

Internal safety can also be aided by re-establishing self-chosen, routine daily tasks. A daily routine can instil a sense of predictability and consistency to ground the survivor. The importance of making time for relaxation and peaceful moments needs to be emphasised as an antidote to the maelstrom of chaos. Taking time to sit and relax, especially with children, without worrying about the abuser or external factors, can provide an oasis in which to restore depleted energy resources. Counsellors can also invite the survivor to set concrete goals to retain a clear focus. Keeping a record of these and recording their accomplishments can help the survivor to keep track of their healing and recovery.

EXTERNAL SAFETY

As the survivor regains control of bodily integrity and vitality returns, energy can be directed to external safety. As safety is undermined if the survivor is in a hostile and non-protective environment, counsellors need to regularly monitor current and potential danger. This includes assessment of all important relationships in the survivor's life to ascertain source and level of danger, along with potential sources of protection, emotional support and practical help. Counsellors need to be aware of the level of entanglement with the abuser, and likelihood of threat and danger. It is crucial to remain objective in assessing this and not to minimise potential danger based on the abuser's assurances, or the survivor's level of fear. It is critical to assess implicit conditions of violence in which the abuser trades cessation of violence for the survivor's compliance and surrendered autonomy. Abusers need to relinquish their wish to dominate, and not just their use of physical force.

Counsellors also need to assess the survivor's relationships with others. Family, friends and neighbours may be coerced by the abuser to take sides, undermining the survivor's sense of safety. One survivor recounted that when ending the abusive relationship, her ex-partner co-opted neighbours and friends, leaving her isolated with no support or place of safety whenever he harassed her. In desperation some survivors may unwittingly turn to potentially dangerous individuals by whom their vulnerability is exploited. Still others withdraw from all social support for fear of being betrayed again.

Establishing a solid support system plays an instrumental role when recovering from DA, and counsellors need to encourage survivors to increase their social support system within healthy boundaries without compromising safety. However, supportive relationships need to be carefully chosen and closely monitored to minimise further betrayal of trust. Many survivors of DA are sustained by seeking support from other survivors, and this is an ideal opportunity to increase their support network. Self-help groups can provide a safe haven for many survivors and should be actively encouraged by counsellors.

To enhance safety, contact with the abusive partner needs to be kept to a minimum. In many cases this may not be possible due to contact orders and legal proceedings. Ideally physical contact must be minimised, and in those instances when it is unavoidable, such as going to court, it is helpful if it is in the presence of a third party, preferably a supportive friend. In such instances the survivor needs to remain at a distance from the abuser and resist eye contact so as to sustain a healthy boundary. If possible the survivor needs to maintain a distance by minimising phone contact, or any kind of social interaction until a level of self-protection has been attained.

It is also helpful to resist trying to ascertain the ex-partner's movements or state of mind as this reinforces enmeshment and prevents the survivor from focusing on personal needs, and re-enacts the abusive relationship.

Counsellors also need to assess the level of safety in the survivor's living arrangement, be it family home, refuge or shelter. In the case of the family home, the survivor may need to change the locks and install panic buttons linked to the local police station, in the event of danger. If the survivor has fled to a refuge or hostel, it is crucial to keep the location secret to ensure safety. This is also the case when seeking temporary refuge with family or friends. One survivor was traced by her husband to a friend's home through incautious comments from a mutual friend. Safety in the larger community may also need to be scrutinised, due to stigmatisation and transgression of social sanctions against disclosing DA. The threat of violence and fear of being found may inhibit the survivor's mobility, which recapitulates the sense of being trapped.

Financial security is commonly compromised when leaving an abusive relationship, and is a recurring threat to external safety. Abusive partners manipulate this in reneging on financial agreements, returning to court to seek changes, or refusing any financial support. This highlights the abuser's level of ongoing power and control, and serves to undermine recovery. Such reminders of the ex-partner's control can destabilise survivors as they struggle to survive financially. It diverts attention away from healing as the survivor has to expend severely depleted energy resources to make ends meet. In the case of claiming benefits, this is often a lengthy process that further undermines the survivor's equilibrium. Many survivors are plunged into debt, adding to their already precarious sense of safety.

As external safety is established, the survivor can resume ordinary activities such as shopping, driving, working and performing routine daily tasks. While each new environment demands some level of assessment of danger, when equipped with self-protection strategies, the survivor can begin to reconnect to daily life. Engagement with such normal and mundane activities heralds the beginning of the survivor rebuilding a life outside the shadow of abuse.

External safety can be compromised by a number of factors, especially when in contact with the abuser. If these become overwhelming, the survivor may need to redirect focus back onto internal safety to restore equilibrium, conserve energy and restore vitality. If stabilisation collapses, counsellors need to assess level of risk and return to crisis intervention. While this may interrupt the therapeutic process, it is necessary to restore inner resources. When energy levels are improved, the survivor can begin to address the external demands again. This will restore control and empower the survivor in dealing with the environmental necessities.

Safety planning

As safety can never be fully guaranteed, survivors need a detailed and realistic contingency plan. Prior to embarking on concrete safety planning, survivors need to have mastered self-protection strategies, and established a level of control over physiological symptoms and affect regulation. In addition, as individual circumstances differ, counsellors need to avoid a one-cap-fits all approach, and ensure that any safety plan is customised to incorporate the specific needs and resources of each survivor.

The aim of safety planning is to prepare, anticipate and plan ahead in crisis situations when the partner is being violent. It is also an opportunity for the survivor to develop practical tools and skills to increase safety. Safety plans are a safe way to take any necessary action, be it raising a specific issue with the partner, or when intending to leave. Focusing on a specific plan also highlights the reality of danger when the partner is violent, and aids recognition of difficulties and limitations around existing protection strategies, for self or children.

A personalised, individual safety plan helps survivors to think about how to increase safety, whether within an abusive relationship, or when leaving. Planning in advance for the possibility of future violence and abuse promotes increased protection for survivors and their children. It also signifies survivors taking proactive control of the abuse. Rehearsing strategies identified in the safety plan, in and outside session, enables survivors to embed skills in the eventuality of danger. In addition, rehearsal will set the plan in mind, and make it more automatic and easier to expedite in actual emergency.

It is important not to make safety plans too complex as it may be too difficult to remember all the intricacies during an emergency. In the face of danger, survival mechanisms will be activated which will prevent the individual from laborious cognitive processing, whereas a simple, well-rehearsed safety plan will be more easily executed. Rehearsal will imprint the plan, making it more automatic and easier to implement, especially when in survival mode.

While there are a number of general principles and standard safety planning techniques, counsellors need to customise them to fit each individual survivor's needs. As each DA situation is unique, with different requirements, any safety plan will have to be tailored to take into account specific circumstances, resources and needs.

In devising individualised safety plans a number of factors need to be considered, such as the specific nature of the safety issues, the survivor's greatest fears, and range of options. The survivor also needs to identify her specific situation, resources and needs goals and how they can be achieved. This includes subtle and implicit cues that precede violent outbursts. Identifying subtle forms of coercive control such as being at the abuser's beck and call, or modulating mood, and changing these represents a shift in the relationship.

Counsellors need to devote time to careful examination to build up a realistic picture and to help set achievable goals. Breaking the plan into small incremental units will make achieving the ultimate goal more manageable. Counsellors are also urged to validate each step to reinforce how the survivor is taking control by prioritising safety rather than focusing on changing the partner's behaviour, for which the survivor is not responsible.

Most crucially, judicious risk assessment needs to accompany any safety planning. While safety planning can enhance safety, counsellors are reminded that the survivor is most at risk when leaving an abusive relationship and any risks must be minimised. When deciding to leave, it is imperative that the survivor does not signal this intention through non-verbal cues or changes in behaviour. The survivor needs to continue to behave as normally as possible to avoid arousing the partner's suspicion. It is also recommended that the survivor does not inform children, or other parties known to the abuser, so as to minimise the risk of exposure of the plan.

If not planning to leave, survivors can still improve safety by increasing self-protection strategies. Ideally survivors need to balance the control the partner has by taking control wherever possible. While survivors have no control in relation to their partner, they do have control over their inner world. Focusing on nourishing themselves by healthy eating, sleeping, exercise and relaxation can maintain energy levels and strength to implement the safety plan. Reducing interactions with the partner, without arousing suspicion or courting danger, can also enable the survivor to maintain a sense of self; to be subject rather than object. In addition, the survivor can be invited to imagine a future outside the abusive relationship. Rehearsing an alternative future can facilitate transforming the limitations of the present by setting specific goals. The more the survivor rehearses an abuse-free future, the easier it will be to achieve that reality.

SAFETY PLAN

While each safety plan needs to take individual circumstances, needs and resources into account, there are some fundamental principles that can be incorporated. Women's Aid Federation (2005) has produced comprehensive guidelines than can helpfully guide counsellors in developing a safety plan with individual survivors (see Table 5.1).

Table 5.1 Guidelines for safety plan

- Keep safe important emergency telephone number, such as local Women's Aid project, or refuge, and other DA services such as the police Community Safety Unit, general practitioner (GP), social worker, and social services emergency numbers. Also children's school, solicitor, freephone 24 hour National Domestic Violence Helpline run in partnership between Women's Aid and Refuge (0808 2000 247). In emergency dial 999: the police will attend the call, even if you are unable to speak. If possible leave phone off hook after dialling.

- Teach children, if appropriate and old enough, to call 999 in an emergency or when they feel in danger. It may help to establish a code word to convey that that is what they should do. Specify what information will be required such as name and address. Rehearsing the procedure with the child can make it easier to execute this in an emergency. However, survivors need to be cautious that the child does not become a target for physical attack or that they feel overly responsible for ensuring safety abuse.

- Attend GP whenever injured to obtain medical notes and photographs of all injuries for later evidence.

- Archive abusive texts and voicemail messages as evidence.

- Keep a diary or log of abusive incidents and store in safe place, preferably not in the home.

- If there are neighbours who can be trusted then it may help to inform them about the violence and abuse. Neighbours can afford an immediate place of safety in an emergency. It is helpful to discuss what you would like them to do if they hear sounds of abusive or violent attack such as calling the police.

- Choose a code word for a neighbour or friend that will trigger a particular action such as calling the police, or coming to the house to visit. Consideration needs to be given to their fears of safety, and only appropriate friends or neighbours should be co-opted.

- Shouting 'fire' is more likely to attract attention than shouting 'help'.

- If in a public place it is helpful to attract the attention of a specific person, who looks most likely to extend help, and be clear what it is they need to do.

- Rehearse escape plan so it is easier to expedite in an emergency without having to think too much.

- If considering leaving or needing to leave in a hurry, it is crucial to have emergency numbers and money put aside, and easily accessible. It is also useful to have access to important documents pertaining to survivor and children such as passports, identification or naturalisation papers. If relevant benefit or rent books, birth certificates and credit cards may be necessary, along with utility bills.

- Try to keep a small amount of money available at all times, including change for phone or bus fares.

- It is important to know where the nearest public phone is located. If survivors have access to a mobile, keep it on them at all times.

- If survivors fear the partner is about to attack, they should endeavour to get to a lower risk area of house or flat where there is a way out, or access to a phone or panic button. Survivors should avoid the kitchen or garage, where there are likely to be knives or other weapons. It is also crucial to avoid rooms where they could be trapped, such as a
  s a cupboard or small space.

  case of emergency.

  order to leave, such as documents,
  value, such as treasured photos or
  each child.

  as clothes, documents and memen-
  ber or women's project.

  essentials and hide it somewhere
  not arouse suspicion.

org.uk (accessed 29 February 2008)

Survivors who have children will also need to include childcare in their safety plan. This is particularly crucial for those with young children. Organising practical aspects of leaving is time consuming and may not be possible with young children. A survivor with three very young children would find it impossible to focus on pressing practical tasks and be fully emotionally available to her children. These competing demands would leave her physically and emotionally drained. Seeking support from health visitors and accessing childcare, even it is only for a few hours a day, can restore a sense of control to address practical tasks, or to rest and restore energy levels.

If survivors are being harassed or stalked by the abuser, then additional strategies will need to be incorporated into the safety plan. Ideally, they need to keep contact with the ex-partner to an absolute minimum, and certainly no more than any legal requirement. If they fear they will be followed, they need to carry a mobile phone or rape alarm, and try to frequent only well-lit or busy public areas. Survivors may need to be reminded that they should carry only legally acceptable objects for self-protection such as keys or spray. If possible, survivors may benefit from attending a self-defence course which can help them evaluate whether self-defence or fighting back is the best option. Knowing that they can defend themselves is often a crucial step in taking control and empowerment.

As internal and external safety increases, survivors can gradually begin to trust themselves again. This trust is strengthened through the therapeutic alliance in which the survivor begins to trust the counsellor and others in the support network. As survivors begin to gain confidence in protecting self, and have control over symptoms, and emotion, they begin to trust themselves and others more than the abusive partner. Being able to rely on a healthy support network enables survivors to set boundaries and resist being drawn into abuse dynamics. This commonly heralds an important shift in the abuse relationship.

This shift is sufficient for some survivors to continue in the abuse relationship, while others begin to seriously consider the idea of leaving. Once self-protection, self-care and appropriate trusting is established, the survivor may begin the preparatory work for leaving.

Preparation to leave

When working with survivors who have decided to leave the abuse relationship, it is imperative that counsellors have an awareness and understanding of the numerous obstacles to leaving. These obstacles will include external blocks as well as internal resistance, and will be unique to each individual. External obstacles usually cluster around lack of knowledge of resources, access to those resources, and availability of practical and emotional support. There are also realistic fears around safety, as many survivors of DA are most at risk of being fatally attacked when leaving or after having left the abuser. In addition there will be genuine fears concerning housing, financial support, child access and legal implications. These all need to be carefully assessed and explored, so that survivors can make informed choices based on their needs and resources.

Counsellors may need to equip survivors with requisite information on DA projects, refuges and emergency helpline numbers, as well as local housing, social services and survivor support groups. It is also useful to have contact details of experienced local family solicitors who may be able to provide legal advice at a nominal or reduced fee. Additional support can be provided by local advocacy projects, which aim to provide information and help, including in-court advocacy for survivors of DA. Such information is often available from local boroughs as leaflets, which counsellors could pass on to the survivor.

While there are many external obstacles to leaving, survivors may also be restricted by internal obstacles. These need to be fully explored and evaluated before continuing work on safety planning. Counsellors need to assess readiness to move on and ensure that survivors are not rushed into premature decisions. Unexplored internal resistance will undermine any safety plan, as survivors may not be able to carry it through, and potentially put them at greater risk. It is crucial to work with each survivor's needs and inner resources rather than implementing leaving strategies prematurely.

Thinking about leaving, making the decision and safety planning can be a long process. It is crucial that survivors direct this at their own pace. It is invariably better to plan slowly and assuredly, and not hurry the process. Counsellors need to remind survivors that they do not have to do it immediately, or indeed at all. What is necessary is to consider all the options and think about how the survivor might overcome the difficulties involved. The process may also be subverted by other pressing factors such as birthdays, holiday periods and anniversaries, or crippling uncertainty and doubts. Counsellors need to tolerate any diversions, be supportive and come back to the process when the survivor is ready.

Ideally the decision to leave should be carefully planned, well in advance. As the risks are greatest when leaving an abusive relationship, the better prepared for all eventualities the survivor is, the safer she and the children will be. If at all possible, it is helpful to set aside a small amount of money each week, or open a separate bank account. Where possible, survivors may also need to establish a separate credit rating, and apply for their own credit card. Documentation pertaining to these and statements need to be carefully hidden so as not to arouse suspicion, which could incur the abuser's wrath and increase danger.

As this is the most dangerous time, the survivor may need extra support, including in between session contact, especially in case of an emergency Counsellors need to be crystal clear in what they can and cannot offer the survivor. During this critical phase, counsellors need to be flexible but need to refrain from making assurances that they cannot fulfil. If counsellors state their availability and then fail to respond to the survivor's call, this will be perceived as being let down or betrayed and will undermine trust. As counsellors cannot be available on a 24-hour basis, it may be necessary to compile a list of other names and numbers to contact. Counsellors need to be realistic and not agree to something that is likely to fail.

If at all possible, the survivor should plan to leave when the partner is not around, to minimise danger. As it may be impossible to return at a later point, the survivor needs to take all essential items including important documents relating to the survivor and the children. It is advisable not to leave any children behind as it may be difficult or impossible to obtain custody in the future. If children are still at school, it will be necessary to inform the head and class teacher, and clarify arrangements of who will be collecting them from school.

Women's Aid (2007) suggest a capsule list of things to organise and pack when leaving (see Table 5.2). A small emergency bag can be packed in advance and hidden somewhere safe in the home, while a larger bag may be kept at a friend's or neighbour's house. It may be safer not to store these at a mutual friend or family member's house as this is where the abuser may try to intercept the survivor.

Protecting self after leaving

The time that survivors of DA are most at risk is when they have left the relationship. Survivors need to continue to monitor their environment for potential danger and evaluate risks. Some survivors may decide not to tell others why they have left their partner and this has to be respected. In cases where the survivor is at risk, it may be judicious to inform trusted others such as family and friends, as well as the children's nursery or school, and employer. To preserve safety, it is necessary to ensure that they do not inadvertently release information to the ex-partner, or allow children to be collected by anyone other than a designated person. It may be helpful to support these measures with appropriate documentation such as court orders, and to establish passwords to emphasise safety.

If survivors remain in the immediate neighbourhood, they need to be vigilant and alert to potential danger. They need to assess their level of vulnerability and avoid isolated localities. Visiting shops or cafes that were frequented together presents a risk of meeting the ex-partner and may trigger painful reminders. If survivors have a regular routine, such as a nursery or school run, or going into work, or regular appointments, they may need to consider altering or varying their routine as much as possible, including form of transport and routes used. This could include counselling appointment times: counsellors will have to consider how flexible they can be to accommodate such measures.

If the survivor stays in the family home, or returns after the partner has left, then it will be necessary to take certain precautions to ensure safety. If the home feels unsafe, survivors may consider changing the locks on all the doors and

Table 5.2 List of items to pack when leaving

- Some form of identification.

- Birth certificates for survivor and children.

- All necessary passports, visas, work permits or naturalisation documents.

- Money, bankbooks, cheque book, credit and debit cards.

- Keys for house, car and work. It is helpful to get an extra set of keys cut to be kept in the emergency bag.

- Cards or benefit books for child and welfare benefits.

- Driving licence and car registration documents, if applicable.

- Any prescribed medication.

- Copies of document relating to housing tenure such as mortgage details, lease or rental agreement.

- Utilities bill which may be needed as additional identification, or for opening a separate bank account.

- Insurance documents, including national insurance number and child health numbers.

- Address book.

- Family photographs, diary, jewellery and small items of sentimental value.

- Clothing and toiletries for survivor and children.

- Small toy for each child.

- Also any documentation pertaining to abuse such as police reports, court orders such as injunctions and restraining orders, copies of medical records if available.

Source: based on resources available at www.womensaid.org.uk (accessed 29 February 2008)

installing window locks. This could be combined with installing motion sensor lighting at the back and front of the property. Counsellors may also direct survivors to any local community alarm schemes that can install rapid response helpline phone lines or a panic button, and advise on additional security measures available in the local area to make the home safe. An added precaution is the installation of smoke detectors and fire extinguishers in case of fire attack.

Survivors may also need to change their telephone numbers, become ex-directory and screen all calls by using an answering machine. Survivors should endeavour to keep copies of all court orders such as injunctions, restraining orders, occupation or protection orders together with dates and times of previous incidents and call outs. To ensure prompt response from the police in case of emergency, it is expedient to ensure that the local police have copies of these on their files. It may also be advisable to inform neighbours of the circumstances and ask them to inform the survivor or police if the ex-partner breaks the terms of any injunctions or restraining orders.

If the ex-partner continues to harass, threaten or abuse, it is crucial to document any incidents, with dates and a detailed account of the situation, and take photographs if there is injury to the person or damage to property. In the case of injury, survivors must attend their GP or go to hospital and request that their visit is documented. In the case of injunctions with power of arrest or restraining order, the police must be informed and asked to enforce them. If the ex-partner is in breach of any court order, the survivor's solicitor must be informed immediately.

Survivors may also need to explore what further decisions they may wish to make such as official separation or divorce. While this can seem yet another external stressor, psychologically it signifies a concrete ending of the abusive relationship. Counsellors must be reminded that such decisions should be carefully assessed as this may provoke a negative reaction from the abuser, who will see this as another way of losing control over the survivor. To restore control, the abuser may escalate threats and become violent, thereby endangering the survivor. Such a decision can evoke ambivalent feelings and generate contradictory advice from friends. Counsellors need to remind survivors not to set unattainable goals as it reinforces sense of failure. It might be prudent to postpone such decisions until strong enough to make informed choices, and internal and external control is well established. Whatever the survivor's decisions, counsellors need to support these even if they are contrary to their own opinion.

If the survivor has moved away from the area and does not want to reveal the location, additional safety strategies may need to be implemented. As mobile phones can be tracked it may be expedient to change the mobile phone and the phone company. If there is a shared email address, it is advisable to change this and establish a separate email account. It may also be prudent to change bank accounts to avoid using joint accounts, or shared credit and debit cards. Any transactions on joint accounts will be logged on statements which will be seen by the ex-partner.

Survivors need to ensure as much as possible that legal documents, court papers or child custody reports that are shared with the ex-partner do not display the new address, subject to legal advice. It is also imperative to screen caller ID when making phone calls to the ex-partner. In the UK this is done by dialling 141 prior to making any calls. Children may also need to be informed of these precautions, and instructed to keep their new address and location confidential.

Leaving DA relationships necessitate major changes and concomitant losses. Many survivors give up everything including their home, neighbourhood, friends, family and livelihood. The enormity of such losses can be overwhelming (see Chapter 9) as survivors recognise that freedom and safety come at a cost.

Counsellors should never underestimate the courage, strength and determination of survivors of DA.

Working with safety

Working with safety can be arduous and demanding, with survivors often wanting to bypass this fundamental stage and rush into deeper therapeutic work. A common error is to precipitate deeper exploration without establishing internal or external safety, or a secure therapeutic alliance. Counsellors need to remind survivors that no in-depth therapeutic work can succeed without establishing safety. In addition, recovery from the trauma of DA is not attained through cathartic expulsion of pent-up feelings and recounting the graphic details of assaults (Herman 2001). Working with survivors of DA is much more painstaking, requiring extensive preparation and practice. Survivors need to regain control of both physiological and psychological disruptions that have accumulated over years of coercive control. These can be restored only gradually, with repetitive practice and embedded internal safety mechanisms.

Central to any therapeutic work is meticulous assessment through evaluation of the survivor's individual circumstances and needs. It is also imperative to assess the level of internal resources, and degree of disruption to psychobiological functioning. In extreme cases, counsellors need to consider medication or residential treatment, and discuss this with the survivor. Counsellors are urged to err on the side of caution and never underestimate the threat or danger.

During assessment, counsellors will need to take into account child protection issues. If children are thought to be in any danger or at risk, counsellors will need to make appropriate referrals. In such instances it is imperative that this is discussed with the survivor, with reasons why. This can be extremely difficult as the survivor may perceive this as punitive, which can undermine the therapeutic relationship. Counsellors need to provide clear evidence of their concerns and the rationale for making the referral.

A crucial aspect of assessment is to evaluate and identify forms of coercive control, including subtle ones such as the survivor's compliance to attending to the abuser's every need, and adjusting mood and behaviour on command. This will help the survivor to recognise the full extent of control and face the reality of DA. It is also a way of assessing level of entanglement with the abuser, and gain understanding of abuse dynamics. This is a time for psychoeducation to enable the survivor to name the abuse, understanding its impact and long-term psychobiological effects. From this counsellors can begin to focus on internal safety strategies.

To engage in therapeutic work with survivors of DA, it is crucial to provide a safe therapeutic space in which a healthy therapeutic relationship can unfold. To achieve this, counsellors need to be aware of the complexities of DA and how it impacts on issues around trust and fear of connection. To ensure safety and trust, counsellors must explicitly state their therapeutic philosophy, what they can offer and what they are unable to provide. This particularly pertains to confidentiality. Survivors often fear that disclosure of information will lead to negative repercussions such as losing their children, being pathologised, or that the abuser may somehow access it. Explicit clarification of ethical guidelines and under which circumstances confidentiality has to be breached must be provided at the beginning of any work. Unless such boundaries are understood the survivor will not feel safe and the therapeutic work cannot begin.

Working with survivors of DA is extremely demanding and commonly involves more active involvement with clients, and a level of flexibility which some counsellors may not feel comfortable with. Counsellors may need to offer extra help such as providing information on practical resources and DA support agencies, writing reports or facilitating survivor's flight to a shelter. It is crucial that counsellors assess their capacity to work with this client group before taking on any therapeutic work with survivors of DA.

Counsellors must also guard against misinterpreting the client's lack of engagement in aspects of therapeutic work, or erratic attendance. Rather than interpreting this as resistance, counsellors need to understand these within the context of DA. There are often genuine reasons as to why attendance is disrupted, not least lack of childcare or transport and other exigent demands. Survivors are constantly faced by the competing demands of practical tasks and emotional needs. Counsellors use such situations as examples of establishing internal safety and encourage survivors to attend regularly as part of their self-care and self-respect. Therapy may be one of the few areas that survivors can take control and be subject rather than object. Counsellors may also need to provide more validation and reassurance than they do with other clients. Validating each positive action and goal attained, however small, is crucial to rebuild self-confidence and self-esteem.

Safety is compromised if the counsellor sees the couple together, or tries to conduct couples therapy. Invariably survivors are not able to speak freely during sessions, and if they do they may be subjected to an increase in violence afterwards. Partners need to seek a different therapist, and most abusers need highly specialised treatment to break their need to control. Cessation of violence is not sufficient to ensure safety, as abusers need to repudiate their need to dominate, coerce and control.

Counsellors must explicitly state that they cannot see the couple together so that the survivor is clear that the therapeutic space is safe and secure. One survivor was coerced by her partner to let him accompany her to her session. The astonished counsellor was unsure how to refuse him entry and capitulated. Throughout the session the survivor was silent as the abuser insisted that she was mentally unstable and prone to make nefarious allegations. The session felt unsafe for both survivor and counsellor and seriously undermined the therapeutic alliance. Had the boundary been established from the outset, the counsellor would have found it easier to refuse entry and reschedule the appointment with the survivor for another time.

In the event that a relationship or couples counsellor suspects when working with a couple that there is DA, the counsellor needs to check the guidelines of his or her governing body or organisation on how to proceed. It may be contraindicated to continue to work with the couple until the abuser has sought specialist treatment. Counsellors should never assume that safety has been established, even if the client believes it, and should never minimise the potential danger. It also sends out a clear message that violence and coercive control are being taken seriously and are not acceptable under any circumstances.

Counsellors need to be careful when survivors set unrealistic or unattainable goals as it reinforces their sense of failure. Counsellors need to support survivors in their decisions, even if they personally disagree with them. Any decision should be fully explored with the survivor to consider all options and outcomes. Once the decision is made, counsellors need to continue to support the survivor in that decision to preserve the therapeutic relationship. It may be at this time that the survivor most needs support, especially if the decision goes against the advice of family and friends. Survivors often fear being seen as idiotic and pathetic if they go back to the abuser, and feel undeserving of support. If counsellors can be constant in their support and focus on enhancing survival and safety strategies, the survivor may be able to reassess the decision until stronger and internal safety and control have been restored.

Working with survivors entails much fear and uncertainty and counsellors must be able to tolerate this. It is crucial that counsellors can contain their fears and uncertainty, and not act out their anger toward the abuser. It is only through such containment that the survivor can be free to permit their feelings towards the abuser. Counsellors must guard against contaminating the survivor's feelings, especially as the survivor invariably has ambivalent feelings which need to be fully explored and expressed. To manage client material and the concomitant responses evoked, counsellors need to ensure regular and robust supervision. On occasions it may be necessary to consult specialist supervisors who are trained in trauma and DA, and are experienced in working with DA (see Chapter 10).

Therapeutic techniques

There are a number of techniques that counsellors can use to aid safety. As DA experiences are unique, counsellors need to be flexible in their approach and integrate a number of modalities into their core treatment philosophy. Psychoeducation can play a potent role when working with survivors of DA.

Knowledge is power and in providing information, counsellors can enable survivors to make informed choices that are empowering. It is essential that counsellors have information about other sources of support in the local community that they can pass on to survivors. Information around the impact and effects of trauma and DA on psychobiological functioning can help survivors to understand their symptoms as normal responses to extreme circumstances. Intelligibility fosters controllability. Such understanding restores a sense of control over their bodily integrity.

To establish internal safety and stabilisation, counsellors can employ behavioural techniques such as biofeedback, relaxation and desensitisation to manage turbulent feelings. Such titration facilitates affect regulation, especially when combined with body awareness techniques. As survivors become more embodied, and able to regulate somatic responses, they are able to feel more in control of physiological arousal. Behavioural techniques can also be employed to re-establish daily routines and engender a sense of stability and predictability.

Cognitive techniques can be used to help survivors name their abuse experiences, recognise symptoms and increased awareness of negative thinking about self, others and the world. Setting realistic goals and manageable homework tasks instils a sense of proactive control over recovery. Daily logs to chart symptoms and adaptive responses along with journal keeping enables survivors to keep a record of their achievements and increased control and safety. Recording any incidents of abuse in a book allows survivors to document patterns of abuse and concrete evidence of outbursts or violent attacks.

Interpersonal strategies are crucial for establishing the therapeutic alliance and to develop trust. Given the betrayal of trust inherent in DA, restoring trust in self and others can be an arduous task. Through building internal safety the survivor begins to trust in self more, which allows for increased trust in the counselling relationship. This in turn can be transferred to trusting others by building a social support system. Mobilising the survivor's support network to include trusted family, friends and self-help groups reduces social isolation and increases external safety.

It is only when internal and external safety is established that deeper psychotherapeutic work can begin. When survivors of DA have established control over physiological arousal and mastered affect regulation they can begin to direct restored energy to external safety. Being able to trust self and others allows for increased safety in the therapeutic relationship and the wider social support system. From this survivors can begin to recount and make sense of the DA experience. During this process survivors can begin to make links between DA and trauma, and how this has impacted on psychobiological functioning. In constructing a coherent narrative, traumatic sensations and fragmented memories are revived, leading to a sense of re-experiencing the trauma of abuse. Chapter 6 examines the relationship between trauma and DA, and how counsellors can alleviate trauma reactions and symptoms to facilitate the integration of trauma.

Summary

- No healing or recovery can take place in the absence of safety. The therapeutic relationship is pivotal in restoring safety, both internal and external. It provides a secure base in which to restore autonomy, and build emotional and social resources.

- Meticulous risk assessment is imperative, and potential danger should never be underestimated. Counsellors need to assess the risk of the abuser's violence as well as the risk of survivor self-harm and risk to children. A safety contract needs to be instituted. Existing safety and protection strategies need to be identified, validated and honed.

- Before any deeper therapeutic work can take place, psychobiological synchrony needs to be restored. Counsellors can start this process through psychoeducation in which physiological responses are viewed as normal responses to trauma. In addition, counsellors need to equip survivors with information about the range of existing resources to provide practical and social support.

- As it is impossible to exert control over the abuser and external environment, the initial focus is on internal safety and control. If survivors can restore control over their physiological arousal, titrate intensity of feeling and regulate emotions, they can develop internal safety. Internal control and safety allows restored energy to be directed to establishing external safety.

- The focus in external safety is assessing potential danger, acknowledging the level of coercive control, both subtle and overt, and honing self-protection strategies. Building a trusted social support can help sustain the survivor, and provide sanctuary when in danger, or in emergencies.

- Self-protection strategies are imperative in managing the abuse relationship, setting boundaries which can be utilised if intending to leave. Survivors and counsellors need to assess individual circumstances and needs, and develop a safety plan. This can be implemented if still in the relationship, and when leaving.

- While safety plans are unique to each individual survivor, there are some general guiding principles, such as a list of helpful contact numbers, emergency escape plans and legal advice. As survivors are most at risk when leaving the abuse relationship, it is important not to rush into making such a decision, or set unrealistic goals. It is at this point that survivors need a clear safety plan including emergency accommodation, financial resources and childcare, and a list of important items to pack.

- Survivors need to continue monitoring potential danger even after they have left the abuser, and continue to implement safety strategies. They need to consider what to do if they are being stalked and how to stay safe if they have gone into hiding. They may also need to make decisions in terms of formal ending of the relationship. These decisions need to be explored so that the survivor can make informed choices.

- To work with survivors of DA, counsellors need to consider their capacity to work in a more flexible way, which may necessitate being more involved in supporting survivors. They need to be sensitively attuned and contextualise erratic attendance or reluctance to engage with aspects of therapeutic work within DA rather than interpret these as resistance.

- Counsellors may also need to employ a variety of techniques alongside their core treatment philosophy, to provide a more holistic approach. With these survivors can restore internal safety, allowing for the building of trust, reconnection to self, and others and begin to rebuild their lives.

CHAPTER 6

WORKING WITH TRAUMA OF DOMESTIC ABUSE

For many survivors, domestic abuse (DA) can be a severely traumatising experience and counsellors need to be cognisant of the complex relationship between DA and trauma symptoms. Increasingly clinicians and researchers contextualise the range of pychobiological symptoms seen in survivors of DA as responses to trauma not personality disturbance, to prevent stigmatisation and pathologising the survivor. Symptoms such as anxiety, depression, self-harm, substance misuse and suicidality need to be seen primarily as reactions to the traumatic effects of prolonged and repeated abuse.

To work efficaciously with survivors of DA who have been traumatised demands a thorough understanding of the essential components of trauma, the extent to which trauma models can explain and describe the impact of DA and how counsellors can work most effectively with trauma-related symptoms. Counsellors also require knowledge of the range of trauma reactions, in particular post-traumatic stress disorder (PTSD), along with the impact on neurobiological functioning. To stabilise the survivor and restore psychobiological synchrony, counsellors need to be aware of how to work with complex post-traumatic stress reactions and dissociation within a safe therapeutic relationship.

Trauma and domestic abuse

The term trauma is often used as a generalised term. When working with survivors of DA, both the client and the counsellor must have a clear understanding of the term 'trauma' so that they can work effectively. This is especially true in the case of survivors who have minimised their traumatic experiences. Commonly survivors do not regard DA as trauma, because they often blame themselves for the abuse and interpret their symptoms as confirmation of their inadequacies. This has been reinforced by some clinicians, who traditionally have understood presenting symptoms and reluctance to leave abusive relationships as indicators of personality disturbances, thereby pathologising survivors.

According to the *Diagnostic and Statistical Manual of Mental Disorders (DSM IV-TR)* (American Psychiatric Association 2000), trauma incorporates both actual and threatened serious injury to the physical self and responses of intense fear, helplessness and horror. This definition proposes that trauma is not only the event but also the enduring adverse response to the experience. As such, for an experience to be considered traumatic, the experience must encompass both an objective event (actual or threat of injury) and the subjective response (fear, help-lessness, horror). The inclusion of threat to the psychological self in the absence of physical contact is particularly pertinent to understanding the impact of trauma in DA.

Some researchers (Allen 2001) propose that clinicians need to distinguish between impersonal trauma, characterised by natural or humanmade disasters, interpersonal trauma, such as assault and rape, and attachment trauma, such as interfamilial sexual abuse and domestic abuse. The impact of these different types of trauma will vary in intensity and range of symptomatology. Trauma that occurs in attachment abuse will consist of betrayal of trust, fragmentation of self-structures and relational difficulties which are not manifest in survivors of impersonal trauma. Some clinicians have proposed that prolonged and repeated exposure to violence in close relationships result in complex PTSD symptoms (Herman 1992b, 2006) which need specific therapeutic attention and focus.

A further crucial distinction is made between Type I trauma, characterised by a single traumatic event, and Type II trauma which involves multiple and repeated trauma (Terr 1991). Commonly, Type II trauma is associated with much greater psychobiological disruption, including complex post-traumatic stress reactions, dissociation, and memory impairment. To account for the diverse impact and trauma reactions, Rothschild (2000) has refined this distinction further to Type IIA and Type IIB trauma. Type IIA consists of multiple traumas experienced by individuals who have benefited from relatively stable backgrounds, and thus have sufficient resources to separate individual traumatic events from one another. In Type IIB the multiple traumas are so overwhelming that the individual cannot separate one from another. The type of trauma most frequently associated with DA is Type IIB (R), in which the person had a stable upbringing but the complex-ity of traumatic experiences are so overwhelming that resilience is impaired, or Type IIB (nR), in which the individual has never developed resources for resil-ience. The latter is characteristic of those survivors of DA who have a history of childhood trauma such as physical or sexual abuse, and adult revictimisation.

Another crucial component in trauma is lack of control and unpredictability. Lack of control is a core aspect of stressful and traumatic events (Foa, Zinbarg and Rothbaum 1992) and is inextricably linked with DA. Control and predictability are important for individuals to feel safe and monitor danger in the environment. Predictably depends on cues that signal danger, and without predictability these fears become generalised and the whole environment appears dangerous. Such generalised fear is associated with persistent increased arousal, heightened conditioned fear responses, numbing and avoidance (Allen 2001). The need to predict enables the individual to take steps to avoid or minimise danger. Clearly, lack of control and unpredictability are core features of DA in which signals as to when the assault will take place are almost imperceptible, and thus demands hypervigilance and heightened arousal in anticipation and readiness to cope with the next outburst.

Research indicates that interpersonal trauma within attachment relationships is likely to have more devastating effects compared with other types of trauma because it not only generates extreme distress but also undermines the mechanisms and capacity to regulate that distress (Allen 2001; Fonagy 1999; Fonagy and Target 1997). Survivors of DA often lose the capacity for affect regulation to manage trauma symptoms and suffer a dual liability in not being able to seek comfort from their partner, as he is also the abuser (Fonagy 2002). This reinforces the survivor's terror and sense of aloneness as the very person who can alleviate the terror is also the source of that fear. The severity of attachment trauma will depend on each individual's experience. In evaluating extent of trauma, counsellors need to assess level of dependency, the extent of coercion and control, intensity of traumatic bonding, the degree of violence experienced, the level of aggression and sadism encountered, and the frequency and duration of the abuse (Allen 1997).

Traumatic bonding occurs when there is an extremely high level of life-threatening stress or fear arousal which evokes fearful dependency and denial of rage in victim. The central feature of traumatic bonding is that the abuser is the source of both preserving life and destroying life. As such it recapitulates early infancy dependency and activates primitive instincts for survival and concomitant psychobiological responses. In order to survive, the survivor needs to conserve energy and move into survival mode activating a freeze response rather than fight or flight, or escape strategies. The survivor cannot afford to access rage or anger as this will elicit further threat and danger, and so it must be denied.

Pivotal to traumatic bonding is intermittent reinforcement in which one person intermittently harasses, threatens, beats, abuses or intimidates and follows this with periods of loving, caretaking behaviour (Dutton and Painter 1981). This cyclical pattern of abusive and loving behaviour results in strong, positive emotional attachment, the superglue that bonds the relationship (Allen 2001). It is important to note that both abuse and loving periods are characterised by extreme intensity. During the abuse there is heightened intensity of fear arousal while during the loving phase the abuser 'love bombs' the survivor by being intensely loving, attentive and caring. Such intensity is often misinterpreted as intimacy and love. Traumatic bonding is motivated by primitive, biologically based survival instincts, which are unconscious and beyond the survivor's control. Along with the myriad biological reactions, the survivor is compelled to change her beliefs about the abuser, to humanise rather than demonise, to aid hope for survival. This invariably involves adopting the abuser's belief system and increased tolerance of the abuse.

Research has demonstrated that traumatic bonding in DA leads to the development of PTSD symptoms, low self-esteem and significant changes in cognitive schemas and cognitive distortions, which threaten psychological integrity (Dutton and Painter 1981). Thus the survivor experiences acute stress reactions including dissociation during the abuse episodes, which are followed by cognitive reorientation and restructuring such as self-blame, which allow the survivor to manage the cyclical nature of abuse. This supports dissociation from the abuse, or compartmentalisation, which permits the survivor to access only the positive aspects of the relationship. Awareness of the betrayal inherent in DA endangers the survivor by threatening the attachment relationship. To ward off such awareness, the survivor activates defence mechanisms, such as dissociation and compartmentalisation. These permit knowledge isolation or 'betrayal blindness' in which experiences are blocked and separated in the mind, preventing integration which aids survival and retains a semblance of functioning. To revoke traumatic bonding, survivors need to explore cognitive disruptions, reduce knowledge isolation and integrate the abuse experiences.

When assessing the impact of trauma, counsellors must also have an understanding of current research on the effects of attachment trauma. Research demonstrates that trauma and stress impact on a number of dimensions, including physiological, neurobiological, psychological, interpersonal and behavioural aspects. Counsellors working with adult survivors of DA will be better equipped in their work if they familiarise themselves with a comprehensive understanding of the impact of trauma and stress and their long-term effects.

Physiological responses to trauma

Counsellors working with survivors of DA need to remember that the trauma of DA is rarely a single occurrence but a series of events in which the individual feels trapped, immobilised and in the grip of frozen terror. The body copes with fear by activating instinctual and primitive defence responses to danger. Activation of the autonomic arousal system instigates a cascade of physiological, biochemical and neurochemical changes that permit the organism to prepare for flight, fight or freeze. Invariably the survivor cannot fight back for fear of even more terrifying consequences; neither can she flee, either because of physical restraint or because she is dependent on the abuser. This leaves only one option – to freeze. Freezing prevents the discharge of energy which becomes trapped in the body with concomitant physiological and psychological symptoms.

THE BODY'S WAY OF COPING WITH FEAR

According to Engel and Schmale (1972), trauma activates two structurally distinct biological defence systems, namely the *sympathetic nervous system* and the *parasympathetic nervous system*. The sympathetic nervous system is implicated in the fight (aggressive) and flight (fear) responses as it mobilises high levels of energy, which enables the organism to be active in its environment. This active response is mirrored in the protest stage in young children as a result of separation. The parasympathetic nervous system is implicated in the freeze (defeat) response, which is most commonly seen in attachment trauma where fight or flight responses are prevented. The freeze response is based on a conservation-withdrawal mechanism (Engel and Schmale 1972) that is 'adaptive for the "exhausted" organism in replenishing energy stores and restoring physiological equilibrium' (Field 1985, p.460). In conservation-withdrawal, the organism experiences 'a relative immobility, quiescence and unresponsiveness to the environment' (Powell and Bette 1992, p.190). During the attack the survivor becomes passive and unresponsive to the environment, which represents the inhibition of the arousal system, characterised by low arousal in emotion.

Physiologically, the freeze response leads to heart-rate deceleration, lowering of the metabolic rate and lowering of activity level. As such, the response consists of inactive energy, carried out passively and expressed passively. The associated physical symptoms are lassitude, weakness, tiredness and fatigue, hypotonia and depressive-type symptoms. The psychological impact of this passive but adaptive response is manifested in feelings of helplessness, emptiness, shame and hopelessness. This frequently leads to submissiveness, the depression of sensory detection in all sensory activities, decreased energy, lack of responsiveness, despair and cessation of being active in attempting to reach personal goals. According to Perry (2000), flight is withdrawal and fight is aggression, but freeze is a defeat and appeasement response that results in immobility and submission. Perry (2000) proposes that in the presence of danger, the survivor freezes in order to allow activation of the fight or flight response, but in the absence of being able to fight or flee, a submission response is evoked.

Activation of the parasympathetic nervous system in which there is no escape underpins many of the features associated with dissociation, in which there is a reduction in heart rate and blood pressure and the release of endogenous opiates. As there is no opportunity for physical escape, the body dissociates mentally and emotionally in order to disconnect from current reality and moves from mobilising combative defence responses to a state of resignation or defeat. Activated biological defence responses interfere with prefrontal cortex and lobe functioning, leading to distraction, disorganisation, impairment in working memory (Arnsten 1998) and an inability to consider other options, limiting capacity to modulate the stress response or make decisions. In effect, the activation of emotional defence responses remains unchecked by objective evaluation or rationality (Lewis 1998), leading to re-enactments of the experience.

Prolonged and frequent activation of the stress response results in the stress response being locked in overdrive. Heightened arousal renders the hippocampus and prefrontal cortex less functional, fuelling the stress response and creating a vicious cycle of escalating arousal and disruptions to psychobiological synchrony. Stien and Kendall (2004) argue that normal stress activates the sympathetic nervous system, leading to a hyperarousal state, whereas overwhelming or repeated stress, such as that seen in DA, activates the parasympathetic nervous system and the endogenous opioid and dopamine systems. This induces bodily and emotional anaesthesia, and inhibits the influence of cortisol, thereby producing a state of apparent calm allowing the survivor to disengage from current reality.

DISSOCIATION

Schore (2001) likens activation of the sympathetic and parasympathetic nervous system in the presence of stress to 'riding the gas and the brake at the same time', whereby the simultaneous activation of hyperexcitation and hyperinhibition results in the freeze response or dissociation from bodily sensations and current reality. Dissociation is therefore seen as an emotion suppression technique when there is no escape from danger. It is also more likely to occur in the presence of lack of control and unpredictability. Ultimately, dissociation leads to impaired self-preservation, with the individual lacking any sense of personal control and self-worth. The individual becomes detached and all responses are shut down.

Some survivors of DA may be able to function to a degree by attaching emotional valence to cognitive evaluations. High functioning survivors usually present with dissociative strategies, such as compartmentalisation of the abuse, allowing them to intellectualise and contain emotions, retain extraordinary levels of focus, and the ability to manage practical and necessary tasks. In essence they present as being extremely functional and relatively unscathed by the DA. Counsellors need to be aware that, while the ability to tolerate abuse and to remain calm in any crisis may be perceived as strength and invincibility, it is indicative of compartmentalisation or knowledge isolation, which needs to be addressed. Such defences enable survivors to tolerate and accept extremely high levels of abuse well beyond normally acceptable levels. In effect, it enables survivors to adapt to the abusive relationship. Some survivors do not dissociate completely but shut down emotionally so that they can still preserve and protect others, such as children.

By dissociating, the survivor blocks all feelings, including anger at the abuse and abuser, which renders the abuse bearable. The splitting of emotions and cognition allows the vulnerable, feeling part of the individual to be protected, but leaves elements of cognitive functioning intact, which sustains the survivor between episodes of DA. The survivor retreats into psychological and emotional escape through dissociation, which aids survival during and after each abuse episode.

In dissociation the survivor becomes out of contact with bodily cues, especially subtle moment-by-moment sensory experiencing and consequent disruption to self-monitoring of affect and bodily cues. As the survivor becomes detached from and loses contact with visceral and emotional aspects of experience, she is able to tolerate increasingly higher levels of abuse, especially emotional abuse. The disruptions to affect monitoring enable the survivor to adapt to the abuse and accommodate to the demands of the abuser. Over time dissociation leads to the development of a self-structure that is defined by abuse and an inability to resist coercive violations due to the lack of a safe system to resist. In this the survivor has no option but to submit to the demands of the abuser through compliance and appeasement. In addition, the lack of safety and betrayal of basic affinitive functions forces the survivor to rely on practical strategies in order to deal with and accept the abuse. Retreating into the safety of cognitive functions, such as intellectualisation and rationalisation, enables the survivor to adapt to the abuse.

A common characteristic of dissociation is the non-verbalisation of feelings, a form of alexithymia (Krystal 1988) in which the individual lacks words for emotions. Alexithymia is a defence against feelings that directs the individual's focus on things rather than people, including operative thinking. Alexithymic individuals tend to be mechanistic in their thinking and solution-focused, rather than incorporating emotions. This allows them to carry on as normal and perform daily tasks, without any emotional expression or reactivity. Once a degree of safety has been established, counsellors can encourage survivors to mentalise their experiences and suppressed feelings to reintegrate emotional responses.

As the survivor is immobilised during trauma, the fear responses become trapped and are not discharged, putting the survivor at risk of going into 'chronic shock' (Kritsberg 1988), or numbness. As a result, the cascade of activated hormones and energy remains trapped in the system, generating more stress, leading to overload. Freezing can have considerable deleterious effects as immobilisation is associated with a sense of deadness and emptiness, whereas the discharge of energy restores aliveness, power and potency. Freezing, numbing and dissociation become the only options for escape, in which the survivor psychologically removes herself from the experience but is unable to leave physically. Once dissociation has been activated, the individual numbs arousal and may become hypovigilant, which may make the individual more vulnerable to further abuse.

The dynamics of DA and trauma also impact on self-regulation, affect regulation and self-soothing mechanisms. Research shows that trauma impacts on the sensory system, particularly the amygdala, and the frontal lobes (Van der Kolk 1994). The amygdala is like a smoke detector that monitors basic features of an event for danger, and modulates arousal states and levels, such as breathing, sleeping, elimination, chemical balances and homeostatic mechanisms. Its role is to register danger, not process it, as this is the function of the hippocampus which contextualises, interprets and labels experiences and controls and soothes the output of the amygdala. The frontal lobes are implicated in more sophisticated detection, including evaluating, planning, rationalising, extracting meaning, problem-solving, using language and making sense of experiences. These systems are distinct, but operate within a feedback loop between the amygdala and frontal lobes. In prolonged and repeated trauma, this feedback loop is disrupted preventing the two systems from communicating with each other, which exacerbates the observed symptoms in PTSD.

This is amplified with frequent high secretion of cortisol and other stress hormones, whereby the physiological system becomes impaired. In particular, essential links and interactions between sensory systems and other crucial areas of the brain can become severed. If an individual is in a constant state of high alert, energy becomes locked in the body, overloading the system and leading to further numbing and dissociation. Brain-imaging techniques indicate that the imprint of trauma is located in the right hemisphere and the limbic system, where the regulation of emotional states and autonomic arousal occurs (Van der Kolk 1994). Constant activation of these systems results in loss of self and affect regulation, and the individual is unable to modulate arousal. In addition, frontal lobes functioning may be impaired rendering the person speechless, and unable to mentalise their experiences. As a consequence, survivors can be described as literally 'taking leave of their senses' (Van der Kolk 1997) in being unable to organize their internal world around the trauma, which is characteristic of PTSD symptoms.

NEUROBIOLOGY, TRAUMA AND DOMESTIC ABUSE

The human brain evolved by retaining primitive structures from evolutionary ancestors and building new structures that have further aided survival. The triune (three-part) brain (MacLean 1990) comprises the reptilian (or visceral) brain, the paleomammalian (or feeling) brain and the neomammalian (or neocortex or thinking) brain. The reptilian brain, which is the oldest part of the human brain, consists of command centres that sustain life, such as the regulation of sleep, waking, respiration, temperature, basic automatic movements and monitoring of sensory input and repetitive functions. The paleomammalian brain includes the limbic system which promotes survival, and refines, amends and coordinates movement and regulates emotional responses and memory. The limbic system holds our feelings, such as excitement, pleasure, anger, fear, sadness, joy, shame and disgust. The neomammalian brain, which is the most recent and sophisticated part of the brain, is responsible for fine-tuning, thinking, reasoning, language, planning and complex problem-solving and is seen as the rational part of the brain.

These three structures are independent but interact in order to maintain equilibrium and survival of the individual. However, the functioning and interaction of the structures can be impaired when the individual is subjected to repeated traumatic experiences. Melzack (1990) argues that the neuronal gating that controls the information in the three brain systems can be interrupted when the emotional pain in the limbic system reaches overwhelming proportions and activates the closure of the gate to the neocortex. This means that the emotional arousal and danger signals do not go away but circulate within the closed circuit of nerve fibres within the limbic system, with no opportunity for discharge. These neurobiological alterations impact on the regulation of emotion, the unified organisation of self-structures and increased risk of PTSD.

POST-TRAUMATIC STRESS DISORDER

The essential feature of PTSD is the 'development of characteristic symptoms following a psychologically stressing event that is outside the range of usual human experience that would be distressing to almost anyone, and is usually experienced with intense fear, terror and helplessness' (American Psychiatric Association 2000). Stressful events in the DSM-IV definition include military combat, rape, assault, kidnap, torture, imprisonment, major accidents and disasters, acts of terrorism, and being diagnosed with a life-threatening illness.

Other features of PTSD include altered threshold of response, especially in terms of readiness, hypervigilance, altered appraisal processes, increased threat appraisal, proneness to re-enactment or re-experience of the event, and lowered stress tolerance thresholds. The individual may display signs of hyperactivity or dysregulation, with increased irritability, proneness to aggression, physiological and psychobiological hyperactivity, elevated startle response, insomnia, avoidance tendencies, and an inability to modulate arousal and affect. Usually, the individual demonstrates altered initial response patterns in the presence of fear or anxiety, decreased safety appraisal, decreased stress tolerance, overreaction to external or internal cues, and heightened proneness to activate the flight, fight or freeze response. This indicates an alteration in the capacity for internal monitoring and increased vulnerability to cognitive and emotional responses. Such response alterations lead to the activation of defence mechanisms, such as avoidance, dissociation, amnesia, hyperarousal and cognitive dysregulation, and somatic expressions of distress, such as insomnia and increased startle response. These changes represent a failure to habituate to the activated stress responses, shut down and restore homeostasis.

Many of the diagnostic criteria of PTSD reflect the observed symptoms of DA, such as flashbacks, lack of specific memories, nightmares, numbing, reduced emotion ('frozenness'), withdrawal, hypervigilance, aloneness and being haunted by intrusive recollections of the trauma. However, the diagnostic criteria of PTSD do not account for all the commonly reported effects such as worthlessness, self-blame and erosion of self-esteem observed in survivors of DA. There are qualitative differences in DA such as shame, guilt, self-destructive behaviours, distorted beliefs about self and others, and fragmentation of the sense of self that cannot be explained solely by PTSD.

Prolonged coercive control and repeated traumatisation results in resignation, in which the individual perceives himself as a victim of others' actions, eliciting victim-type behaviour and reduction of self-efficacy. The survivor becomes overly compliant, turning anger and hostility towards the self. This can manifest in a sense of despair, hopelessness, depression or self-destructive behaviours. The inability to control aversive events, accompanied by fear and anxiety, results in dissociation, nightmares, phobias, hypervigilance, somatic complaints, eating and sleeping disorders, and vulnerability to subsequent victimisation.

Working with trauma

Prior to embarking on working with trauma, counsellors need to assess the impact of trauma and range of effects. In particular counsellors need to evaluate both processes responses and symptom responses. Process responses are the impacts of trauma that can be easily determined during diligent assessment interview, whereas symptom responses are classic markers of psychological disturbance. Commonly process responses include activation responses such as sensory re-experiencing, emotional arousal, revival of memories and cognitions, and avoidance responses such as lack of affect, detachment, dissociation and deflection. Survivors may activate effortful avoidance through thought suppression, emotional numbing, denial or self-medication, without obvious intoxication.

Counsellors need to distinguish between avoidance responses and resilience to stress which has built up over years of abuse. Explicit signs of avoidance include visible dissociative symptoms such as spacing out, fixity of gaze, disconnected motoric responses, or different identity states. Some survivors are able to self-report on dissociative features such as depersonalisation, or 'out-of-body' experiences, or derealisation wherein they feel like they are in a dream. Other signs include visible intoxication through drugs or alcohol, or cluster of PTSD symptoms such as avoiding people, places, situations or discussing material in session for fear that might trigger PTSD symptoms or distress. Such avoidance commonly indicates a greater likelihood of PTSD, increased chance of chronicity, and potentially greater difficulties dealing with exposure component of therapy.

Such avoidance strategies must be seen as coping responses that maintain psychological stability in the face of destabilising trauma memories and indicators of PTSD rather than deliberate resistance. It is crucial that counsellors understand these within the context of trauma responses and not misinterpret or judge the survivor. This is particularly the case with distress avoidance strategies such as self-medication, self-harm, impulsivity or paralysis. Distress avoidance strategies need to be addressed in a sensitive manner and worked through until the survivor feels safe enough to relinquish them and integrate more adaptive ones.

Affect dysregulation makes it harder to process trauma without being over-whelmed and counsellors must titrate such work as survivors may experience this as a retraumatisation. Counsellors must have a good understanding of the classic signs of affect dysregulation in order to implement appropriate therapeutic inter-vention. Common signs are rapidly fluctuating mood states that seem to resolve spontaneously, and sudden extreme emotional distress during session with diffi-culty calming down or shifting into a more positive emotional state. Acting out is often associated with affect dysregulation especially self-injury, self-medication, heightened aggression, suicide attempts, sudden tension reduction behaviour when upset and dissociative responses.

To restore affect regulation counsellors need to titrate exposure to traumatic material and co-opt existing capacity to regulate painful feelings. The aim of affect regulation is to develop affect tolerance in which the survivor can tolerate painful internal states through affect modulation. The focus in affect modulation is the ability to internally reduce stress without resorting to dissociation or other avoidance resources. Such work needs to be carefully paced by the survivor and must not be rushed. As survivors become more skilled at affect regulation, inter-nal safety is restored and they will feel more in control of their trauma responses (see Chapter 5).

Skilful emotional regulation requires mentalisation in which the individual is able to fathom mental states such as emotions, feelings, in self and others. The ability to mentalise also allows the individual to remain in conscious contact with needs, desires, motives, intentions, hopes, fears, thoughts, beliefs and fantasies. Mentalisation is most likely to occur during optimal arousal states when the indi-vidual is alert and relatively calm. In DA and trauma the capacity to mentalise is blocked due to hyperarousal, or diverted to mentalising the motives, thoughts and feelings of the perpetrator. As all available energy is diverted into survival, there is no time or space for self-reflection, especially of own feelings, experience or needs. The more the individual becomes out of contact with feelings and needs, and the more isolated he becomes, the less he is able to mentalise. The fur-ther these mental states are pushed out of awareness, the less they can be mentalised, which allows continued tolerance and acceptance of abuse. In addi-tion, impaired mentalisation reduces the capacity to problem solve and make informed decisions, exacerbating feelings of being trapped.

Counsellors need to provide a safe haven for survivors to mentalise implicitly and explicitly. Implicit mentalisation is awareness of internal states, while explicit mentalisation is being able to identify and articulate these internal states, and have them acknowledged by others. Such mentalisation enables survivors to self-regulate, seek support and problem solve more effectively. Most importantly the more intelligible emotions become, the more self-awareness increases. When this is combined with greater awareness of others within appropriate boundaries, the individual is more able to relate to others and form healthy attachments.

Self-regulation and affect modulation enable survivors to tolerate and contain feelings appropriately rather than vacillating between the extremes of dissociation in which no feelings are experienced, and hyperarousal in which they are overwhelmed by feelings. Survivors may benefit from learning how to monitor their level of arousal and emotional feelings. This is facilitated by keeping a mood diary and plotting levels of emotional arousal on a scale of zero to ten. It must be noted that many survivors of DA are unable to tolerate positive affect and this can be experienced as overwhelming as aversive affect. Counsellors need to be aware of this and work towards tolerating the full range of affect.

During assessment of the impact of trauma, counsellors need to consider the survivor's degree of resilience, as this will demand a different therapeutic focus (Rothschild 2000). Survivors with Type I and Type II trauma will require less emphasis on integrating trauma and those with Type IIB (R) or Type IIB (nR). Those survivors with Type IIB (R) will require particular emphasis on reacquainting themselves with eroded or lost resources or resilience, and need to resurrect these. Survivors who present with Type IIB (nR) trauma, who have never developed resilience, will need the therapeutic focus to be on acquiring resources and building resilience. When working with survivors of Type IIB (nR) trauma, counsellors also need to devote close attention to the therapeutic relationship as it is through the strength of this that such survivors are able to build trust, and build resilience.

WORKING WITH PTSD

To enable the survivor to have a semblance of control over PTSD symptoms, counsellors are advised to increase the survivor's awareness and understanding of the relationship between trauma, DA and PTSD. Understanding these symptoms and normalising them within a trauma framework will enable the client to feel more in control and to understand that she is not 'going mad'. Offering psychoeducation on the psychological impact of trauma and its relation to PTSD symptoms may allow the survivor to gain an understanding of her symptoms and, ultimately, a greater sense of control. The counsellor can explore the nature, function and development of symptoms such as avoidance, psychic numbing, denial, emotional constriction, self-harm, substance abuse, social isolation, estrangement and detachment and link these to the DA experience. Psychoeducation enables the survivor to make links between her trauma responses and DA experiences and to see that her responses are a normal reaction to trauma. Restoring some sense of control can improve survivor's self-esteem, self-confidence and self-efficacy, reduce feelings of helplessness and restore a sense of mastery over the trauma.

A common effect of trauma is altered thresholds of response in terms of readiness, hypervigilance, altered appraisal processes, proneness to re-experiencing of trauma, and lower levels of stress tolerance. This can lead to a range of PTSD symptoms including psychobiological dysregulation, hyperactivity, insomnia and avoidance tendencies. Such alterations in response patterns result in decreased safety appraisal, decreased stress tolerance, overreaction to external or internal cues, and proneness to flight, fight or freeze responses. The altered capacity of internal monitoring decreases the capacity for accurate self-monitoring and increases the individual's vulnerability to distorted cognitive and emotional responses. Altered feedback based on distorted information further decreases the capacity for accurate monitoring of interpersonal events and effects on others, altered cognitive schemas and erroneous cognitions of self and the world.

Continuous alteration in such responses leads to an increased proneness to dissociation, knowledge isolation, hyperarousal and hypoarousal, cognitive dysregulation and somatic expressions of distress. This represents a failure to habituate to the trauma or restore homeostasis, which leads to fluctuating levels of arousal, emotional lability, somatogenic expressions of PTSD and vulnerability to stress and illness. Panic attacks indicate an oversensitive alarm system triggered by internal physiological sensations in which the amygdala is tripped. The hippocampus can rein in the response of the amygdala by labelling the initial surge of panic as benign, but if the hippocampus misinterprets the response it is unable to exert control over the amygdala, thereby fuelling the initial response. The counsellor can help the survivor to challenge hippocampal misinterpretations and desensitise the amygdala by gradual exposure to alarm reactions associated with traumatic material, enabling the survivor to face her fear of re-experiencing the trauma in a safe environment.

It is useful to track and identify any dissociative symptoms from the outset of treatment so that these can be monitored. The counsellor should encourage the survivor to keep data on the triggers, frequency, intensity and duration of flashbacks and dissociative episodes so that these reactions can be monitored and worked with. Survivors who experience flashbacks will need to work on safety and grounding exercises. A powerful feature of flashbacks is the client feeling as though she is re-experiencing the trauma in the present. The counsellor needs to help the survivor to develop strategies and techniques to ground her in the present rather than the past. If the survivor lives with another person, then the counsellor may consider educating this partner or carer in simple grounding techniques. Throughout the treatment focus is to re-establish normal stress responses and to normalise PTSD symptoms. It may be necessary to consider medication to stabilise some of the symptoms, so that the survivor can engage fully in the therapeutic process. In this case, the counsellor must liaise with either the client's general practitioner or psychiatrist in order to provide a comprehensive treatment package and ensure full collaboration between all professionals involved with the survivor.

It is important to restore the survivor's internal control mechanisms, through biofeedback and relaxation. The counsellor should work with the survivor to identify triggers that activate debilitating emotional and somatic responses. To gain mastery over fear and distress responses, the survivor may need to practise grounding techniques (see below). that can alleviate symptoms. Other defence mechanisms may have to be explored in order to gain insight into their function and development. In exploring PTSD symptoms the survivor is more able to control them than be controlled by them. As the DA experiences are integrated the survivor is able to restore shattered self-structures. This can strengthen the survivor's self-concept and self-identity and repair fragmented ego states, allowing the survivor to move from self-blame to a more accurate assessment of the DA experience.

Survivors often blame themselves for their DA experiences in order to claim an illusion of power, in which they see themselves as active participants rather than passive victims. This illusion of power may serve to retain a sense of self, but is counterproductive by suffusing survivors with shame, guilt and self-blame. Such cognitive distortion needs to be appropriately explored and restructured in order for survivors to develop healthier cognitions about self, restore self-esteem, personal integrity and vitality. Assimilating trauma and DA experiences into the appropriate cognitive schemas decreases the survivor's sense of vulnerability.

Counsellors must also enable survivors to identify and explore the function of self-destructive behaviours in relation to trauma to decrease suicidal ideation, or self-injurious behaviour and restore a more positive, grounded sense of self. In addition, increasing survivors' awareness of cues that trigger dissociative states and disruptions in cognitive processes facilitates more effective management of symptoms.

The interpersonal dimension of PTSD also needs to be addressed, including working on restructuring the client's interpersonal world. This involves identifying and tracking interpersonal stressors that can fuel disturbing recollections. Prolonged attachment trauma generates difficulties around trust, relational dynamics, and fears of loss and abandonment. In working with the interpersonal dimension of PTSD, the counsellor needs to help the survivor restore healthy relationships, learn to establish boundaries and confront emotional feelings associated with vulnerability in relationships. Such difficulties need to be explored in order for the survivor to evoke an increased capacity for self-trust so as to reduce detachment, estrangement and emotional isolation. The survivor of DA can then learn to relate to others without worrying about personal vulnerability in relationships to allow for intimacy to be developed. Much of this work can be achieved in the therapeutic process, whereby the survivor learns to be in a relationship with the counsellor in a safe environment in which healthy boundaries are maintained.

When working with adult survivors of DA who are not embodied, counsellors may need to consider additional ways of working, such as body work. Counsellors who do not offer body work may need to collaborate with body therapists to provide additional therapy. In this case, the counsellor must ensure the survivor's readiness to engage in body work. The survivor must feel safe before engaging in such work. Body work can allow the survivor to become more embodied and help her 'keep hold of [her] senses' (Van der Kolk 1997). Similarly, Levine (1997) also proposes that safe somatic experiencing and education of body sensations are a powerful aid to embodiment and recovery from trauma. It is imperative that body work is conducted in a safe, appropriately boundaried setting.

Counsellors should budget for relapses, as working with adult survivors is rarely a linear process. Both the counsellor and the survivor should be aware that aspects of trauma not been integrated during the therapeutic process may be reactivated after the completion of therapy. This reactivation cannot be planned for, but it is important that during therapy the survivor acquires sufficient understanding and techniques to minimise the impact of these life events in order that she is not overwhelmed by the reactivation. It may be useful to offer a return to therapy for a period of time to offer support during such crises, rather than the survivor starting again with a new counsellor.

Therapeutic interventions and techniques

There are a number of other therapeutic interventions and techniques that may prove valuable to the survivor in the amelioration of PTSD symptoms, including traumatic incident reduction (TIR), cognitive behavioural therapy (CBT), grounding techniques and crisis management. However, these should not supersede the importance of the therapeutic relationship in which to repair attachment trauma.

The counsellor must identify and address the survivor's fears before implementing any changes in the therapeutic approach. Many adult survivors fear change as they cannot conceptualise a different way of being. They may fear that if they reduce long-standing symptoms and reactions, especially those that have been their constant companions, then they will be replaced with something worse. Invariably, fear and confusion have been such a central part of survivors' existence that they cannot imagine or conceive of life without them. These are genuine fears that the counsellor must respond to sensitively.

Counsellors should be aware of survivor compliance, whereby the survivor does not wish to challenge the therapist. It is crucial that the counsellor does not assume that the survivor exists in a reasonably functional environment outside of the therapeutic setting and understands that the way the survivor acts in session may not reflect the survivor's world outside of therapy. The counsellor needs to be realistic with regard to the anticipated length of therapy, goals of therapy, and the survivor's and counsellor's evaluation of the effectiveness of therapy. In order to prevent relapse, the trauma work must be undertaken at a manageable pace for the survivor and should include time for the survivor to process the trauma. Survivors need to know that these are best done in short, manageable chunks by setting aside regular time periods in which to write about the trauma and talk to supportive friends.

TRAUMATIC INCIDENT REDUCTION (TIR)

TIR is a guided cognitive imagery procedure (Gerbode 1989) in which the survivor is invited to confront the trauma by exploring recent traumatic incidents and linking them to past experiences. The survivor is encouraged repeatedly to imagine the traumatic incident as if watching a film and to talk through it until some level of resolution has been attained. Resolution is measured by a cognitive shift in thinking, significant physiological relaxation or a return to the present. This can be conducted only in a safe environment in which the client feels held and listened to intently without interpretation or verbal feedback. This allows the survivor to connect with feelings, discharge them and make cognitive shifts by taking a different perspective on the trauma.

While TIR is helpful for many types of trauma, it may have a limited value when working with survivors of DA who are not ready to tolerate exposure due to lack of safety and the absence of a good support network. Counsellors should ensure that they do not sacrifice the importance of the relational therapeutic work necessary in attachment trauma by replacing them with prescribed protocols and procedures. The latter may indicate that the counsellor is trying to avoid being in a relationship with the client and thus represent a form of protection for the counsellor by disconnecting counsellor from survivor (see Chapter 10). TIR may be used as an adjunct to relational work in specifically contracted sessions, but it should not be used in isolation.

COGNITIVE-BEHAVIOURAL THERAPY

Counsellors working with trauma may find a number of CBT techniques to help with affect regulation and cognitive restructuring as an adjunct to more relational work. Before undertaking CBT work, the counsellor should explain to the survivor the interplay of cognitions and emotions and how a CBT approach can be helpful by providing interventions that increase the survivor's self-efficacy and reduce PTSD symptoms. MOOD management consists of four components:

mood, observe, objective, decide. In the *mood* stage, the survivor is asked to monitor changes in her mood and ask of herself questions such as 'What is it that I am feeling?' and 'What effect is it having on me or others?' This allows the survivor to label and describe the intensity of mood states on a scale of one to ten. The *observe* component consists of the survivor observing her thinking and the content of any self-talk. In the *objective* component, the survivor develops greater objectivity about her thinking and what she is saying to herself. This can also be plotted on a scale of one to ten by asking questions such as 'How true is it?', 'How useful is it?', 'Does it get me what I want?' and 'Would others look at it differently?' Finally, the *decide* component involves the survivor in making decisions about beliefs to invest in and alternative beliefs, which can lead to cognitive restructuring.

Trauma can distort the survivor's perception, leading to a propensity for cognitive bias and distortion. There are a number of cognitive distortions which underpin and maintain symptoms of PTSD which need to be restructured, as these distortions underpin and maintain symptoms of PTSD. These cognitive distortions need to be challenged and explored by the survivor and the counsellor to enable the survivor to restructure them and to generate alternative, more objective, and realistic beliefs. Cognitive restructuring may at first sight seem relatively easy, but it is often very difficult for the survivor and needs to be constantly practised and validated with each achievement, no matter how small. Systematic desensitisation techniques can be used to enable the survivor to tolerate exposure and master relaxation skills. Encouraging the survivor to develop a greater sensory awareness allows her to establish a hierarchy of triggers that trip the alarm system and to develop coping strategies, thereby aiding self-regulation.

EYE MOVEMENT DESENSITISATION AND REPROCESSING (EMDR)

EMDR has been shown to benefit survivors of trauma, although we do not understand fully how it works (Shapiro 1995). Underpinning the approach is the theory that the brain freezes the trauma in its original form, complete with concomitant emotions, images and negative self-assessments. The series of rapid eye movements in EMDR allow the frozen material to be unfrozen and processed, thus easing the symptoms of PTSD. EMDR may be of benefit to survivors of DA although there has not been enough research with this client group. Counsellors should consider EMDR only for those survivors who have reached a considerable level of stability and should work in collaboration with an EMDR specialist.

GROUNDING TECHNIQUES

There a number of grounding techniques that can help survivors to manage overwhelming feelings and PTSD symptoms, especially dissociation. Counsellors must familiarise themselves with these as they can assist survivors to reorient themselves and remain in the present. These techniques can be introduced during the therapeutic session, and subsequently practised at home, or whenever intense feelings arise. The techniques prevent dissociation, reorient survivors when they experience intense feelings and anxiety, to regain mental focus. Ultimately they can also help survivors with remaining embodied, facilitating affect regulation, and reduction of self-injurious behaviour.

Initially, survivors need to identify the triggers that lead to dissociation and recognise the signals that indicate its onset. Some triggers may be consciously known to the individual survivor, but others may be outside awareness. It is important that survivors recognise that identifying and understanding dissociative process can empower them to feel more in control of them, reduce the number of triggers, and make it easier to deal with automatic reactions. To facili- tate the identification and naming of triggers to dissociation, counsellors may ask questions such as 'Where were you at the time of the abuse?', 'What were you like at that time?', 'What was the abuser like?', 'What was happening inside your body?', 'What were your emotional experiences like?' and 'Can you describe any other sensations, feelings and thoughts that you experienced at the time of the abuse?'

Counsellors should ensure that the survivor understands that automatic reac- tions can be thoughts, feelings or somatic sensations that disrupt current func- tioning. Many survivors are confused and feel out of control in the presence of dissociative symptoms and counsellors need to normalise such reactions that operate below the level of conscious awareness. It may be necessary to explain that some automatic reactions last for seconds but others for hours, and that the reactions usually occur in a series, whereby one triggers another. Links must also be made between dissociation and self-injurious behaviour. Commonly survivors self-injure either to induce a dissociative state, or to jolt themselves out of dissociation and permit feeling.

Together counsellor and survivor need to generate as many viable grounding skills as possible, and identify those that are most helpful and effective. These can include sensory awareness grounding skills such as amplifying sensory channels, or cognitive awareness skills that promote mentalising the dissociative episode (Sanderson 2006). It is helpful to make a list of the most effective techniques so the survivor can refer to it when necessary. Grounding skills enable the survivor to master intrusive symptoms, flashbacks and automatic reactions. To implement grounding techniques survivors must have some degree of somatic awareness and recognition of automatic reactions. A powerful way for the counsellor to ground the client and reorient her into the present is to change the sensory experience by encouraging the client to utilise all five senses.

Kinaesthetically, the client may reorient herself in space by moving around, jumping, stretching and waving her arms; this revokes numbness and 'frozenness' and discharges trapped energy (Levine 1997). Discharge of energy in a proactive, rather than reactive, way can also be achieved by engaging in self-regulatory activities such as yoga, t'ai chi, martial arts or dance. Such activities enable survivors to become more embodied and remain grounded when in distress. The counsellor can calm the client by encouraging him to breathe slowly and deeply, relax the muscles, and repeat a refrain such as 'I am safe: no one can hurt me now'. Gradually survivors can begin to choose new responses such as different reactions and actions in order to feel more in the present. These can be self-protective actions and corrective messages of reassurance and comfort to counteract traumatic re-experiencing.

Given the extra support that dissociative survivors may need, some therapists may need to collaborate with and seek assistance from other agencies. Counsellors must consistently monitor personal safety in the home and be aware of the danger of dissociation. Survivors who dissociate and have children must develop strategies to help keep their children safe during dissociative episodes. To some extent, this can be facilitated by ensuring that the survivor has a good support network through other agencies, or support worker, in order to maintain appropriate levels of childcare.

Working with adult survivors who dissociate may involve a degree of crisis intervention, with a focus on building up internal support mechanisms and resources and external sources and support networks. A helpful strategy is to enable the client to establish routines for basic self-care, such as sleep, nutrition, exercise and use of alcohol or drugs. In some cases, short-term medication may be indicated, as long as this is fully discussed with the survivor and with the full cooperation of their general practitioner (GP) and/or psychiatrist.

WORKING WITH SELF-HARM

Many survivors of DA who dissociate also self-harm. Counsellors should ensure that they have a good understanding of the function of self-harm. Self-harm may be a release from internal pain or pressure or a distraction to prove the 'aliveness' of the individual. Some survivors self-harm in order to avert suicide, while others find this is the only area of their life where they can exert control and feel empowered.

When working with survivors of DA who self-injure, it is essential to create a safety contract in relation to their self-harming behaviours. This should incorporate being honest about any self-injurious behaviour that takes place and a commitment to replace such coping strategies with more healthy forms of expression. It may be impossible for the survivor to cease all self-injurious behaviours immediately, and to expect this might be counterproductive therapeutically. Instead, it may be necessary to develop a safety contract around minimising the injury and strategies such as distraction, avoidance, deterrents and a degree of commitment to self-care. Safety contracts must be mutually agreed, and include clear boundaries around confidentiality and under which circumstances the counsellor will inform the survivor's GP or other professionals.

Once such a contract has been agreed, the counsellor needs to help the survivor to identify the self-injurious behaviour, make the behaviour conscious, understand its function, and link this to trauma and DA. The counsellor must explore the functions of self-injury without shaming the client, as decreasing the guilt and shame will remove some of the pressure to self-injure. In combination with reducing the self-injurious behaviour, the counsellor must explore with the client alternative coping strategies. Such strategies vary between survivors but might include minimising the self-injurious behaviour by making a small rather than a large cut, using a less harmful implement, cutting earlier on in the cycle before the distress has built up in intensity, or finding an alternative that does not result in wounding, such as plunging a hand into a bowl of ice. Counsellors must encourage survivors to restore a general level of self-care through diet, exercise and self-nurturing, which can be built upon to cease self-injury. As the survivor discovers more appropriate coping strategies and builds upon these, the self-injurious behaviour will subside.

If the survivor is self-medicating, the counsellor will need to assess the level of dependency and discuss any concerns with the client. In the case of high-level dependency, the counsellor will need to consider referring the survivor to specialist addiction programmes or a residential treatment facility. This may be necessary until self-medication is under control and the survivor can fully engage in the therapeutic process. Such decisions must always be discussed with the survivor and GP, or psychiatrist, in the light of any negative ramifications.

WORKING WITH TRAUMATIC MEMORIES

Metabolising trauma commonly results in the activation of nightmares and flashbacks, and evokes a range of sensory or somatic memories, all of which can trigger overwhelming emotions. The counsellor must listen and attend to all aspects of the survivor's memories, especially if the traumatic material increases in intensity, as the latter may lead to an increase in self-harming behaviours, distraction and avoidance behaviours, substance misuse, suicidal ideation and suicide attempts. Counsellors must have considerable understanding of the dynamic nature of memory and how traumatic memories become lost to consciousness and are recovered (Mollon 2002b; Sanderson 2006). It is crucial that counsellors do not contaminate recovered memories or direct their content through suggestibility. Counsellors will need to familiarise themselves with the range of techniques that aid recall, such as verbal and visual timelines, recognition, and familiarity tasks (Sanderson 2006).

SUPPORT NETWORKS

Given the alienating and isolating nature of DA, a critical component in trauma recovery is the survivor's access to a rewarding support network. The counsellor needs to actively encourage the survivor to access external resources and build a solid support network. External support networks, personal, social and professional, can be crucial in stabilising the client. Such networks might include trusted family and friends, the GP and other professionals, as well as members of DA agencies. During certain crises, the counsellor may need to consider contacting some people within the survivor's support network, but only ever with the survivor's permission and within the boundaries of confidentiality.

CRISIS MANAGEMENT

Working with trauma is not a linear process and is characterised by fluctuations in stability and safety. Survivors of DA encounter frequent crises in which safety is undermined. Counsellors need to tolerate such fluctuations and contextualise these within a trauma framework. Such crises are often accompanied by reactivation of PTSD symptoms such as flashbacks and panic attacks, as well as spontaneous regressing, switching into angry or hostile mode, escalation of self-harm and suicidal feelings. Crisis management involves identifying and recognising triggers to crises and managing these triggers through appropriate support networks, and grounding techniques that maximise the survivor's inner resources. This encourages growth of trust in self, self-efficacy and self-reliance. It is important to continue to link these difficulties to trauma and DA to keep the survivor focused on the consequences of the abuse. Many survivors feel ashamed of setbacks as they fear failure, and thus it is crucial that counsellors validate their progress and link crises as outside their control.

The role of counsellor when working with trauma

Working with trauma can be very difficult for both survivor and counsellor. In order to integrate the trauma and alleviate the associated trauma reactions and symptoms, the counsellor must remain engaged and connected with the survivor. The counsellor needs to understand DA specifically in terms of attachment trauma, not just trauma, and to work with the survivor in a healthy relational way and not hide behind protocols or solely cognitive techniques. While such techniques ameliorate some of the symptoms, they will not restore the survivor's trust in relationships. The therapeutic relationship is often the most powerful component in recovering from attachment trauma.

Counsellors need to be cognisant that many of the dynamics present in DA can be brought into the therapeutic relationship. Clinicians must be aware of the potential for re-enactment of such dynamics, and set clear boundaries to ensure the safety of the survivor. This necessitates appropriate exploration of power and control issues without relinquishing empathy, to minimise the re-enactment of abuse dynamics. The dynamics of DA prevented the survivor from experiencing a sense of control over what happened to her and her body, and so she must be given some sense of control over her therapeutic process. The counsellor thus needs to demonstrate a good understanding of the client's world, both before and after the DA, and ensure that the survivor is exposed to the traumatic material at the survivor's pace. The counsellor should also appreciate the survivor's 'lost identity' and see the client as a whole person, not just as a victim or a survivor.

Pivotal to a consistent and caring therapeutic relationship is clear boundaries. Safety is established through the consistent and reliable behaviour of the therapist, who provides sensitively attuned listening within a climate of openness and honesty. Counsellors need to be able and willing to apologise for insensitive interventions, and openly acknowledge their own limitations. When working with trauma, counsellors need to be interactive and engaged with the client with an appropriate use of silence. This is especially pertinent with survivors of DA who have been silenced by the abuser or experienced a resounding silence from others who did not acknowledge the DA.

ISSUES FOR THE COUNSELLOR

It is crucial that the counsellor develops appropriate knowledge of DA through education, training and continuous professional development. Clinicians need also to be aware of and to challenge their own beliefs about the nature of DA, survivor and perpetrator dynamics and difficulties around leaving, and dispel any erroneous belief or myths. They need to be aware of their own experiences around power, control and abuse. Given that DA is predicated on power and control, clinicians need to be acutely aware of their own needs for power and control, and how such needs can be misused or abused. An exploration of the counsellor's own 'internal abuser' and attachment issues such as feelings around needs and fears of being connected or disconnected is of paramount importance. If counsellors are unable to explore such issues themselves, they should seek professional support, such as supervision or a return to therapy. If counsellors experience inordinate fascination, voyeurism, preoccupation, frustration, admiration, fear, inadequacy or vicarious arousal, they need to know that these may be indicators of secondary traumatic stress (STS), and should seek appropriate help in order to avoid STS and counsellor burnout.

Most importantly, when working with trauma, counsellors must not recoil from the terror of DA and remain emotionally engaged and empathically attuned to the survivor. They need to be flexible in their approach and be able to implement a range of effective strategies and techniques rather than adhere rigidly to a single monolithic theory. The therapeutic relationship is critical in restoring trust and enabling survivors to reconnect to self and others. Counsellors must be confident in working with power and control dynamics as they arise in the therapeutic process, and feel comfortable in being connected with their clients.

Summary

- Prolonged DA can be a severely traumatising experience and counsellors need to be cognisant of the complex relationship between DA and trauma symptoms. Increasingly clinicians and researchers contextualise the range of psychobiological symptoms seen in survivors of DA as responses to trauma not personality disturbance, or survivor pathology.

- Symptoms such as anxiety, depression, self-harm, substance misuse and suicidality need to be seen primarily as reactions to the traumatic effects of prolonged and repeated abuse. Complex post-traumatic stress symptoms are also a feature of DA and need to be understood as such.

- To work efficaciously with traumatised survivors of DA demands a thorough understanding of the essential components of trauma, and how this impacts on survivors. Counsellors require knowledge of the range of trauma reactions, in particular PTSD, along with the impact on neurobiological functioning.

- Prior to embarking on trauma work, counsellors need to conduct a thorough assessment of trauma-related symptoms and establish an optimal level of external and internal safety. In the absence of safety any therapeutic work will be contraindicated. To effect these the counsellor needs to stabilise the survivor and restore psychobiological synchrony through mentalisation and affect regulation.

- These skills will facilitate managing the complex post-traumatic stress reactions and dissociation associated with DA. As traumatic material is explored and painful memories are evoked, trauma symptoms will be reactivated. Counsellors will need to have a good knowledge of the range of interventions and techniques that facilitate managing the material and concomitant symptoms.

- Counsellors need to incorporate a variety of interventions into their core practice such as traumatic incident reduction, cognitive behavioural techniques and crisis management. They need an appreciation of grounding skills to minimise dissociation and self-harm, along with alternatives strategies that survivors can develop. Survivors must be encouraged to develop a healthy support network to revoke isolation and reconnect to others.

- The role of the counsellor and therapeutic relationship is pivotal when working with attachment trauma. Counsellors must provide a safe therapeutic space in which they are emotionally engaged and do not recoil from the terror of abuse. To remain connected to survivors, counsellors need to explore their own experiences of power and control, and monitor their responses to such dynamics within the therapeutic setting.

CHAPTER 7

WORKING WITH SELF-ASPECTS OF DOMESTIC ABUSE

The self develops in relation to others through attachment, care giving, intimacy, love, connectedness and cooperation. It is through healthy attachment that the individual can safely separate, and develop autonomy, self-definition and individuality. From these, the person learns to take initiative and responsibility, and acquires a sense of achievement. Relatedness also plays a critical role in the development of self-concept, self-worth, self-efficacy, self-agency and self-continuity. The chaotic and contradictory nature of attachment in domestic abuse (DA) serves to undermine these self-structures, and engender a fragmented sense of self. To reclaim self-identity and develop a coherent sense of self, the survivor of DA must integrate fragmented self-structures and engage in more accurate self-appraisals and rebuild self-worth. In essence, recovery from DA entails healing the self.

This chapter examines the central aspects of self by exploring the development and interaction of self-worth, self-efficacy, self-agency and self-continuity and how these promote a coherent sense of self. The complex nature and impact of DA is explored to provide a deeper understanding of how abusive relationships erode and undermine self-structures, and fragment the self. To restore a cohesive sense of self, survivors need to reclaim self-identity through mentalising their experiences and develop more accurate self-appraisal. This needs to be combined with actions that restore self-agency and self-efficacy, in order to reconnect to self, others and life. The therapeutic relationship is crucial in the restoration of self and counsellors need to adopt a positive model of post-traumatic growth and be sensitively attuned and responsive to the survivors striving for connection and relatedness.

Aspects of the self

The self develops within an attachment framework in which the individual is in relation to others. The nascent self is organised in early infancy through interactions with significant others, such as the primary care giver. For a healthy sense of self to develop the individual needs to experience positive mirroring. If the mirror does not reflect, or distorts the reflection, the individual develops a negative view of self. These early experiences facilitate the organisation of self-structures which allows for a cohesive sense of self to unfold (Sanderson 2006). These self-structures are threatened in the face of trauma and abuse, which can result in the fragmentation, or shattering of the self. In DA, abusers commonly annihilate the survivor's cohesive sense of self, creating a lacuna upon which they can project a false or alien self. As self-structures are shattered, the survivor has no choice but to incorporate the abuser's distorted reflections. Over time the false self obscures the authentic self, and compensatory self-structures emerge that feel fraudulent and fake, and evoke existential angst. Counsellors need to understand the complex dynamics that give rise to a cohesive sense of self, how this can be shattered, and the concomitant defences such as the development of compensatory self-structures and the incorporation of a false self.

The self is complex and multifaceted and evolves in relation to others throughout childhood (Fonagy 2001; Stern 1985) and into adulthood. Empathy and positive mirroring is crucial, as what is mirrored back provides the structure for the nascent authentic self. Positive mirroring provides a guidance system of ideals and values in which the individual can develop self-esteem, self-confidence, self-agency, self-efficacy, autonomy, mastery and competence. This promotes the organisation of self-structures that lead to a cohesive sense of self-identity that is stable, consistent and coherent. The self is initially structured through the internalisation of the responses received from significant others, which form internal working models (Bowlby 1977) or schemas, which promote an internal locus of control and evaluation rather than relying on external sources of evaluation and control provided by others.

There are a number of crucial aspects of self that need to be considered to understand how these interact to create a cohesive sense of self. These include self-worth, self-efficacy, self-agency, self-continuity and self-stability. It is important to note that when considering these aspects of self, they appear to exist as separate and distinct entities; they are nevertheless experienced as a coherent whole. A fundamental distinction is made between 'I' and 'me'. The 'I' represents the subjective self, or self-as-subject, while the 'me' represents the objective self or self-as-object.

The 'I' is active and is made up of the self-as-agent in taking initiative, making choices and achieving desired needs and goals, and a sense of self-efficacy. A crucial aspect of 'I' is a sense of continuity in which the sense of 'I' is relatively stable and enduring over time and situations. In contrast, the 'me' is how the self is seen from the outside and others, and as such represents the social construction of self. While the 'me' is greatly influenced by interactions and relationships with others, these can be incorporated into the 'I'. This is highly beneficial if the quality of the relationship is predicated on positive responses from others, but can become maleficent when suffused with negative responses. In many respects the 'I' is the private self or inner core, which is hidden and may never be revealed, while the 'me' is the public self or outer aspects of self which is displayed to the world.

The 'me' is reflected in both the self-concept, which is how the individual thinks about the self and self-worth which is how the individual evaluates the self. Both these are highly dependent on how others view the individual, respond to them, and relate to them. These reflections can contain overt verbal messages, and can be inferred from actions, behaviour and responses, or lack of them. Providing the self-structures are well integrated, any discrepancies in reflections can be incorporated into a unified whole without shattering the self. The healthy self-concept contains and balances both positive and negative reflections based on accurate and realistic self-appraisal. If this delicate balance is interrupted through negative evaluations or reflections of the self, then the self-concept is undermined giving rise to a lowered sense of self-worth.

Self-worth is dependent on how the individual evaluates, thinks and feels about the self. The foundations of self-worth originate in childhood through caring and affirming relationships. In the presence of positive relationships, which reflect relational worth, the self emerges predicated on a relatively stable feeling of being of value. Harter (1999) proposes that the *baseline self-concept* derives from what is reflected by others and is associated with a stable and global sense of self-worth, while the *barometer self-concept* is based on situational factors, competence and who is present. This would indicate that self-worth relies on both a sense of connectedness and a sense of competency. The barometer self-concept is vulnerable to fluctuations depending on situational demands in which competencies are being tested. Despite these fluctuations, the stable baseline self-concept can act as a counterbalance to retain a healthy self-concept and retain self-worth.

In DA the baseline self-concept is commonly eroded by the negative projections and evaluations emanating from the abuser, while the barometer self-concept is impacted by restrictions on opportunities to demonstrate competencies. The abuser's negative projections are absorbed by the survivor and over time coalesce to disrupt any semblance of balance in the self-concept. In the absence of a social support network the survivor is prevented from challenging the validity of the abuser's projections. This leaves the survivor with no option but to introject these negative evaluations and come to believe them. Furthermore, the coercive control and lack of autonomy prevents the survivor from exercising choices, taking initiative and developing, or testing competencies. In combination the survivor is prevented from making realistic or accurate self-appraisals, which leads to lowered self-esteem and self-worth.

Self-worth is supported by *self-efficacy* which is the sense or feeling of being able to influence the external environment, or make an impact on others, and internal experience, such as the regulation of emotions. Self-efficacy is also associated with being able to meet needs and achieve intentions, which underpins the sense of competency. Competency and self-efficacy is inextricably linked with a sense of potency, power and control. It is through self-efficacy that survivors can experience that they have value and the capacity to make an impact on others, especially in intimate relationships. It is self-efficacy that enables survivors to know that their partner has their welfare in mind. In DA the survivor's needs, sense of self-efficacy and competency are largely ignored by the abuser. The control and domination does not allow for any sense of self-efficacy which serves to further undermine self-worth. The more the survivor's basic needs and competencies are dishonoured, the more potency, power and self-efficacy are eroded so that the survivor comes to believe that she has no influence over her own actions, intentions or life. This results in profound feelings of helplessness, hopelessness and resignation.

Intertwined with self-efficacy is *self-agency* in which the individual is a self agent, who is active in initiating, organising, choosing and interpreting experiences. Self-agency is a core facet of the self (Stern 1985) which evolves in interactions with emotionally sensitive and responsive care givers (Meins 1997). In DA, self-agency is inhibited or erased, as the abuser is in total control and will not permit the survivor to take initiative or be a self agent, as this undermines his authority and power. The survivor is not allowed to organise her life, or choose, or act of her own volition. The abuser also seeks to control the survivor's interpretation of experiences by distorting her reality by insisting she is crazy and is misinterpreting his behaviour. This further prevents self-agency in being free to make accurate interpretations.

A crucial aspect of self-identity and the experience of a cohesive self is the sense of *self-continuity*, which provides the individual with a sense of self-unity and integrity. Self-continuity allows the individual to have an enduring sense of self at different times, and in different situations. This enduring sense of self is retained despite external changes allowing the individual to experience integrity and coherence. As self-continuity is inextricably linked with self-agency and self-efficacy, it promotes a sense of individuality and sense of separateness. Self-continuity is disrupted in DA as the abuser dictates what the survivor is permitted to feel or how she can behave. Discontinuity in self-experience can lead to confusion and a sense of fragmentation. Discontinuity in self is often manifested in how the survivor's behaviour changes when she is with the abuser and when with others. This can sometimes be so radically different that the survivor can barely recognise herself. Many survivors are compliant, biddable and subservient when with the abuser, and yet outgoing, humorous and feisty when with family or friends. Continuity of self is especially undermined in contradictory attachment relationships which give rise to internal conflict as the individual tries to reconcile loving behaviour with abusive behaviour, or feelings of anger with the need to protect the abuser. To manage such discontinuity, the survivor is compelled to compartmentalise feelings and experiences, which leads to fragmentations of the self.

Alongside self-continuity, individuals need to experience a degree of *self-stability* in which they feel able to control, regulate and manage the full range of emotions giving them a sense of internal safety. Self-stability is enhanced when the environment is relatively predictable and consistent. Unpredictability and lack of consistency prevent the individual from being able to relax, mentalise or reflect on experiences as they are in a constant state of alert or hypervigilance. This impedes the individual's ability to make sense of his or her experience or create a coherent narrative, leaving the survivor in a state of internal chaos. In DA, the abuser thrives on unpredictability and chaos as it strengthens his control and dominance, and engenders the survivor's total surrender.

The presence of all the above aspects of self and the internalisation of good working models allows the individual to evoke an internal locus of evaluation and control, which further reinforces self-efficacy and self-agency. It also allows for congruence between the person's self-concept and the organismic or experiencing self. Crucially it promotes being in contact with inner experiencing, needs and desires, being able to accept and express these, and seek satisfaction from these. In DA these are cruelly oppressed by the abuser, and introjected by the survivor leading to self-loathing and shame. Paradoxically this renders the survivor even more dependent on the abuser as an external source of evaluation and control. This increases the chasm between the authentic self and the false, or imposed self to such a degree that survivors can no longer recognise themselves. The loss of self epitomises the total surrender of the survivor's identity and strengthens the bond with the abuser.

A crucial component of working with survivors of DA is to rebuild the shattered self through mentalising the abusive experiences and develop an in-depth understanding of how abuse erodes and annihilates any vestiges of self-esteem and self-efficacy they may have possessed. Awareness of abuse dynamics and their impact on survivors will enable them to understand the origins of the inchoate mass of imposed aspects of self. Once identified, survivors can reject these imposed alien aspects of self, and restore the authentic self into an organised and coherent whole. This will restore the authentic self and permit survivors to connect to and rebuild a relationship with the self.

Impact of domestic abuse on self

Trauma, psychological abuse and DA lowers self-worth and impacts on self-esteem. Persistent exposure to humiliation and degradation undermines self-worth. This is evoked through not only words but also actions and how survivors are treated. To defend against the pernicious effects of DA and preserve some sense of control, survivors frequently take responsibility for the abuse, and blame themselves. This false illusion of power and control rescues the survivor from total surrender and helplessness to the detriment of low self-worth, which further undermines the self. The brutalisation in DA impedes the capacity to mentalise self-experiences, which leads to self-loathing and lack of self-compassion, whereby the survivor no longer has the self in mind.

DA also impacts on self-efficacy and self-agency because the person is overpowered and rendered helpless. Loss of predictability squashes self-efficacy and the ability to influence one's own life. Trauma also disrupts self-continuity through changes in consciousness, such as dissociation, detachment and withdrawal. Continuity of self is further undermined by heightened internal conflict such as tumultuous and contradictory feelings of rage and love. As anger can rarely be safely expressed in the face of DA, the survivor's destructiveness collides with protectiveness (Allen 2006a) as the individual vacillates between desiring to express anger, and wanting to preserve the relationship. The survivor fears hurting the attachment figure, and fears punishment for expressing anger. Continuity of self is compromised in the presence of contradictory attachments which oscillate between abuse and affection, as it is nigh impossible to reconcile dramatic contradictions: to believe that the self is worthy of love and affection and yet also deserving of abuse and neglect. Such intense conflicts can tear the self apart, leading to compartmentalisation and fragmentation (Allen 2001).

The abuser may also attempt to destroy positive changes in self-identity such as triumphing over early childhood adversity, or post-traumatic growth by consistently reminding the survivor of previous victimisation in part to rationalise the present abuse but also to prevent acknowledgement of growth and change. Such reminders serve to underscore the abuser's assertions that the survivor is worthless, unstable and suffering from mental health issues. This can be used as a threat against the survivor to colour professionals' assessment of her by claiming that she is crazy or an unfit mother.

As the survivor relinquishes the authentic self, she may also relinquish family, friends and other attachments that could act as transitional objects to enable her to counterbalance the abuser's projections. In the absence of positive mirroring from friends, the survivor comes to rely solely on the reflection from the abuser, no matter how distorted. The fear of betrayal, rejection and abandonment lead to an overwhelming terror to be left alone, and equal terror to be with others. This disrupts the survivor's connection with others and access to social support. In the absence of self-connection or connection with others, the survivor starts to disconnect from life and the world. The survivor begins to repudiate once treasured beliefs and values, and adopts those of the abuser. This reinforces her sense of being trapped, which diminishes hope and vitality. This enhances the abuser's control and power, and leads to the total surrender of the survivor.

The erosion of identity is a pernicious long-term effect of DA. Initially the survivor may have a cohesive sense of self, and an internal locus of evaluation and control, which is wrested from her by the abuser, who seeks to control every aspect of the survivor's self. Abusers commonly dictate how the survivor should be, feel, think and behave, and seek the total surrender of the self. The obliteration of the self leaves a vacuum where the core self should be (Kohut 1972), which is then impregnated by the abuser's projections to create an alien identity. Like an incubus, this imposed identity takes possession of the survivor, who is forced to absorb it to replace the shattered self-structures. This is enforced not only through the abuser's direct, negative verbal evaluations but also from the negation and rejection of the survivor's basic needs. The abuser renders the survivor's authentic self invisible, giving rise to a reduction in self-continuity and existential uncertainty.

To manage such fragmentation, compensatory self-structures are evoked which serve to oppress the authentic self. Compensatory self-structures such as invincibility, invulnerability and self-sufficiency give rise to a fallacious sense of omnipotence, which, while giving the impression of being able to cope, actually increases danger. To be in contact with the fear and danger inherent in DA is overwhelming as the survivor is in constant survival mode. By blocking out the terror and fear, the survivor finds temporary respite which enhances her ability to tolerate increasingly higher levels of abuse and danger. The abuser's oppression and the demands of being in survival mode impede the development of higher self-structures such as creativity, inspiration, joy or vitality. It also compromises the necessary cognitive capacities to plan and execute alternative outcomes and decision making. In addition, the false illusion of invincibility and invulnerability enforces self-sufficiency and prevents the survivor from seeking or asking for help.

The alienation from the authentic self extends out to alienation from others. This along with shame leads to isolation and withdrawal from others, which reduces access to alternative sources of evaluation, reality testing or help. This increases the survivor's dependence on the abuser, rendering her even more susceptible to his control and projections. As the survivor internalises the abuser's projections, she incorporates them into shattered self-structures and comes to perceive these as her own, even long after she has left the relationship. In essence the internal self ceases to exist, and the imposed identity is perceived as 'self'. All authentic feelings have to be concealed as they do not fit the abuser's fantasy of how the survivor should be. The abuser's lack of empathy for the survivor is also internalised and becomes part of the imposed self, leading to a marked lack of self-compassion and self-empathy. In effect the survivor has become dehumanised, and devoid of feeling for the destroyed self.

The internalisation of the abuser's projections and lack of empathy necessitates the creation of defences to protect split-off internal vulnerability, and promotes attacks on the self. This can lead to self-derogation, self-mutilation and self-destructive behaviours. Such violence against the self is thought to be a way of managing damage to self-esteem and mastering inner fragmentation and annihilation anxieties. Some survivors of trauma and DA oscillate between traumatophobia, or fear of trauma, and traumatophilia, an attraction to trauma as a way to manage the internal effects of violence (Sanderson 2006).

Violence against the self is closely linked to the brutalisation inherent in interpersonal trauma, and the obliteration of the authentic self which can generate intense shame (Fonagy *et al.* 2002; Mollon 2002b; Sanderson 2006). Shame is multifaceted and affects not only emotions but also cognitions and behaviours. The central conflict in shame is the attempt to *suppress* the self and *express* the self (Mollon 2002b) which gives rise to a number of coping strategies. This is especially the case in DA where the survivor desires to be visible in her pain and yet needs to be invisible to avoid further assaults. The need to conceal shame leads to avoidance, detachment and withdrawal, and disruption to self-continuity. As the survivor becomes invisible the anguish of lack of intimacy, fear of abandonment and aching aloneness is so overwhelming that the survivor seeks closeness to the abuser, even if it means being assaulted or vilified for reaching out.

The five main strategies to manage shame are avoidance, concealment, compensation, aggression and heightened attentiveness to being exposed. In avoidance the individual withdraws, and avoids intimacy in order to avoid exposure of shame. In concealment the individual seeks to cover up the shame through pride or the use of self-medication such as alcohol or drugs to oppress the authentic and vulnerable part of the self. Compensatory strategies to manage shame manifest as self-blame, self-reliance, the repudiation of feelings such as neediness, weakness and vulnerability or inadequacy. The survivor replaces shame with a facade of strength, self-confidence and invincibility which belies the vulnerable and dependent aspects of the self. As it is dangerous to express rage and aggression towards the abuser, many survivors have to suppress this only to enact these against themselves, or in some instances, their children. Fear of exposure of shame promotes heightened attentiveness to being exposed and manifest in reduced interactions with others, and impaired relational dynamics.

Damage to self-structures invariably leads to feelings of helplessness, hopelessness, powerlessness, defilement, expectation of danger and persistent fear of recurring abuse. Survivors are commonly suffused with a sense of detachment, demoralisation, dispiritedness and a profound loss of bonding capacity to anyone other than the abuser. To protect damaged self-structures dissociation is evoked along with unconscious disposition to self-destructive defences such as self-mutilation and suicidal ideation. The pervasive loss of self-identity incurs loss of vitality and futility in living, which impacts on willingness to thrive, preoccupations with death, loss of belief system, seeing the world as an essentially dangerous, untrustworthy and unpredictable place.

The more the survivor's core identity is annihilated, and all needs and emotional vulnerability are repudiated, the greater the desolate psychological space onto which the abuser can project and impose a false identity. This renders the survivor vulnerable to the introjection of the abuser projections. The survivor is compelled to organise the self-structures around the abuser's reflection of the denigrated, bad and unlovable aspects of the self. This leads to oppressive mental structures that while offering containment, are cruel, oppressive and self-condemnatory. As the false self emerges it obscures any vestiges of the authentic self, concealing vulnerability and deeply felt shame. The survivor seeks cognitive meaning in what is inchoate and cannot be understood, which further compromises control, self-agency and self-efficacy.

These alterations in self-identity, and the adoption of a false self, can result in deep psychological fissures in self-structures which persist long after leaving the abusive relationship. Many survivors find it extremely hard to relinquish the imposed identity as they are plagued with memories and feelings of the enslaved self that was humiliated and subjugated. Such survivors find it difficult to reject the abuser's projections and continue to oppress and conceal the authentic self through self-condemnation and lack of self-compassion. It is only through identifying the function, dynamics and processes of annihilation of the self that survivors can acknowledge this rape of the self and begin to dissemble compensatory and imposed self-structures. Through the therapeutic process survivors can abandon the dehumanised identity and begin to access the remnants of the authentic self.

Many survivors of trauma find that the restoration of the authentic self allows for the emergence of a post-traumatic self that is more empowered and has enhanced personal meaning and appreciation of life. Post-traumatic growth allows for increased control, self-worth and confidence that were not present before the DA. This is often accompanied by increased awareness, wider ranging choices, enhanced spirituality and reconnection to life. As survivors reclaim a sense of their own identity, in which they can set boundaries and become figure rather than ground, they can begin to rebuild their life outside the shadow of abuse.

Working with self-aspects

The primary aim when working with self-aspects is to provide a safe and secure therapeutic space in which to build or rebuild structures, through the therapeutic relationship. An uncontaminated therapeutic environment permits the exploration of damaged self-structures, the opportunity to discard false identities, rebuild new self-structures, and the restoration of an authentic, cohesive self. To facilitate this, clinicians need to provide genuine, and authentic empathic attunement in which the survivor feels understood and accepted in expressing such needs. The quality of the relationship is critical to allow the unfolding of new self-structures, free from dread and shame.

Counsellors need to be aware that by entering the therapeutic relationships, survivors are expressing hope and courage in not repudiating their needs for connection and that they are willing to risk connection, despite previous betrayals. It also demonstrates that the authentic self has not been totally annihilated and that there is opportunity to repair the shattered self and allow the authentic self to unfold. However, this can be extremely painful and painstaking work, as survivors begin to relinquish their compensatory self-structures, or imposed identities and fear disintegration.

Below the veneer of containment and high functioning, many survivors are tormented by self-condemnatory beliefs and a terror of disintegration. Disintegration anxiety is activated in close intimate relationships, including counselling, and can lead to psychic agony and fear of fragmentation. The opportunity for change through the therapeutic process may be feared rather than welcomed, which can increase psychic and body armour and engender increased bodily tension. Survivors need a safe and secure therapeutic environment in which to lower defences and allow for the shedding of the abuser's imposed identity. It is in such a space that the survivor can safely confront disintegration anxiety and restore authentic self.

Counsellors need to adopt a warm, empathically attuned therapeutic stance in which the survivor is visible and appropriately mirrored without being shamed. Counsellors need to guard against being too intrusive or charismatic, as this has the potential to re-enact abusive elements of the DA relationship. The survivor must always be subject, not object; figure, not ground. The focus of the therapeutic work needs to be on the restoration of a coherent and cohesive self in which the authentic self can unfold in order to restore self-stability and self-continuity.

The counsellor needs to enable the survivor to identify the false self, and facilitate the shedding of the imposed identity. Some survivors may actively resist this, especially if the imposed self-structure has promoted survival. It may take a considerable period of time for survivors to feel safe enough to shed what has been deeply embedded and provided a semblance of safety and control. Counsellors need to be patient and allow survivors to go at their own, manageable pace to relinquish these self-structures. Survivors' resistance may activate abuse re-enactments which counsellors need to understand within the context of abuse and carefully monitor their own counter-transference reactions. The emphasis must be on containing destructive acting out and exploring their meaning and function.

Counsellors must work towards enabling survivors to assimilate the DA experiences and integrate them into restored self-structures, and facilitate the development of more positive self-schemas in order to rebuild self-worth and self-esteem. Exploring and understanding the origins of self-blame, guilt and self-recrimination will facilitate a reduction in such cruel oppression. Understanding the origins of damaged self-structures and how the abuser's projections are introjected are crucial to healing. In clarifying these, the survivor can expunge these projections and redirect them to their original source, the abuser. This will allow self-compassion, empathy and self-tolerance to emerge that are necessary in reclaiming the self.

To ensure safety, counsellors must also help survivors to identify and modify self-destructive behaviours, such as alcohol, or drug abuse, self-harm and suicidal ideation. Triggers that activate dissociation and detachment must also be identified so that survivors can be more present and in contact with internal and external cues. Counsellors need to validate existing coping strategies, and encourage survivors to consider a range of alternative healthy strategies and options.

In working with the restoration of self-structures, counsellors must support the survivor's autonomous strivings for self-definition and self-agency in order to promote the restoration of internal locus of evaluation and control. Counsellors must refrain from defining the survivor so as not to impose yet another identity. The survivor needs to be given time and space to develop self-definition without being directed by the counsellor. Throughout this process counsellors must encourage the survivor to rebuild competencies, provide opportunities to practise these, and restore self-efficacy and self-agency. This allows the survivor to feel more grounded and centred, restore personal meaning, vitality and spirituality in order to reconnect to self, others and life.

To heal from DA necessitates an understanding of the development of self-aspects, mentalising experiences, and the creation of a coherent narrative out of chaos. This will facilitate internal and external safety, the restoration of continuity of self and the reconciliation of powerful internal conflicts. Reconstructing the self-narrative and evaluating negative self-thoughts can allow for greater self-acceptance and self-worth. This is enhanced through rebuilding and engaging in close attachment relationships, such as the therapeutic relationship. It is through connecting to the counsellor, being validated, and responded to in a care-giving, growth-promoting way that the survivor can begin to connect to self and others, and reconnect to life and the world.

RESTORING THE SELF THROUGH MENTALISING

Mentalising allows for the deconstruction and reconstruction of unquestioned and unevaluated beliefs and attitudes towards the self. Mentalising permits a fresh perspective on experiences, in which the survivor can mentalise the abuser's negative assessments, and allows for more objective self-appraisal. In mentalising the survivor reclaims control and the freedom to think and feel autonomously without being dictated to by the abuser, or anyone else. This is initially unfamiliar and terrifying, but ultimately liberating (Allen, Bleiberg and Haslam-Hopwood 2003). It is crucial that counsellors encourage the survivor to mentalise positive and negative self-beliefs, as this engenders a more open-minded, balanced and productive definition which permits both praise and criticisms. Through this the survivor can adopt a more objective and benevolent view of the self.

Mentalising also facilitates self-awareness and enables the individual to derive meaning from emotions, making them more intelligible. Mentalising also enhances awareness of others which leads to improved relational dynamics and healthier attachments. Mentalising can also be applied to identifying needs, desires, motives, intentions, hopes, goals, fears, thoughts, beliefs, attitudes, fantasies and dreams. Mentalising is blocked in DA as the survivor is in survival mode, leaving insufficient time or energy to reflect. Survivors commonly subsume their needs under those of their abusers and divert any meagre energy resources to mentalising their abuser's needs. The lack of opportunity for self-reflection and mentalising of unmet needs, emotions and experiences means that these become blocked and pushed further away from awareness, which increases tolerance and acceptance of the abusive behaviour. Counsellors need to actively encourage mentalising as this will enable the survivor to move from survivor mode to taking control, restore self-stability and self-continuity and adopt a more solution-focused stance.

RESTORING SELF-STABILITY

Through mentalising, survivors can learn to regulate and modulate their emotions, which is critical to restoring a sense of internal control and safety. Mentalising facilitates more skilful emotional regulation and self-regulation in which the individual can monitor and calibrate emotions. The capacity to modulate tumultuous and overwhelming emotions allows for a greater sense of self-stability. In learning to modulate emotions the survivor will be less susceptible to self-destructive behaviours, dissociation and self-attacks to enhance self-continuity. Mentalising and self-regulation leads to feeling more in control, and increased capacity to manage and greater opportunity to feel more competent. Mastery over emotions and other competencies enhances self-efficacy, self-care, self-agency and self-compassion, allowing the survivor to reconnect to the self.

CHANGING SELF-CONCEPT AND SELF-WORTH

Mentalising can facilitate changes in self-concept and self-worth. While this is not easy when self-worth has been eroded, it is possible to develop more accurate self-appraisals through mentalising the abuser's negative assessments. As a healthy self-concept is a balance of both positive and negative attributes, realistic appraisal is crucial. If anything a slight tilt towards positive attributes is associated with improved mental health and is considered to be adaptive (Allen 2006a). To increase self-worth and self-esteem, counsellors must encourage the survivor to amplify positive aspects of self, while not denying negative aspects, but to tone these down slightly. To facilitate this, survivors need to identify negative self-talk and self-criticism, and replace these with more accurate evaluations.

RESTORING SELF-EFFICACY AND SELF-AGENCY

The antidote to the erosion of self-efficacy and self-agency is empowerment, the restoration of control, both internal and external, and providing opportunities to practise competencies. The survivor needs to take control over her own life through increased awareness and understanding of abuse dynamics, and increasing a sense of predictability in her environment. Once a degree of safety has been restored (see Chapter 4) the survivor can start to set personally meaningful goals and work towards achieving them. Counsellors can help this process through short, medium and long-term goals, and to set tasks that will enable the survivor to attain these. The setting of mutually agreed homework exercises will give the survivor the opportunity to practise competencies. It is also useful to encourage the survivor to revive skills that she has been prevented from using during the abusive relationship, or to develop new ones. Choosing, practising and developing competencies and skills will restore much needed self-efficacy and self-agency.

RESTORING SELF-CONTINUITY

To restore self-continuity counsellors need to enable the survivor to reclaim her personal history, experiences, capabilities and cohesive sense of self. A powerful exercise that can restore self-continuity is a timeline, on which the survivor plots significant positive and negative life events. This can include photographs and mementos that evoke poignant self-experiences. Timelines frequently also aid the recall of previously blocked memories, which when integrated into the self-structure, further increases self-continuity. The reduction of post-traumatic stress disorder symptoms such as dissociation also facilitates self-continuity. The conscious management of internal conflicts and overpowering ambivalent feelings also allows for a greater sense of self-continuity. Reconnecting to others and re-establishing healthy relationships in which the survivor can permit the presence of the authentic self can also be hugely beneficial to the restoration of self-continuity.

RECLAIMING SELF-IDENTITY

Along with restoring self-continuity, the survivor can rebuild self-identity through identifying and reawakening dormant needs, beliefs, values, desires and interests. It is imperative to explore the survivor's pre-abuse identity, and to rebuild those aspects that have not been destroyed by the abuser. The survivor can be encouraged to access these aspects, build upon them and begin to integrate new aspects that emerge as a result of post-traumatic growth. The counsellor needs to enable the survivor to identify, evaluate, reject and accept those aspects that fit the authentic self and consolidate these. It is important during this process that verbal affirmations are accompanied by opportunities to demonstrate self-efficacy and self-agency. Reminding the survivor that he or she is in total control of autonomously chosen self-definition and self-identity can be exhilarating, enthralling and liberating.

COGNITIVE RESTRUCTURING

Cognitive techniques enable survivors to become more aware of automatic negative self-thoughts and demoralising narratives. In cognitive restructuring these need to be identified, challenged and replaced with more constructive alternatives. Changing such negative thoughts such as 'I am helpless' to more positive ones such as 'I am resilient' can impact on a more positive view of the self. This is compounded when the positive statements are supported with evidence, and reinforcement from others. Friends and the survivor's support network are powerful reinforcers in validating and confirming a more positive view of the survivor. Cognitive restructuring not only allows survivors to think more positively about the self, but also will change how they feel and behave.

A useful technique to restructure the survivor's thinking is the use of self-narratives. Counsellors can encourage survivors to write success or failure narratives and challenge the thinking contained in them. This is critical as the way that survivors think about the self fuels how they then feel and behave. In the presence of negative and self-critical thinking, survivors are more likely to fuel despair, self-abuse and negative self-assessments. Negative thinking needs to be constantly challenged, evaluated and reconstructed so that survivors can take more control over these negative cognitive schemas, and their concomitant negative impact on the self. Taking control of these allows for increased level of internal locus of control and evaluation.

ROLE OF ACTION

The role of action is central in rebuilding damaged self-structures. While positive affirmations are desirable, they are not always trusted by survivors of DA. Many abusers shower the survivors with positive affirmations during the reconciliation phase of the cycle of abuse only for those to be obliterated during the abuse phase. This means that many survivors learn not to trust words, but to look for evidence in actions. In essence, as abusers use words to enthral and manipulate the survivors, they cannot be fully trusted. The therapeutic process should incorporate the importance of action by encouraging survivors to engage in activities that are pleasurable and rewarding and which allow competency, self-efficacy and self-agency. Active engagement in pleasurable activities should not be restricted to the public self, but needs to include the private self in which survivors can reclaim self-pleasure and self-compassion and meet previously unmet needs.

The therapeutic environment can provide a secure and safe place in which to explore unmet needs and to find healthy ways to satisfy them. The expression of these basic needs requires empathic non-shaming responses from the counsellor, rather than interpreting them as childish or narcissistic. The counsellor needs to view the expression of unmet needs as welcome indicators that they have not been destroyed, and that the survivor still has life energy and a willingness to grow, and has not abandoned hope that these needs can be met. The counsellor must understand that it is important for the survivor to express these basic needs to fully complete the healthy development of self.

WORKING WITH SHAME

Shame is a protective strategy against psychic devastation, and is common when self-structures are damaged through interpersonal relationships. Working with shame can be extremely difficult as the persistent conflict for the survivor is the need to *express* and *suppress* the self. This is enacted in the therapeutic process whereby the survivor vacillates between engaging and retreating; wanting to be visible and wanting to be invisible. Such withdrawal can manifest in session through withdrawal, dissociation or disappearing into silence. Counsellors need to understand that this is fuelled by the survivor's fear of exposure and need to preserve invisibility. Outside of therapy shame may manifest in fierce self-reliance, self-attacks, self-harm, self-sabotage and self-criticism. To fully engage in working with shame counsellors need to have explored their own experiences of shame and be sensitive to not reshaming the survivor (Mollon 2002b; Sanderson 2006). Counsellors must contextualise the survivor's shame and be aware of their counter-transference reactions to ensure that the therapeutic relationship is preserved.

POST-TRAUMATIC GROWTH

Recent research has shown that survivors of trauma can go beyond recovery and experience what is known as *post-traumatic growth* (Allen 2006a; Tedeschi 1999; Wilson 2006) allowing for an enhanced experience of being alive. Surviving trauma can also increase self-reliance, awareness of mortality, promote closer ties to others, and increased empathy and compassion. Many survivors report developing a clearer philosophy of life, renewed appreciation of life, a deeper sense of meaning and spirituality. This is often accompanied by enhanced self-efficacy, persistence, courage and openness. Survivors also report that they are able to cultivate a full range of feelings, in particular pleasure, enjoyment, humour and vitality. Post-traumatic growth can also engender a greater capacity for caring and intimacy which enhance close relationships. Most significantly, post-traumatic growth restores hope and allows reconnection to self, others and life in an enriched way.

RELATIONSHIP WITH SELF

To fully recover from DA, survivors need to develop a healthy relationship with self. To effect this the survivor needs to exorcise the internalised abuser, abandon attacks on the self, and repudiate the abusive relationship with the self. To develop a more supportive relationship with the self, counsellors need to enable survivors to identify self-attacks, improve self-care, self-compassion and self-nurturing. This can be developed through positive self-talk, permitting positive feelings about self, and becoming more benevolent and compassionate towards the self. While many survivors yearn for a loving, caring relationship with someone special, it is critical that they can develop such a relationship with the self. In creating a secure attachment to the self, which is encouraging and supportive, the survivor can create a much deeper sense of self-stability, self-worth and internal locus of evaluation. This can feel much more secure as this stability is under self-control and not dependent on the evaluations and affirmations from others, which can fluctuate and undermine self-stability. By providing pleasure, comfort, soothing and positive affirmations to the self, the survivor not only develops self-empathy, but also becomes more open to compassion from others.

BUILDING CONNECTIONS

Relationships which are secure and safe and which offer positive reflections promote healthy self-structures and enhance relational dynamics. Healthy relationships are a powerful antidote to DA as they provide better reflections, acceptance and compassion. To facilitate improved relationships, survivors need to be encouraged to develop well-bounded relationships in which needs can be expressed, acknowledged and accepted rather than judged, ridiculed or dismissed. Survivors of DA initially find it hard to accept positive regard from others due to mistrust and fear of being abused, especially if the abuser alternated between love and affection and abuse. A significant effect of DA is the destruction of the survivor's relational worth. In order to rebuild this, the survivor needs to invest time and energy into those relationships that enhance self-worth, while minimising contact with those who diminish it. This can be hard for the survivor as it is more familiar to be stripped of self-worth than it is to be validated, respected and be treated with compassion and empathy. Many survivors initially find themselves gravitating towards familiar relational dynamics than to develop new ones, and counsellors need to understand this within the context of DA.

Counsellors need to encourage survivors to take risks in expressing themselves in close relationships, set healthy boundaries and challenge difficulties in order to develop trust, self-efficacy and self-acceptance, and learn to accept validation and affirmation from others. It is also helpful to encourage the survivor to actively evaluate the quality of relationships and find ways to enhance them rather than withdraw. In developing relatedness to others, survivors can begin to engage in relationships in which they are treated with compassion, they can learn to trust and permit self-acceptance. Rebuilding a good social support network consisting of a variety of healthy relationships allows for connection to others which is a crucial component of healing from trauma and DA.

Role of counsellor

As the therapeutic relationship is central in healing trauma, counsellors need to be responsive, affirming and respectful of their clients within clear boundaries around self, so as not to become enmeshed. To this effect, counsellors must be fully engaged, present and empathically attuned. It is crucial that the therapeutic relationship offers a real connection between counsellor and client in which trust can flourish. In the presence of such a relationship the survivor can reconnect to the authentic self, and begin to connect to others. Counsellors need to provide a holding environment in which damaged self-structures can be explored and restored, without further judgement or shame. To facilitate this, counsellors must be visible and emotionally available but guard against being overbearing, intrusive or too forceful as this could be reminiscent of the abuser. This will revive the survivor's fear that her core identity will not be accepted or annihilated, making her vulnerable to introjecting any perceived projections, and the adoption of a false identity. Counsellors must refrain from being too charismatic or providing too much positive mirroring, as this is invasive and diminishes the survivor's visibility. Moreover, it is likely to evoke existential angst and is indicative of the counsellor's own need for visibility.

Too much positive mirroring can be counter-therapeutic as the counsellor flatters or defines the survivor, thereby undermining autonomous striving for self-definition, and seeing the client within the counsellor's frame of reference. Flattering or defining the survivor provides only temporary relief and prevents the survivor from developing her own self-definition. Most crucially, counsellors need to provide healthy mirroring and not use the survivor to affirm their own reflection. To seek gratification of the counsellor's own unmet needs from the survivor is tantamount to abuse, and repeats the survivor's abuse experience. This will be experienced as yet another betrayal in which another part of the self is destroyed. Counsellors need to constantly balance containing damaged self-structures and supporting the survivor's striving for autonomy and self-definition.

Counsellors must also adopt a non-defensive stance in which they contextualise therapeutic battles and understand these as underlying latent desire to connect. In addition clinicians must let go of assumptions, preconceptions and rigid theories to release full capacity for empathic understanding, and openness to the survivor's revived self-structures. It is paramount that counsellors do not fit the survivor to the theory but to understand the survivor's experience as fully as possible (Sanderson 2006).

To facilitate this, counsellors need a high level of self-awareness and ability to identify and understand their own damaged self-structures such as compensatory self-structures, such as the need for omnipotence, omniscience and invincibility. They also need to examine the degree of cohesiveness, own feelings of being fake, the adoption of false self, identity diffusion, compartmentalisation, shame and attacks on self. It is crucial that clinicians understand any negative counter-transference reactions, especially vacillation between idealising survivors and devaluing them. Counsellors must not hide behind an austere or clinical mask but allow humanity to show. This is critical when working with the dehumanisation seen in DA. It is the human qualities of empathy, warmth and compassion which are restorative alongside an open, engaged stance, which exudes emotional availability. The emphasis and focus needs to be on engagement and connection, not theory or cognitive analysis. Feeling heard and understood can be life-changing for survivors of DA, especially when accompanied with respect for the individual and each unique experience.

Counsellors need to consider the role of post-traumatic growth and focus on the positive outcomes when healing from trauma and DA. Counsellors must genuinely believe in the capacity for positive growth rather than pay lip service or seek to merely replace negative experiences with positive ones. It is integrating both positive and negative experiences that truly underpins post-traumatic growth and is beneficial to healing. Such a positive approach needs to be balanced with realism, and to be assessed in relation to each individual survivor. The presence of hope, strength and courage is evident in entering counselling, as survivors demonstrate their willingness to trust again despite the betrayal in DA. This is testament to tremendous courage to risk trusting again, which needs to be validated from the outset not only in words but also in deep recognition and understanding of how difficult and costly this can be to the survivor. It is a clear indicator that the survivor has not abandoned hope and that the self has not been totally annihilated, and that vitality and life energy is still present to allow for growth. As the therapeutic relationship is critical in providing opportunities for reconnection, counsellors need to constantly monitor the quality of the therapeutic relationship. It is when the survivor is in a safe and secure therapeutic environment that self-structures can be rebuilt and the survivor can reconnect to self, others and life.

Summary

- The self develops in relation to others through attachment, care giving, intimacy, love, connectedness and cooperation. It is through healthy attachment that the individual can safely separate, and develop autonomy, self-definition and individuality. From these, the person learns to take initiative and responsibility, and acquires a sense of achievement.

- Relatedness also plays a critical role in the development of self-concept, self-worth, self-efficacy, self-agency and self-continuity. The chaotic and contradictory nature of attachment in DA serves to undermine these self-structures, and engenders a fragmented sense of self.

- To reclaim self-identity and develop a coherent sense of self, the survivor of DA must integrate fragmented self-structures and engage in more accurate self-appraisals to rebuild self-worth. In essence, recovery from DA entails healing the self.

- Counsellors need to enable survivors to link the complex nature and impact of DA to the erosion and fragmentation of self-structures. It is through mentalising DA experiences that survivors can begin to understand how abusive relationships can destroy and undermine self-structures, and how these are then impregnated with the abuser's projections and imposed identity.

- To restore a cohesive sense of self, survivors need to reclaim self-identity through more accurate self-appraisal, objective self-evaluation and autonomous striving for self-definition. This needs to be combined with actions that rebuild self-agency and self-efficacy in order to restore internal locus of evaluation and control. With this in place, survivors of DA can begin to reconnect to self, others and life.

- The therapeutic relationship is crucial in the restoration of self and counsellors need to adopt a positive model of post-traumatic growth and be sensitively attuned and responsive to the survivors striving for connection and relatedness, both to self and others.

CHAPTER 8

WORKING WITH RELATIONAL ASPECTS OF DOMESTIC ABUSE

The need for connection and support from others is important in human development, especially in the development of coherent self-structures, the regulation of emotional states and ability to relate to others. Attachment aids survival and allows for the formation of affectional bonds which are necessary for mental well-being. Attachment also allows for the development of trust in others and a belief that the world is a relatively benign and benevolent place. When under threat or in the presence of trauma, survival mechanisms are activated which prompt individuals to seek refuge and security in the safe haven of attachment relationships. The complex nature of domestic abuse (DA) disrupts attachment relationships and undermines the bedrock of trust in others and the world, and causes a loss of confidence that others will provide protection.

Lack of trust evokes relational apprehensiveness which compels the individual to disconnect and withdraw from others, leading to a reduction in seeking social support. In DA this is compounded when the abuser restricts the survivor's access to family, friends or work colleagues through enforced isolation. Some survivors also come to distrust professionals, which can impede access to emotional, psychological and practical support to help them at a time when they most need it. The lack of connectedness with others serves to bind the survivor even more to the abuser, rendering the survivor totally dependent on the abuser. This increases the abuser's power and control over the survivor and ensures total submission and surrender. Over time the survivor feels increasingly isolated and alienated from others, reinforcing feelings of being trapped and a profound sense of hopelessness.

Research has shown that an integral part of healing and recovery from DA is the reduction in social isolation and the rebuilding of social support networks (Dutton 1992; Herman 1992a). This can be a painstaking task as the survivor needs to learn to trust again and begin to reconnect. To facilitate reconnection to others, survivors need to identify abusive relational dynamics and their impact on relational schemas. Once these have been identified they can be modified and replaced with healthier relational schemas and relational patterns. This can occur only within a predictable and consistent relationship such as that offered in the therapeutic process. The therapeutic relationship can provide a safe and secure environment to discover new, healthier ways of relating that will enable the survivor to connect to others. It is also a safe haven to identify and express needs, set healthy boundaries, learn conflict resolution and experience relational worth. Equipped with an enhanced relational repertoire, the survivor can begin to trust again, and build, or rebuild, healthy, satisfying relationships without fear of revictimisation.

This chapter examines the importance of connection to others, how DA impacts on relational dynamics, and the individual's attachment style. It will propose that in order to rebuild connection to others, the survivor needs to understand the origin of relational difficulties, and develop new relational schemas. To facilitate this, clinicians need to adopt a relational framework when working with survivors of DA. The chapter will also look at the importance of assessment and the necessity of a good understanding of the survivor's attachment history and current relational style, and how these manifest in the therapeutic relationship. It will consider the pivotal role of the working alliance as a fertile environment in which to explore current relational dynamics and discover new ways to form and sustain connection. This reparative work is an integral part of the therapeutic process as the survivor explores and shares relational experiences and is understood and valued. The emphasis is on the centrality of the therapeutic relationship to model healthier relational dynamics, revise relational schemas and develop relational worth. To facilitate this, counsellors need to ensure a warm, engaged and sensitively attuned therapeutic stance in which the survivor can learn to trust self, which is an essential ingredient in trusting and reconnecting to others. From this the survivor can form, sustain and rebuild satisfying relationships based on respect, relational worth and mutuality.

Relationship models

As social animals, humans need to attach and form bonds with others to aid survival (Bowlby 1969, 1973). In our evolutionary past, a lone human was more vulnerable to predators than one who was part of a group. Thus, to be in close proximity to others is adaptive and promotes safety and security, especially when under threat. When in danger, individuals seek protection from others to subvert annihilation, which suggests that attachment relationships are a critical part of human survival. To live in social groups that enhance safety, requires relational skills of affiliation, protection, cooperation and collaboration. These relational skills are acquired in early infancy, initially through the attachment bond to the primary care giver, which provide the foundation for later relationships.

Models of relationships are based on recurrent patterns of attachment interactions, which generalise and become more diverse, and complex over time. Early attachment bonds are thought to provide relational schemas or templates for all later relationships (Bowlby 1973). Although relational schemas are highly resilient, they can be changed, modified and reshaped depending on later relational interactions or new relationships. Thus, someone with a secure relational style may experience disruption to this as a result of being held captive in an abusive relationship.

Relational schemas not only shape relationship experiences but also determine an individual's behaviour towards others. Two pivotal factors in this process are the individual's expectations of how others will respond, and the view the individual has of self as worthy of attachment. In effect, the expectations of accessibility and responsiveness of others is inextricably linked with the individual's degree of relational worth. Therefore, if an individual is neglected he or she will feel unwanted and come to believe that they will always be unwanted by others, thereby compromising their relational worth. In addition, as relational schemas contain expectations of how others will respond, they also have the capacity to shape the behaviour of others. Most relationship interactions are synchronous in which relational patterns are repeated and reciprocated by others, especially when the relational styles between two individuals is mutually compatible and complementary. A pertinent example of this is when one individual is in pain and the other responds with comfort and soothing behaviour. In DA this synchrony is disrupted and inconsistent. The survivor who has been assaulted and in pain is rarely comforted by the perpetrator, but is vilified and neglected thus prolonging the pain. Thus when the survivor most needs comfort, it is denied.

Bowlby (1969) proposed that relationship models are developed in early infancy in the relationship with the primary care giver. Attachment facilitates the responsiveness and availability of others as a protection from threat, danger or overstimulation, and provides a secure base or place of refuge. It also plays a pivotal role in regulating physiological arousal and emotions, which becomes a template for the healthy development of relations to others. The absence of affectional bonds and a secure base has detrimental consequence for future attachment relationships, especially when the individual experiences violence, abuse or neglect. Research has demonstrated that relational misattunement, or relational trauma, promotes insecure attachment which can have severe impact on neurophysiological functioning and impair the capacity to relate to others (Allen 2001; Schore 2003a, 2003b).

These early experiences of attachment, responsiveness and affectional bonds are internalised and represented as an *internal working model* (IWM) of relational worth (Bowlby 1973). Although these IWMs are thought to be moderately accurate reflections of how the infant was related to, they are also influenced by the infant's temperament, perceptions and reactions to these relational experiences. Thus IWMs are not entirely passive introjects but represent the organisation of experiences and perceptions into coherent schemas which will inform and shape future expectations and behaviour towards others. Most importantly, IWMs are unconscious repetitive relational patterns, or *implicit procedures* for interacting with others (Fonagy and Target 1997), which are commonly evoked outside conscious awareness. One way to become more aware of these implicit procedures is to mentalise them in order to modify them and develop new procedures that promote more satisfying relationships, which are less generalised from past experiences and more responsive to present relationships (Allen 2006a).

While IWMs are resilient, they can be modified and adapted depending on the quality of relational experiences. In DA, the expectation of a secure relationship is shattered and replaced with mistrust and wariness. The abusive and uncaring relational reactions of the abuser lead the survivor to come to believe that she is not worthy of a loving and caring relationship. Over time this lack of relational worth and mistrust is projected onto all other relationships, including the therapeutic relationship. Mistrust is further exacerbated by some abusers, who subvert and undermine the quality of relationships the survivor has with family and friends. This can evoke relational anxiety which compels the survivor to withdraw even more from others and become increasingly socially isolated. When this is combined with the enforced seclusion commonly seen in DA, the survivor experiences both external and internal barriers to intimacy. The internal barriers of shame, secrecy, mistrust and fear of betrayal reinforce the survivor's feelings of being trapped, and increase the dependency on the abuser.

Social isolation also leads to estrangement and alienation from others increasing the survivor's sense of detachment. This restricts the survivor's range of emotions towards self and others which further undermines relational dynamics. Despite the palpable fear of others, survivors nevertheless commonly yearn for connection but are too terrified to risk such connection. This compounds the trauma of DA as the critical factors thought to ameliorate trauma, namely protection, supportive relationships and social support, are denied (Bowlby 1969; Wortman, Battle and Lemkau 1997). Given the distorted and inconsistent relational dynamics inherent in DA, survivors may also come to have discrepant and ambivalent expectation of others, leading to further disappointments and emotional wounding. Over time relational interactions and IWMs become organised into attachment styles which are generalised to all relationships.

A number of researchers have attempted to measure how Bowlby's (1969) IWMs and their concomitant cognitive and emotional representations of self and others form the basis of behaviour, and act as templates to organise responses (Ainsworth *et al.* 1978; Main 1999). To date four categories of attachment style have been identified: *secure, insecure-ambivalent (resistant), insecure-fearful/avoidant* and *insecure-disorganised/disoriented.* It is the last attachment style that is most likely to thwart healthy relational capacities and appears to be most closely associated with severe complex trauma such as DA. In addition, some researchers propose that the insecure-disorganised/disoriented attachment style is linked to dissociative identity disorder and borderline personality disorder and as such could be denoted as insecure-disorganised/dissociative attachment (Anderson and Alexander 1996; Fonagy *et al.* 1995; Liotti 1992).

Individuals with a secure attachment style display higher levels of self-esteem, cognitive organisation and consistency, and are better able to express emotions and resolve conflicts, making them generally more successful in relationships. Individuals with an insecure-preoccupied attachment style tend to display a high level of affect-based behaviour, a reduced capacity for cognitive organisation accompanied by strong affect anxiety, dependency, anger and jealousy. Such individuals commonly vacillate between extreme idealisation and deprecation of others, and engage in risk-taking and addictive behaviours to manage intense affect, yet paradoxically cling to unhealthy relationships to avoid being alone.

Those individuals with an insecure-dismissive attachment style frequently display extreme discomfort with intimacy and present as highly defensive, hostile and self-reliant. They commonly deny and minimise feelings, are highly oppositional to others, and report no relational distress and as such rarely seek treatment. The insecure-fearful avoidant-unresolved (disorganised-disoriented-dissociative) attachment style is the one most associated with complex trauma and characterised by dysregulated emotions, relational instability, underdeveloped self-capacities and use of approach-avoid behaviour patterns. This attachment style is suffused with highly defensive strategies leading to a disjointed and discontinuous relational style with high levels of dissociation and relational impairment.

Although attachment styles are shaped in infancy, and are highly resilient, they can change throughout the lifespan. When relationships are inadequate or abusive as in DA, previously secure attachment style can be undermined and transformed. This is especially the case when relational interactions are suffused with negative beliefs about self and others, and where there is no sense of reparation (Pearlman and Courtois 2005). By the same token, IWMs and insecure attachment styles can be updated and revised in the presence of new, more healthy and positive relational experiences (Kohut 1971, 1977; Winnicott 1965). Thus, connection to benevolent others can increase the relational repertoire and facilitate a more a secure attachment style. The therapeutic relationship offers the survivor of DA an opportunity to explore developmental and relational difficulties (Ford and Kidd 1998), and examine clients expectations of therapist and significant others. In devoting explicit attention and responses to attachment issues, IWMs and attachment styles can be strengthened and changed from insecure and disorganised to secure (Schore 2003b; Siegel 1999).

The impact of domestic abuse on relational difficulties

Trauma and danger evoke primitive self-protective mechanisms to aid survival such as seeking security in the safe haven of attachment to others. However, if the safe haven is also a war zone, then internal working models are distorted leading the individual to lose confidence in the protectiveness of attachment relationship. This is especially the case in DA, where trauma is embedded in the very relationship that ought to provide a feeling of security. The complex nature of DA disrupts cognitive schemas about the self and relational self-worth, leading the survivor to doubt the motivations of others (Pearlman 2003). In essence, chronic and pervasive trauma and abuse have a deleterious impact on relational capacities leading to significant alterations and disruptions in relational security and stability, and expectations of others (Pearlman and Courtois 2005). This impedes the formation of healthy relationships, while compelling the abused individual to seek the familiarity of relational patterns that are characterised by instability, abuse, and victimisation (Van der Kolk *et al.* 2005). Critically, survivors find themselves vacillating between polarised positions of seeking closeness and retreating into isolation which further undermines relational stability.

Counsellors need to be aware that many survivors of DA may be drawn to relationships which are predicated on unresolved trauma or loss, or which feature complementary relational deficits and needs. These can lead to re-enactments of the abuse relationship, making the survivor more vulnerable to revictimisation and continued traumatic bonding. This in turn intensifies mistrust, betrayal and abandonment, while frustrating the need for connection and support. Counsellors need to understand these difficulties and address them sensitively and empathically in the therapeutic relationship. It is only with such understanding that relational styles can be revised and new relationship skills learned, thereby expanding the survivor's relational repertoire so that she can make healthy informed choices in future relationships.

RELATIONAL DYNAMICS OF ABUSE

In order to control and dominate every aspect of the survivor's life, the abuser resorts to coercive and violent behaviour to establish power and control (Dobash and Dobash 1979). To do this he creates an illusion of omnipotence which in reality masks his profoundly deep feelings of inadequacy, helplessness, fear of abandonment and self-contempt. In order to rid himself of these unacceptable feelings, he denies them in himself and through projective identification (Klein 1946) identifies them in his partner. This is an interactive process in which the perpetrator evacuates denigrated parts of the self unto the partner. The recipient of projective identification has no choice but to absorb these projections and thus feels helpless, vulnerable, weak and terrified of abandonment. As these are absorbed they become integrated into the self-structure and the survivor takes ownership of them, thereby losing touch with her own feelings and adopting the imposed identity. Concomitantly, the abuser, in seeing these projections in his partner, despises, vilifies and denigrates her.

The more the survivor adopts the imposed identity and loses touch with her own vulnerability, the more she is able to accept and tolerate the abuser's aggressive and abusive feelings and behaviour. This eradicates any vestiges of relational worth, with the survivor believing that she deserves to be abused and vilified. Consequently the survivor has to deny her own feelings of murderous rage leading to polarisation of feelings: unbearable vulnerability and fear of abandonment, or overwhelming rage. This split is incorporated into the relational schema with both the survivor and abuser oscillating between paralysing fear and murderous rage. As the survivor is too terrified of the abuser to express her rage, this is invariably internalised and results in self-attacks (see p.183).

As these relational dynamics are an active and interactive process, the counsellor needs to explore this polarisation in a sensitive manner to ensure that the survivor does not misconstrue this as a form of blame. To ensure transformation of relational schemas, it is crucial to understand the complex nature of relational dynamics, including the abuser's fear of abandonment and dependence on the survivor and that his power derives from her devotion to and fear of him. Through projective identification the abuser treats the survivor like a helpless child, as he once was, and which she ultimately becomes. In this process, the survivor frequently adopts a maternal role towards the abuser by indulging and excusing his behaviour, thereby becoming the ideal mother that the abuser yearns for. In addition, the survivor needs to recognise that by infantilising the abuser, she is making him more manageable.

Understanding the abuser's IWMs, recognising his fears as re-enactments of insecure attachment, and her reactions to them, enables the survivor to dissemble projective identification. Such unravelling of relationship dynamics will enable the survivor to acknowledge her role in the relational dance and focus on how to change the underlying relational schemas. In exploring the survivor's own IWMs the counsellor can enable her to set healthy boundaries with which to resist identifying with the abuser's fear of abandonment. This will promote focus on the survivor's own fears rather than those imposed by the abuser and become more aware of the complex interplay of both the abuser's and her own IWMs and the concomitant unconscious needs.

POLARISATION AND ALTERNATING STATES

A pernicious effect of DA is the destabilisation of relational schemas in which internal representations are no longer secure with survivors oscillating between yearning for closeness and recoiling from intimacy. This results in alternating states of intense attachment and terrified withdrawal. Such alternating states represent distorted perceptions and disruptions to internal locus of evaluation which undermines accurate appraisal of genuinely healthy relationships and those that are abusive. Survivors of DA frequently cling to others who they believe will rescue them, only to find that they are potential abusers, while avoiding and denigrating genuinely healthy relationship. In addition they often show extraordinary loyalty and devotion to those who are abusive while pouring scorn on those who are benign.

Such alternating states are extremely labile and are subject to rapid fluctuations between two diametrically opposed positions. This is commonly seen when survivors tolerate extremely high levels of abuse, and yet can be devastated by minor disappointments from a benign friend. This represents the degree of distorted perception instilled by the abuser, whereby the survivor assesses the quality of relationships through the abuser's locus of evaluation and appraisal rather than her own. This results in increased vulnerability to returning to the abusive relationship, or entering unhealthy or dangerous relationships and revictimisation. Rapidly alternating states also lead to disruptions to self-continuity and relational stability which can manifest in the therapeutic relationship.

Commonly survivors of DA oscillate between intense and anxious attachment and terrified withdrawal, which can persist for years after the DA relationship has ended. The desperate need for closeness and intimacy compels survivors to invest too quickly in relationships as they seek to restore hope, belief and trust, only to find that they have invested in potentially unhealthy and dangerous relationships from which they need to retreat. These relational dynamics commonly emerge in the therapeutic relationship in which the survivor clings desperately to the counsellor as the perceived rescuer, and then flees due to profound suspicion of the counsellor. Invariably survivors unconsciously test out these fears through assiduous monitoring of the counsellor's empathic attunement and experience intense disappointment in the presence of the slightest lapses of empathy or misattunement. These prompt retreat and withdrawal from the therapeutic relationship, which leads to further isolation. Counsellors need to be aware that such fluctuations are a result of abuse dynamics and not indicative of personality disorder. It is crucial that the survivor is able to make links between alternating and polarised states and abuse dynamics to ensure relational stability and the development of more accurate relational appraisals.

RE-ENACTMENT OR COMPULSION TO REPEAT

Survivors of DA often oscillate between hope and disillusionment which is enacted in relational patterns in which hope for rescue spirals into withdrawal and isolation. Allen (2001) proposes that survivors of abuse commonly enact three common relational patterns: *rescuing–rescued, abusing–abused, neglecting–neglected*. These become manifest in the hope for rescue, feeling abused and retreating into isolation. These enactments are not conscious but represent implicit procedural patterns of relating, which are overgeneralised to all relationships. In the case of DA, survivors are vulnerable to traumatic re-enactments in which they are highly sensitised to the smallest slights, or failure in empathy, leading to sense of abandonment and neglect, and concomitant withdrawal as a form of self-protection. These relational dynamics are activated even though they do not match the actual relationship, but represent traumatic re-enactments in the presence of ordinary or healthy relationships. Such intense re-enactments are confusing to both the survivor and others, and serve to undermine new relational patterns.

Re-enactments can also be directed towards self through attacks on self. These can be direct such as self-harming behaviours, or indirectly through unwittingly promoting others to attack, either through provocation or permission by not defending against attack. Counsellors must be careful not to misconstrue or misinterpret such indirect self-attacks as a form of masochism and making the survivor responsible for their abuse, but need to look at past and current relational dynamics which have evoked such re-enactment. Clinicians need to be mindful that trauma can engender familiarity of punishment, and that this can elicit self-punishment, or punishment by others, to reinforce the lack of self-worth. Thus direct or indirect self-attacks must be contextualised within distorted self and relational schemas and lack of relational worth rather than pathologising them as personality disturbances or indicative of masochism. This is crucial as such traumatic re-enactments can occur in the therapeutic relationship in which the survivor may unwittingly invite, or permit attacks on the self by the counsellor.

Re-enactments or the compulsion to repeat (Freud 1914) is considered to be effort for mastery, and a way for the individual to triumph over trauma. Many clinicians believe that through re-enactment the individual seeks to assimilate, digest and overcome unresolved trauma allowing for integration. While this appears to be a plausible and viable mechanism, there is very little evidence that repetition of trauma consistently leads to mastery or resolution. Indeed, some clinicians argue that it may merely lead to further suffering (Allen 2006a). Allen (2006a) proposes that rather than the compulsion to repeat, the individual experiences the compulsion to relate in which the survivor recreates familiar relational patterns and repeats what has been learned in previous relationships. Thus when the survivor returns to the abusive relationship, or enters a new potentially abusive relationship, the survivor is re-enacting what has been learned too well.

TRAUMATIC BONDING

There is considerable animal and human research evidence that abuse and mistreatment can accentuate attachment (Scott 1987) and strengthen relational bonds (Dutton and Painter 1981; Walker 1979; see Chapter 3). It is thought that the combination of isolation and imbalance of power is highly conducive to traumatic bonding as it renders the abused to feel completely dependent on the abuser. Domestic abuse generates intolerable conflict in which the secure base of the attachment relationship is also a terrifying source of danger. As the survivor is terrorised and abused, the need for comfort and protection escalates, and yet these needs cannot be satisfied as the very person who could provide comfort is also the abuser.

The dynamics of the cycle of abuse (Walker 1979) in which the abuser vacillates between abuse and reconciliation seen in DA superglues the bond (Allen 2006a) by combining momentary relief, comfort or affection with abuse and assault. This intermittent kindness is a powerful reinforcer which cements the survivor to the abuser. In addition, being spared even more harm, or being reprieved from injury or terror engenders inordinate gratitude. Such gratitude transforms the abuser from perpetrator to protector, or abuser to saviour (Herman 1992a) albeit momentarily. Believing that the abuser is also the protector forces the survivor to cling even more tightly to the abuser to ensure continued safety. In this dynamic the survivor is not able to see that it is the abuse, and therefore the abuser, that is responsible for the heightened need for safety and security, not something that is lacking in the survivor. The power of the abuser is further enhanced as he appears to be the only one who can gratify these heightened security needs. The powerful dynamics in traumatic bonding are highly resilient and resistant to change, which is why survivors find it so hard to extricate themselves psychologically and emotionally, even after they have physically left the relationship. Thus, traumatic bonding goes some way to explaining why many survivors find it difficult to leave, or return to abuse relationships (Henderson et al. 1997) thereby perpetuating the abuse cycle.

The traumatic bond is further strengthened by enforced isolation, which precludes other sources of attachment, making the survivor even more dependent on the abuser. Lack of access to other relationships also impedes self-efficacy and the acquisition of relational worth and development of healthier relationship skills. As the survivor feels increasingly helpless and hopeless, the more she comes to rely and depend on the abuser. The absence of other relationships also reinforces the belief that any relationship, even an abusive one, is better than no relationship at all. The complexity of traumatic bonding also prevents the survivor from recognising that the power and control exerted by the abuser masks the abuser's weakness, dependency needs and fear of abandonment (Dutton and Painter 1981).

RELATIONAL AVOIDANCE, WITHDRAWAL AND ISOLATION

Isolation from others can be either overt, as a result of enforced isolation by the abuser, or covert through stigma, secrecy or shame, which create internal barriers to intimacy and closeness. Survivors often retreat into emotional distance for fear of accidently disclosing the abuse, or because of a profound sense of shame. This can be seen primarily in the superficiality of their relationships with others, avoidance of all relationships, or through retreating into an inner fantasy world. While initially such withdrawal may appear to be adaptive as a protection from further betrayal, as the DA escalates it is no longer adaptive. Paradoxically the more isolated that survivors feel, the less they have access to safety and the more vulnerable and dependent they become on the abuser. In addition the more isolated that survivors feel, the more they are in survival mode thereby reducing opportunities for reality testing, problem solving and reflecting. This can render survivors more trapped, alienated and dehumanised.

ELEVATED YEARNING FOR CONNECTION

As has been demonstrated, a corollary to relational avoidance is increased yearning for closeness, affection, comfort, protection and relational connectedness. Thus, paradoxically DA fuels attachment needs (Allen 2006a) which generates profound longing for much needed care giving, closeness and intimacy. This yearning for connection is commonly expressed in the therapeutic relationship and counsellors need to explore the origins of this and enable survivors to sustain healthy connections.

Yearning for connectedness can propel survivors back into the abuse relationship or to seek comfort from those who are not benign, or who have manipulated and exploited them in the past. This is in part due to the comfort found in familiar relational patterns, and the perceived safety of the known rather than the unknown. This is compounded by internalised distorted perceptions in which healthy relationships are seen as dangerous, while abuse relationships are perceived as benign. In essence, these represent the total distortion and destruction of healthy IWMs and relational schemas which render survivors vulnerable to revictimisation. Yearning is often accompanied by pervasive fearfulness and distrust.

PERVASIVE RELATIONAL FEARFULNESS

Pervasive fearfulness and distrust can prevent survivors of DA from connecting to others. Commonly survivors fear injury, domination and control, and avoid entering relationships to ensure that they do not become trapped, smothered, terrorised, humiliated or degraded. Survivors also fear that they have no relational worth and cannot conceive why anyone would wish to have a relationship with them other than to manipulate or exploit them. Some survivors become so highly sensitised to further betrayal or abandoned that they cannot risk connection again and therefore avoid all relationships. This can result in being resigned to a life devoid of any relationships, especially in older survivors who believe that they are unable to change their relational schemas and do not wish to risk future relationships. Many survivors also fear that they cannot trust themselves to choose healthy relationships, and thus avoid all socialising. In contrast, some survivors actively choose not to engage in intimate relationships. Counsellors need to understand this and enable survivors to trust in themselves to make decisions that are right for them which are based on informed choice rather than fearful avoidance.

EXCESSIVE DEPENDENCY NEEDS

Lack of trust disrupts an individual's capacity to depend on others. It is important for counsellors to convey to survivors that dependency is a strength that is necessary for healthy attachment and not a weakness. In extreme cases of abuse, or traumatic bonding, excessive dependency is evoked that can lead to relational difficulties. Such excessive dependency is also associated with control, domination and lack of self-efficacy and self-agency. Survivors of DA are forced to relinquish all control and self-efficacy, and through enforced isolation, become increasingly dependent on the abuser. In effect, excessive dependency is characteristic of insecurity and is usually fuelled by fear of abandonment. Excessive dependency needs also to breed resentment, hostility and render the individual vulnerable to feelings of being controlled and trapped. Such dependency is quite different from the dependency that characterises healthy relationships. Counsellors need to distinguish between healthy and excessive dependency and explore these with the survivor so they can modify their relational schemas that permit the expression of dependency in healthy relationships.

DISSOCIATION

Excessive dependency and fear of abandonment can outweigh the pain of abuse. To tolerate prolonged and repeated abuse, dissociative defences are activated which numb the physical and psychological pain incurred in DA. Through dissociation the survivor attempts to regulate intense relational and emotional states (Pearlman and Courtois 2005). While dissociation is initially adaptive it is associated with huge long-term relational cost. Counsellors need to assess the degree of dissociation and identify the emotional and relational triggers such as fear, terror, disappointment, despair, shame and rage that trigger such powerful defences. As these triggers can be subtle and outside of conscious awareness, and therefore are not easily identified, counsellors will need to monitor their own affective state, confusion or somatic counter-transference reactions, as a source of valuable information about the survivor's somatic state.

Dissociation allows survivors to adapt to the abuse environment by retreating into psychological and emotional escape which permits the survival of each episode of abuse. By dissociating, survivors are able to stay out of contact with tumultuous feelings, including anger at the abuse and abuser, and appear to be unaffected as all emotions are suppressed. Dissociation numbs the individual and renders the abuse bearable, resulting in a splitting of emotions and cognition that allows some parts of the individual to be protected, commonly the vulnerable 'feeling' parts, but leaves some cognitive functioning in order that the survivor can get through the periods between episodes of violence and attack. Dissociation can result in self-structures that are defined by abuse which leads to an inability to resist coercive violations due to the lack of a safe system to resist. As basic affinitive functions are disrupted, survivors believe that they cannot turn to people but must rely on practical strategies in order to deal with and accept the abuse.

This allows for increased levels of tolerance of abuse and renders survivors vulnerable to returning to the abuse relationship, or to further revictimisation. Counsellors need to enable survivors to link dissociation to increased tolerance of abuse and aim to explore more active defence strategies. Herman (1992a) suggests encouraging survivors not to see themselves as victims and thus vulnerable to revictimisation, but rather to emphasise blocks to self-protection. This facilitates a more solution-focused approach which calls for equipping survivors with more appropriate self-protection strategies. This can be achieved through increasing the survivor's relational repertoire through enhanced relationship skills such as setting appropriate boundaries, conflict resolution and the expression of needs. In the secure and safe therapeutic relationship the survivor can relinquish dissociative defences and allow new relational patterns to emerge and develop more secure relational schemas.

POWER AND CONTROL

Abuse relationships are predicated on power and control, in which the survivor is at the mercy of the abuser. This leads to a pervasive fear of any relational interactions in which the survivor is forced to minimise or relinquish control. This includes interaction with professionals and authority figures such as clinicians. As a reaction to feared loss of control, survivors are commonly averse to the setting of boundaries as these are perceived as mechanisms of control rather than healthy parameters that promote safety. Many survivors of DA find it hard to comply or submit to the desires of others, especially those in authority, even if there is no real danger or harm. Consequently they engage in power struggles to avoid being controlled by others, and in turn exert considerable power over others. Exerting active control and domination over others allows survivors to triumph over trauma, ensuring that they will not be controlled or dominated ever again. This can lead to conflicted relationships based on power struggles for control, which are ultimately unsatisfying. Such power and control dynamics frequently emerge in the therapeutic relationship and need to be sensitively managed.

AGGRESSION

Survivors of prolonged and repeated trauma frequently identify with the abuser (Freud, A. 1936) and thereby transform being abused into abusing others. This can sometimes manifest as overt or covert aggression towards the abuser but can also be directed at safer targets such as children, or others such as professionals. Such aggression may also manifest in future relationships as a way of ensuring that the survivor will not be taken advantage of. A characteristic of IWMs and relational schemas is that they can incorporate both the abuser and the abused, which enables the survivor to switch roles between aggressor and victim.

When survivors identify with the abuser, and incorporate aggression into their relational schema, they are attempting to reclaim the power that was denied them in DA. In many respects such power is perceived by the survivor to be the perfect antidote to feeling helpless and weak. However, the power and control obtained through identification with the aggressor is a false illusion of empowerment as aggression merely begets aggression and in reality the survivor is as weak and fearful as the abuser. It is worth noting that identification with the abuser is most likely to occur in those survivors who exert a high level of denial of the abuse, and who tend to idealise the abuser (Allen 2006a). Some survivors do not attack others but internalise this aggression, and direct it against the self through self-attacks and self-harm (see above, p.183). Counsellors need to enable survivors to mentalise such dynamics in order to transform these defences and reduce aggression towards others, and self.

TRUST

The impact of DA is not only on disconnection from self but also from others. This is achieved through either enforced isolation or through the abuser poisoning the survivor against others. By instilling a fear of others into the survivor, abusers ensure an increase in their power over the partner. Abusers commonly undermine the survivor's trust in others by intimating that others cannot be trusted. The survivor incorporates this belief into relational schemas and generalises this to all relationships. This is compounded by the betrayal of trust at the hands of the abuser. Such total lack of trust in others makes it virtually impossible for the survivor to trust others. This can be ameliorated in the safety of the therapeutic relationship in which the survivor can learn to trust the self and others, enabling the survivor to reconnect.

Working with relational aspects

The antidote to the impact of DA and distorted relational schemas is engagement in healthier relationships which are predicated on relational worth and more positive relational dynamics. This allows for the revision and transformation of IWMs and restores a sense of self-agency in relationships. This allows the survivor to extend the relational repertoire which permits more healthy connections to others and more satisfying relationships.

As relational deficits are at the heart of pervasive trauma and DA, counsellors are urged to incorporate an attachment-relational approach (Courtois 1988, 1999; Pearlman and Courtois 2005; Pearlman and Saakvitne 1995a; Saakvitne *et al.* 2000) which incorporates an understanding of complex trauma and its impact on self-capacities and relational dynamics. This requires particular focus on the therapeutic alliance, the provision of a consistent, reliable and well-bounded therapeutic relationship in which a clear treatment frame is maintained to explore the survivor's relational history and identify behavioural re-enactments of past attachment experiences. Counsellors need to examine and assess the survivor's attachment history, concomitant attachment style, identify relational schemas and complementary relational behaviours. In order to change IWMs, clinicians need to enable survivors to explore their expectations of significant others, including the counsellor, and focus explicit attention to relational responses. In identifying the survivor attachment style, the counsellors can permit requisite changes to be made.

Counsellors need to identify relational perceptions and capacities, and acknowledge that these are rarely static but dynamic and labile, or 'kaleidoscopic' (Davies and Frawley 1994). Pearlman and Courtois (2005) propose that a relational framework must employ the principles of their RICH model, which is predicated on *respect, information, connection* and *hope*. The emphasis is on the therapeutic relationship as both a catalyst and secure base in which to explore and evaluate the survivor's relational history (Pearlman and Courtois 2005). It is only within a safe relationship that relational schemas can be revised, and different ways of relating can be refined, tested and tuned in order to develop a greater repertoire of self-capacities and relational skills. Along with the principles of RICH, counsellors also need to ensure that they are reliable and consistent in their approach, have a strong sense of integrity and feel comfortable with their own relational style in order to establish a supportive connection with the survivor. A number of researchers (McCann, Sakheim and Abrahamson 1988; Pearlman 1998; Pearlman and Courtois 2005) also emphasise five key domains in self and others that facilitate a healthy relational treatment framework: *safety, trust, esteem, intimacy* and *control.* Such a treatment framework will allow for the development of self-capacities, affect tolerance, self-worth and connection to benevolent others.

The therapeutic relationship also plays a pivotal role in enhancing awareness of both the abuser and survivor relational dynamics, mentalising these to gain a greater understanding of relational schemas and relationship patterns. Such exploration will enable the survivor to begin to define, redefine and change relational patterns, allowing for greater flexibility and self-agency in relationships. This is enhanced through the identifying and expressing of needs, setting healthy boundaries and practice in conflict resolution. Equipped with heightened awareness, understanding and new relationships skills, the survivor can seek connection to others and allow the formation of new relationships outside the shadow of abuse.

ASSESSMENT OF RELATIONAL DIFFICULTIES

When working with relational difficulties, it is critical that counsellors are able to assess the degree of relational disruption. Survivors who present with hypervigilance and hyper-alertness to aggression, boundary violations, unfair criticism and interpersonal danger, including in the therapeutic process, may be indirectly expressing relational anxiety (Herman 1992a). If a survivor displays fears that she is being followed to therapy, the counsellor will need to assess the evidence for this and to what degree this could represent the survivor's fears. Some survivors may be so terrified they fear that their counsellor is in cahoots with the abuser, and that the counsellor is in direct communication with him. Such fears may manifest in preoccupations with the counsellor's motivation and intentions, relevance of assessment and confidentiality, all of which indicate relational apprehension and fear of evaluation and interaction with authority figures. Counsellors must be mindful that such fears represent relational schemas which are sensitised to danger and betrayal, and which are evoked in interpersonal relationships. They may also indicate post-traumatic stress reactions which need to be stabilised.

Survivors of DA may also present with pervasive themes of loss and abandonment, and chronic fears of rejection. These manifest in the therapeutic process as constant vacillation between neediness, clinginess and dependency and anger, despair and hostility. Survivors of DA are highly sensitised to any perceived failures in attunement or if the counsellor is insufficiently caring, supportive or physically unavailable. This can lead survivors to oscillate between idealising and denigrating the counsellor, which resemble borderline personality type features. Counsellors must be assiduous in contextualising these relational dynamics as symptomatic of traumatic bonding and relational trauma rather than pathology or personality disturbance. It is crucial that counsellors avoid labelling clients as difficult, manipulative, demanding or suffering from a personality disorder. Instead, counsellors must reframe such dynamics as indices of relational schemas which are organised around fear, ambivalence, trust, intimacy and withdrawal, in order to remain therapeutically attuned. In essence they represent the continued striving of the survivor to connect, and must be honoured as such.

Relational anxiety may also manifest in the survivor's need for safety and control in interpersonal relationships. Commonly this is expressed as negative responses to any perceived control and insistence for autonomy through micro-managing interactions with others so that safety and determination are preserved. Survivors of DA are highly sensitised to perceived manipulation or influence from others which are interpreted as attempts to control. This is often acted out in the safety of therapeutic setting as a reaction to the degree of control experienced in DA and other relational interactions. It is only within the safety of a secure base that the survivor can reclaim control and challenge others relational interactions. Such survivors present as feisty, speaking continuously without allowing for counsellor feedback, ignoring counsellor interruptions or letting the counsellor speak.

Any attempts by the counsellor to challenge the survivor may result in intense anger or irritation. Counsellors must ensure that they do not personalise such responses but see these as indices of relational anxiety, fear of revictimisation, interpersonal rigidity, and compulsive self-protection. In addition they must be seen as evidence of previous exposure to highly controlling, abusive encounters, and trauma, not personality disturbance. Counsellors are advised to employ patience and reassurance to focus on the survivor's attempts to engage and sustain the therapeutic relationship rather than constantly challenging the survivors need for interpersonal control. It is critical that the counsellor consistently assesses the degree of relational engagement and capacity for relinquishing relational control, especially as the therapeutic relationship can trigger flashbacks and conditioned fears, and evoke threat-related cognitions. This is especially as the therapeutic relationship evolves and intensifies. Survivors will vary enormously in their ability to engage fully in the therapeutic relationship, with some not feeling safe to do this for many months, sometimes years, while others risk connection almost immediately. Counsellors need to assess each survivor individually and be alert to potential difficulties around boundaries, trust, control and safety before working with trauma-related material.

IDENTIFYING RELATIONAL SCHEMAS

In assessing relational difficulties, counsellors will begin to identify specific relational schemas. In survivors of DA these commonly incorporate self-beliefs that they are bad, inadequate and helpless and lack relational worth, while they perceive others as dangerous, rejecting and unloving. These beliefs and concomitant expectations may also be projected onto the therapist, who is perceived as critical, hostile, emotionally absent and potentially abusive. Counsellors need to identify the unique relational schema for each individual survivor and take into account each client's preponderant schemas for self and others and how these manifest in the therapeutic relationship (Pearlman and Courtois 2005). It is the relational patterns, transference and counter-transference reactions that provide a fertile source of information which assists understanding of relational schemas, which can then be identified, explored and changed (Alexander and Anderson 1994). From these counsellors will also be able to identify the survivor's particular attachment style.

ATTACHMENT STYLES

Once relational schemas have been identified, counsellors can begin to assess the survivor's attachment style and how this impacts on relational dynamics both within the therapeutic relationship and with others. While research has identified four main categories of attachment style – *secure, insecure-ambivalent (resistant), insecure-fearful/avoidant* and *insecure-disorganised/disoriented* (Ainsworth *et al.* 1978; Main 1999) with the latter attachment style most commonly associated with survivors of DA.

While it is highly unlikely that survivors of DA will present with a secure attachment style, counsellors must assess to what degree the client had secure attachment experiences prior to DA. Some survivors may have entered an abusive relationship with a secure attachment style, only for that to have been undermined during DA. Providing that these early secure attachment experiences have not been completely annihilated, such survivors require less relational work as these early relational schemas are easily revived to restore self-esteem, cognitive organisation and consistency, and ability to resolve conflicts. These survivors can most easily go on to develop secure attachment in future relationships despite the abuse.

In contrast, survivors with an insecure-preoccupied attachment require ongoing therapeutic attention to relational reliability to lessen anxiety and enable the survivor to acquire interpersonal security through internalising a more organised and consistent relational pattern. This will increase cognitive organisation and develop self-capacities to reduce vacillation between idealisation and denigration, decrease addictive behaviours and facilitate a more healthy less dependent relational style. Survivors with an insecure-dismissive attachment style will attempt to alienate the clinician by being hostile, dismissive, condescending and contemptuous to avoid connection. Counsellors must look beyond this behaviour and concomitant counter-transference reactions (CTR) of anger, avoidance and rejection to minimise the risk of re-enactment of traumatic rejection. It is vital that counsellors understand the survivor's attachment style, and the elicited CTR, as self-protective functions to thwart profound fears of rejection and abandonment, in order to remain empathically attuned and not compromise the therapeutic relationship. Survivors with this attachment style require counsellor equanimity and supportive psychotherapy rather than a defensive or austere therapeutic stance, if they are to reverse relational dynamics predicated on fear of rejection, abandonment insecurity and rigid self-sufficiency. Counsellors must also not retreat into pathologising the survivor in interpreting the vacillation between idealisation and denigration as indicative of a fully-fledged personality disorder.

Perhaps the most frequently encountered attachment style when working with survivors of DA is the insecure-fearful/avoidant-unresolved or disorganised-disoriented-dissociative attachment style. As this style is highly correlated with complex trauma it is not surprising that clients will perceive the counsellor as a contradictory source of comfort and danger, and approach the counsellor with both deep longing and pervasive fear. Survivors with this attachment style often present as more overtly distressed, depressed and disorganised self-structures with elevated levels of dissociation, self-harm, self-loathing and social impairment (Ford *et al.* 2005). Given the high level of dysregulated emotions, underdeveloped self-capacities and absence of relational stability, survivors with this attachment style require more complex treatment within a highly structured and organised therapeutic framework. It is imperative when working with survivors with this attachment style that attention is directed to internal and external safety, affect regulation and mentalising experiences and feelings. A considerable amount of attention must also focus on the therapeutic relationship as place of consistency and support, where feelings and needs can be named, understood and not judged, to minimise retraumatisation.

RELATIONAL INVENTORY

Counsellors are urged to encourage the survivor to take an inventory of attachment style and predominant relational schemas to ascertain which models are most frequently employed, which need to be pruned, which need to be abandoned, and which can be developed, cultivated and nurtured. This can be achieved through asking and exploring question such as: Which individuals in the survivor's life go with which models? What are the patterns and sequences of interactions that characterise your relationships? How stable and steady are these interactions? How changeable, consistent and turbulent are they? In identifying these the survivor can choose which ones to keep and which ones to jettison.

DEVELOPING NEW RELATIONAL MODELS

The evolutionary imperative for close attachment ensures that the desire for secure attachment, despite abuse and trauma, remains a powerful drive and is highly resilient to prolonged attacks and attempts at annihilation. It is also why it is possible to change attachment styles and replace with new, more healthy relational models and schemas. It is through the safe, secure and consistent therapeutic relationship that survivors of DA supplant old relational models with new ones, and learn more healthy ways of connecting to others which can generalise to other relationships, and inoculate the survivor against future relational abuse. While these new ways of relating do not lend themselves to simple instructional or didactic protocols, they are acquired through insight, mentalisation and procedural learning by connecting, relating and interacting with others who are nurturing, reliable and trustworthy. In essence new relational models are learned in the same way that abusive models were originally acquired, procedurally.

Healthy relationships based on trust, kindness, consistency and respect can reverse the sense of being devalued and lack of relational worth. In the presence of benign relational experiences, survivors can begin to feel more confident, respected and valued. This will enable them to identify, assert and express their needs and increase relational worth. Pivotal to developing new relational schemas is the acceptance that relationships are not perfect and that they are subject to fluctuations in closeness and distance. Counsellors must keep survivors grounded in realistic expectations and encourage them to measure relationships with others on a 'good enough' (Winnicott 1958) basis rather than yearning for a 'perfect' relationship. In addition, survivors need to be aware that no relationship is foolproof and that all individuals are susceptible to being deceived or overpowered. Survivors need to be able to accept that all relationships are flawed to some degree and that with more realistic expectations and increased behavioural repertoire, they are more able to tolerate and manage the limitations of relationships and not be overwhelmed by disappointment.

The therapeutic relationship also offers an opportunity to risk connection, communication and acceptance which can be affirming and develop and learn new relational skills. To facilitate this, counsellors can provide models for intimacy, affection, confiding, cooperation, helping, teaching, supporting, collaborating, sharing and giving, alongside models for conflict resolution, confronting, challenging, contesting and asserting. The therapeutic relationship not only promotes the learning of new skills, but also provides a safe space to practise these so that they can be integrated and restore relational competencies and self-efficacy. Most crucially, it can model having fun and permission to seek and take pleasure in relationships. Finally, counsellors are urged to remind survivors that trauma can promote growth, in promoting compassion and empathy for others, which is an essential ingredient for healthy relationships. Thus, recovery from trauma and DA can promote models of secure attachment and enhance the survivor's capacity to provide comfort, nurture, protection and care for self and others.

REBUILDING SOCIAL SUPPORT NETWORKS

The social isolation associated with DA makes it extremely difficult for the survivor to engage in close relationships. Counsellors must acknowledge what a monumental task it is for the survivor to engage in a single relationship, let alone build a social network. To facilitate the rebuilding of a social network, counsellors need to encourage the survivor to start small and build upon each new connection and relationships. For some survivors a single close relationship may be too risky, frightening and intense with too many expectations that cannot be fulfilled. To minimise the risk and disappointment, survivors may be advised to develop a small network rather than one close relationship. In such instances survivors may benefit from joining a self-help group or enter group therapy rather than the intensity of individual counselling. Stein, Allen and Hill (2003) propose a flexible approach to developing relationships which can meet a diverse range of relationship needs, at different levels of closeness, and in several domains. Counsellors need to explore the many different ways the survivor can form healthy social support networks and be open to the potential for a myriad of creative ways for meeting attachment needs.

Initially survivors may benefit from focusing on *social contact* relationships that restore a sense of belongingness which are not overly intimate but could provide a gateway to deeper relationships. Social contact relationships can be built through regular contacts in the community such as frequently visited shops, cafes, parents at school, religious services or playing sport. Although such relationships are initially predicated on small talk, they provide opportunities to practise and develop valuable relationship skills. Most importantly, social contact relationships provide pleasurable social contact, which foster a sense of familiarity, safety, and predictability to counter feelings of isolation and alienation. From social contact relationships, survivors can develop *friendships* based on shared circumstances and shared interests such as going to the theatre or cinema, or attending concerts or sporting events. Such friendships are rarely exclusive and do not require deep sharing of confidences, but do provide stability and emotional and practical support. As friendships require reciprocity and maintenance, they provide opportunities to explore relational worth and have the potential to develop into special friendships that can meet a variety of attachment needs.

If the survivor is in employment, *work relationships* can provide opportunities for social support and have the potential to develop into friendships or romantic relationships dependent on the amount of closeness and contact. While generally work relationships can be supportive, they can also be fraught with conflict, competitiveness and difficulties with authority figures such as supervisors or line managers, and as such require a considerable degree of interpersonal skills. A further source of support for survivors of DA is through *professional relationships* such as doctor, counsellor, refuge workers, social and welfare workers as well as those involved in the professional support of the survivor. Providing professional relationships are appropriately bounded to provide safety and predictability, they can enhance confidence and trust, and enable the survivor to move from dependence to independence. This is particularly the case in the therapeutic relationship, which can be the bridge to forming other close relationships (Allen 2001).

Family relationships often provide the widest, most readymade network of social support and have the potential for nurturing and satisfying relationships. However, some families can also be war zones consisting of extreme conflicts which render the survivor defenceless. Counsellors must never assume that immediate or extended families are necessarily sources of support: they can at times be the most dangerous relationships. Careful assessment of the quality and safety of family relationships is crucial before the survivor embarks on rebuilding such relationships.

Similarly, *romantic relationships* can be the most satisfying and the most dangerous relationships. Romantic relationships are primary attachment relationships which meet many relational needs such as closeness and intimacy that usually involve love and sexual affection. However, romantic relationships can also entail intense conflict which requires considerable negotiating skills, and conflict-resolution skills to manage any conflict in constructive ways. It is often romantic relationships that survivors of DA fear the most as it is within these relationships that abuse has occurred. As a result it often takes a long time for survivors of DA to develop healthy romantic attachments and to build trust in such relationships again. Some survivors may choose not to enter such relationships again, with others becoming romantically involved too quickly before trust has been fully established. Counsellors need to be supportive of survivors striving for connection and balance this with the requisite relational therapeutic work.

INTERPERSONAL SKILLS TRAINING

The therapeutic process also provides the opportunity to take an inventory of interpersonal skills to identify existing skills, and highlight areas that need to be improved. To facilitate this, counsellors can use transference and countertransference reaction as rich sources for assessment of interpersonal skills. Some survivors of DA may benefit from specific interpersonal skills training which may be addressed in the counselling process or through undertaking specific training courses. Counsellors can implement psychoeducative techniques to enhance non-verbal communication, especially increased eye contact and less submissive body stance, to exude greater confidence and improve the full range of interpersonal skills. Through the therapeutic process, survivors can become visibly less compliant and more confident, hold themselves better, smile, and begin to adopt a more open stance rather than a submissive or defensive one. When combined with appropriate boundary setting, conflict resolution skills and assertion training, survivors of DA are able to negotiate relationships in increasingly more effective ways.

SELF-DEPENDENCE

A crucial component when working with relational aspects is to establish a balance between self-development and relatedness, closeness and distance, openness and privacy, and togetherness and solitude. The therapeutic task is that individual survivors need to find an optimal blend that suits them alongside developing self-dependence (Lichtenberg 1989). A danger of overinvestment in independence is that when taken to extreme it can lead to counter-dependence and a sense of needing anyone, and a life resigned to isolation. Lichtenberg (1989) proposes that self-dependence is a way of balancing autonomy and attachment, retaining a sense of continuity in relationships, which prevents being subsumed under others. This can be achieved through the internalisation of relational schemas associated with an individual so that the individual does not need to be in the continuous presence of the other person to feel secure, as the internal image bridges the gap between separation and reunion. This can be done through mentalising, remembering and imagining the person, so that the secure attachment can be preserved. While the reunion refuels the attachment the individual can operate autonomously without overreliance on others.

Self-dependence can be hard to achieve, and to some degree is a lifelong process, which can be severely impaired through DA. To acquire self-dependence requires mentalising, having access to comforting attachment relationships to sustain the survivor during separations and being able to supplant the fears associated with being connected to others with pleasurable feelings. It is only through such secure attachments in current relationships that self-dependence can be strengthened and integrated, to increase relational worth.

The therapeutic relationship

When working with trauma and abuse, clinicians need to adopt a relational and attachment perspective, in which they can provide relational guidance and allow the survivor to experience more healthy ways of relating. Dozier and Tyrell (1998) liken this to the critical features of early attachment relationships by suggesting that

> the therapist's work with a client is similar to, yet more difficult than, the mother's with her infant ... The mother's task is easier than the therapist's because she need not compensate for the failures of other attachment figures...exploration of prior working models cannot wait until after a secure base is established, rather, the processes occur in tandem. (Dozier and Tyrell 1998, p.222)

A number of researchers, most notably Pearlman and Courtois (2005), have iden-tified four essential elements that are necessary in the therapeutic relationships when working with survivors of abuse: respect, information, connection and hope (RICH). This needs to be accompanied by integrity, reliability and a high level of self-awareness in the therapist. Pivotal to this is the counsellor's own capacities for connection, access to support network and self-care (Sanderson 2006). A secure therapeutic relationship provides an opportunity to examine attachment difficulties, revise self-capacities, rebuild relational schemas and learn a broader range of interpersonal skills which can generalise to other relationships.

Working with relational patterns can be the most rewarding and the most challenging therapeutic work, especially when in the case of working with survi-vors of DA who commonly present with labile relational patterns, with borderline features (Allen 2001; Bromberg 1993, 1998; Chu 1998; Dalenberg 2000; Davies and Frawley 1994; Magnavita 1999; Olio and Cornell 1993; Pearlman 2001; Pearlman and Courtois 2005; Putnam 1989; Ross 1997; Saakvitne *et al.* 2000; Schwartz 2000). Given these demanding challenges, clinicians need to be genuine, emotionally available and able to tolerate the many relational and per-sonal challenges characteristic of such work. To ensure that they are able to face this challenge, counsellors need to pay particular attention to the therapeutic stance, therapeutic alliance, therapeutic frame and boundaries, re-enactments and shifting relational states.

THERAPEUTIC STANCE

Given the relational anxieties as a result of DA, counsellors need to ensure that they present a positive, non-intrusive therapeutic stance which is predicated on respect for the survivor's individual and unique experience. Counsellors must honour the survivor in risking connection despite previous betrayals of trust and abuse. Domestic abuse dehumanises the individual and counsellors must ensure that they are capable of showing human qualities of warmth, genuineness, empa-thy and compassion. Counsellors need to acknowledge the survivor's immediate situation, whether visibly distressed, or shut down, and assess both internal and external safety. It is crucial that the counsellor is clear and explicit in discussing the therapeutic process, including assessment, confidentiality and boundaries, what can be expected and the level of therapeutic contact. To minimise demean-ing or interrogating the survivor, counsellors need to avoid excessively direct or intrusive questions which might be perceived as threatening or derogatory. Counsellors must show respect for the survivor by allowing her the autonomy to pace the therapeutic work in terms of what is most helpful to her at any particular point, be that with practical support, provision of information, emotional support or disclosure. A full appreciation of the relational disruptions experienced and how hard it is to risk connection will enable the survivor to feel understood and permit engagement at her own pace.

Counsellors must guard against shaming or humiliating the survivor by ensuring that they do not patronise or pity her, or claim to know how she really feels. To rebuild relational worth, counsellors need to maintain a positive and consistent therapeutic relationship in which the survivor is respected, accepted, validated and taken seriously. To facilitate this, the counsellor needs to ensure a non-judgemental, empathically attuned stance and tailor the therapeutic process to the specific characteristics of the survivor and her unique experiences (Briere and Scott 2006).

Dalenberg (2000) proposes that clinicians need to be authentic and emotionally available in relational interactions, and possess emotional integrity. In addition, they need to be authentic, genuine and aware of their own feelings and needs, be able to link these to their own experiences, and use them to understand and assist the survivor. Counsellors must be emotionally available, be open about their motives and goals in the therapeutic relationship, and answer any questions honestly and sensitively. Such transparency must however not be confused with overt self-disclosure of personal information, or engagement in dual relationships (Pearlman and Courtois 2005). Clinicians working with survivors of DA must remember that such boundary violations are particularly damaging to, and counter-therapeutic to individuals who have experienced relational abuse as there is a high potential for retraumatisation, no matter how well intentioned or rationalised.

Counsellors must be capable of secure attachments themselves, possess appropriate relational skills and feel comfortable being in emotional and psychological contact with their clients. They must also be able to maintain and regain equanimity and tolerance in face of the survivor's relational inconsistency and understand these as strivings for connection rather than indices of personality disturbance, or deliberate attempts at hostility or rejection. The use of counter-transference reactions can enable counsellors to understand and name their clients' relational states and manage their own emotions as they arise, either as a response to real issues posed by the survivor, or as a result of projective identification, or direct provocation (Bromberg 1993; Davies and Frawley 1994; Gabbard and Wilkinson 1994; Pearlman and Courtois 2005; Pearlman and Saakvitne 1995b; Schore 2003b; Schwartz 2000). It is imperative that clinicians remain open and engaged with survivors of DA in order to create the optimal therapeutic alliance to explore relational difficulties, and ensure a non-defensive stance.

THERAPEUTIC ALLIANCE

Survivors of DA commonly present with relational difficulties due to the betrayal of trust, distorted relational schemas, and relational lability (Dalenberg 2000;

Herman 1992a; McCann and Pearlman 1990; Pearlman and Courtois 2005). To ensure a strong therapeutic alliance, counsellors need to have a penetrating insight and understanding of the survivor's attachment history and current relational difficulties with which to empathise rather than stigmatise the client. Counsellors must not take relational interactions and skills for granted as the survivor may have pervasive relational deficits, especially if there is a history of childhood abuse, and may have little or no knowledge of relational skills, or how to maintain relational continuity. As survivors of DA have no organised way of responding to consistent relationships, they may find a well-bounded therapeutic relationship incomprehensible or threatening. As they are unable to gain solace or comfort from relationships, powerful defensive strategies may be evoked that the counsellor needs to contain and hold.

Dissociation can also impact on establishing the therapeutic alliance especially if accompanied by fluctuations in perceptions of self and others, and relational alternations. These alternations are volatile, dynamic and 'kaleidoscopic' (Davies and Frawley 1994) rather than static. In order to remain empathically attuned, counsellors need to tolerate such vacillation and contextualise these as self-protective and self-regulatory functions, and explore these sensitively. Counsellors need to be prepared to expect defensive strategies and not personalise them and remain reliable and consistent in their responses. It is crucial that, rather than reacting in a defensive way, counsellors assess the survivor's relational style and give sensitive feedback in tolerable doses which are appropriately titrated in order to promote changes in relational perceptions and enhance relational stability.

THERAPEUTIC FRAME AND BOUNDARIES

Given the myriad boundary violations inherent in DA, it is vital that clinicians negotiate and maintain professional boundaries at all times. When working within a relational-attachment framework, counsellors must provide clear and explicit boundaries which include clarification of the aims of therapy and the therapeutic process, issues around informed consent, and confidentiality. In addition survivors need to be clear about the therapeutic goals, the duration, length and frequency of session, fees if privately funded, form of address, therapist availability and limitations, safety and procedures for crisis management. While these need to be addressed during the initial contract, they may need to be reiterated, revised or sensitively renegotiated during the therapeutic process.

When working with trauma and DA, it is critical that clinicians provide firm but not rigid boundaries. As discussed in Chapter 4 counsellors need to be able to tolerate some flexibility around rescheduling sessions, out-of-session contact and the provision of information, and yet must ensure that the therapeutic boundaries do not collapse. It is not uncommon when working with survivors of DA that boundaries are challenged. Many clinicians working with survivors of abuse report compelling counter-transference reactions urging them to rescue or reparent their clients in an attempt to make-up or compensate for the abuse. The need to rescue or reparent is accompanied by overinvolvement, over-giving and over-identification of the clinician, which alternates with frustration and irritation as the counsellor becomes exhausted and resentful of the survivor. The consequent oscillation between over-solicitous care-taking behaviours and hostile rejection becomes a reflection of the relational dynamics associated with DA, and renders the therapeutic relationships vulnerable to collapse while reinforcing negative relational schemas and experiences. To minimise this, counsellors need to ensure that boundaries are maintained in order to prevent yet another negative relational experience.

RE-ENACTMENTS

The lack of organised relational patterns associated with DA tends to manifest in the therapeutic relationship as re-enactments of previous relational dynamics. These re-enactments represent explicit or coded repetitions of unprocessed trauma attempts at mastery (Chu 1991; Van der Kolk 1989) and are expressed psychologically, relationally or somatically, often outside conscious awareness. Counsellors need to understand these as re-enactments as a replaying, or non-verbal 'remembering' (Pearlman and Courtois 2005) of dominant relational patterns and attachment style. These re-enactments may also be habitual repetitions of familiar behavioural and relational sequences such as victim–perpetrator–rescuer–bystander. Commonly these familiar roles are re-enacted in the therapeutic relationship with both survivor and counsellor enacting these roles in a complementary way. Counsellors need to conceptualise such re-enactments within transference and counter-transference reactions which provide incisive information about previous relational patterns. If sensitively attended to and identified, these can provide the basis for exploring and changing relational dynamics.

ALTERNATING AND SHIFTING RELATIONAL STATES

The volatility of rapidly alternating and shifting relational states can be destabilising for both survivor and counsellor and must therefore be addressed in the therapeutic relationship. Counsellors need to have a clear understanding of the origins of these and their self-protective function. To manage these alternating states, counsellors need to be able to tolerate survivors' relational lability, contain them and their own responses, and remain consistent in their responses. In retaining equanimity and providing a reliable and consistent relationship, survivors will gradually be able to organise relational patterns into a more coherent and stable framework. This will enable survivors to rebuild trust in themselves and others, and begin to acquire more secure and stable relational schemas. Equipped with healthier relational schemas and an enhanced relational repertoire the survivor can begin to risk connection to others and rebuild relationships outside the shadow of abuse.

Role of counsellors

To work with survivors of DA within a relational framework, counsellors need to have a thorough understanding of the importance of attachment, relational dynamics and schemas, and range of attachment styles. It is also necessary to have an understanding of the impact of complex trauma on self-capacities and relational difficulties both in and outside therapy, as well as the centrality of the therapeutic relationship in recovering from relational abuse. Most importantly counsellors need to respect and validate the survivor in risking connection despite the abuse and provide a safe and secure environment in which to rebuild relational skills.

Critical to the formation of a beneficial therapeutic relationship is counsellors' self-awareness of their own relational history and attachment style. Counsellors need to be aware of how their relational style may impact on survivors of DA and how relational dynamics can enhance or hinder the therapeutic alliance. Most importantly, counsellors must be actively engaged in connecting to the survivor and not fear psychological and emotional contact. Counsellors need to be open and warm and to relate to the survivor in a human way to offset the dehumanisation encountered in DA. The more the counsellor can risk connection, the more the survivor will be able to connect, and permit a more healthy relational style.

In order to fully relate to survivors of DA, counsellors need to explore and understand their own relational experiences and anxieties, especially in relation to power, control and domination, fear of abandonment or rejection, and relational worth. Alongside these, counsellors need to explore any fears around helplessness, hopelessness and vulnerability, and how these may inform counter-transference reactions or defences. The use of the relational self can be a vital part of the therapeutic process and counsellors must ensure that they monitor their own relational responses and how they impact on the survivor. Counsellors must also challenge their potential for denial, emotional or cognitive avoidance, and detachment (see Chapter 10). Such defences reduce emotional attunement and avoidance of discussing trauma material, which reduces therapeutic contact and evokes the survivor's abandonment fears and relational anxieties.

Counsellors must avoid being theory driven and relate to the individual survivor's unique experience. Working with survivors also requires an acute awareness of the potential for the abuse of power in the therapeutic relationships, especially through defining or pathologising the survivor. To provide a holistic therapeutic approach, counsellors need to ensure that they contextualise DA within a socio-political framework and have an adequate knowledge of DA resources in the community and establish appropriate links with relevant organisations. Such links can be critical in providing a social support network not only for the survivor, but also for professional support to the counsellor. Being in contact with other professionals working in the field of DA can enable the counsellor to refer a survivor to appropriate services or treatment options as well as providing an important source of professional support through specialist consultation or supervision.

Research has shown that an effective antidote to secondary traumatic stress (STS) is access to both a good professional support network, and a broad social support network outside of abuse and trauma. It is imperative that counsellors look after themselves physically, emotionally, cognitively, socially and spiritually (Saakvitne et al. 2000; Sanderson 2006) as no professional involved with trauma or relational abuse is immune to STS (McCann and Pearlman 1990; Pearlman and Courtois 2005; Wilson and Lindy 1994). Counsellors working with survivors of DA need trauma sensitive supervision and access to specialist consultations (Pearlman and Saakvitne 1995a; Saakvitne and Pearlman 1996) within a safe and supportive environment which promotes open discussion of all aspects of the therapeutic process that does not harm either therapist or client (see Chapter 10).

In order to work in a relational framework, counsellors need to ensure relational health in their personal lives by ensuring they have regular access to satisfying and nurturing personal relationships. Counsellors must also ensure that they are connected to others and to life by engaging in a range of activities outside of abuse and trauma that replenish and enrich them, to maintain vitality and hope. Spiritual nourishment can enable counsellors to appreciate the resilience of the human spirit and honour survivors of DA, who despite their betrayal, continue to risk connection.

Summary

- In working with relational aspects of DA, counsellors need to have an in-depth understanding of the adaptive need for connection and attachment to others as a fundamental aid to survival and mental well-being. Although the need for connection is highly resilient, clinicians need to recognise that attachment needs can become disrupted in relational abuse such as DA.

- To restore such disruptions, counsellors require considerable knowledge about the myriad ways that DA impacts on relational dynamics, distorts relational schemas, and the concomitant attachment style. Pivotal to this is an awareness of the deleterious effects of disconnection from others and social withdrawal.

- To rebuild connection to others, counsellors need to understand survivors' relational difficulties, distorted relational schemas and attachment style, identify the origins of these and develop new relational schemas.

- As relational schemas are implicit procedures that exist outside of conscious awareness, counsellors need to adopt a relational framework when working with survivors of DA, which emphasises the importance the therapeutic relationship as a medium to restore connection to self, and others and enhance relational worth.

- This necessitates sensitive assessment and profound understanding of the survivor's relational schemas and relational deficits, and how these manifest in the therapeutic relationship. Along with assiduous assessment, counsellors need to view the working alliance as a fertile environment in which to explore relational dynamics and provide the opportunity to risk, form and sustain connection as experiences are explored, shared, understood and resolved.

- The emphasis is on the importance of the therapeutic relationship to model healthier relational dynamics, revise relational schemas and develop relational worth. This will allow for the development of new relational skills which can increase the relational repertoire which can be practised in session, and then adopted outside in relationships with others.

- This will enable survivors to rebuild their social support network, with enhanced interpersonal skills, improved boundary setting, and effective conflict resolution capacities. Through this social support network survivors can begin to build healthier relationships in which they can identify and express needs without fear of abuse.

- To facilitate this, counsellors need to ensure a warm, engaged and sensitively attuned therapeutic stance in which the survivor can learn to trust self and others, and begin to reconnect to others and life.

- A fundamental component of working in a relational framework is counsellors' self-awareness of their own relational history, attachment style, and relational worth. Counsellors must be willing to risk connection, in order to be truly engaged with their clients and feel comfortable in maintaining emotional and psychological contact. This is greatly enhanced through regular access to professional and personal support networks. These are not only an antidote to STS but also a testament to the counsellor's self-care and ability to connect to others, and ultimately the survivor. This promotes a healthy therapeutic relationship in which the survivor can connect to self, others and life outside the shadow of abuse.

CHAPTER 9

WORKING WITH LOSS AND THE RESTORATION OF HOPE

Grief is a response to loss or change, and is a sign that healing can take place. The trauma and multiple losses experienced in domestic abuse (DA) resemble a 'massive bereavement' and will require considerable attention. To fully heal and recover from DA, survivors need to permit mourning. As there is no typical loss, or response to loss, with each loss experienced differently, counsellors need to be sensitively attuned to each individual's grieving process. Accepting the significance of mourning and its integral role in the therapeutic process enables survivors to grieve, transform loss and restore hope.

Recovery from massive bereavement (Worden 2003) is complicated by a variety of factors. This is particularly the case in DA, where the loss is ambiguous because no death has occurred, and the lost person may still play a role in the survivor's life through children or contact orders. In addition, there are no accepted cultural practices around mourning the loss of an abusive relationship. Indeed, prevailing socio-cultural attitudes may impose sanctions on grieving by implying that survivors should be relieved to have escaped the abusive relationship and rejoice, not grieve. Similarly, survivors of DA rarely see their abuse experience within a context of trauma or loss, and may need permission to grieve.

A further complication is the sheer intensity of turbulent and ambivalent feelings, which threaten to engulf the survivor and are difficult to reconcile. Additionally, the loss experienced in DA is rarely singular and usually involves multiple losses. As these multiple losses frequently impinge simultaneously, the experience of loss and expression of grief becomes overwhelming. Current losses often reawaken earlier or previous losses that have not been fully mourned. As these losses meld and fuse, survivors become further overwhelmed, which reinforce anxieties around grieving.

The enormity of accumulated losses is excruciating and exhausting and can prevent some survivors from engaging in grief work. The concomitant tempestuous emotions emerge at various stages in the therapeutic process, often in waves of intensity, with survivors frequently vacillating between wanting to grieve and wanting to resist. This is exacerbated by severely depleted energy reserves which are needed to manage essential practical tasks entailed in ending an abusive relationship. As a result, many survivors are unable to mourn until many months, sometimes years, after the DA has ended.

This chapter will look at loss and the restoration of hope through the grieving process, and examine the ways in which counsellors can facilitate mourning. To actualise the loss, survivors need to identify the multiple losses incurred through DA, explore their meaning, and grieve them. To facilitate this, counsellors need to have an appreciation of the stages of grief, and the factors that can complicate mourning in DA. This must be accompanied by an understanding of the commonly experienced losses, including the re-emergence of previous losses, and the range of therapeutic techniques that can aid grieving. As the losses are transformed, healing can occur and survivors can begin to rebuild their lives outside the shadow of abuse.

Mourning and grieving

The losses associated with trauma and DA mirror bereavement. The term bereavement denotes the circumstances in which someone has lost a loved one, usually through death. While in DA this is generally not the case, this does not invalidate the major changes and losses incurred when ending an abusive relationship. Bereavement is inexorably linked to the experience of grief and mourning. Grief represents the personal experience of loss which includes emotional, psychological as well as somatic responses, whereas mourning refers to acts of expressive grief shaped by the mourning practices of a particular culture (Stroebe and Stroebe 1987; Worden 2003).

As grief is the subjective experience of loss, it is usually seen as a process that the individual goes though that is not linear or progressive. It is characterised by fluctuations in intensity of focus, disruptions and detours, with clients oscillating between current and previous losses. In survivors of DA the process may become disrupted by pressing practical tasks or contact with the abuser. Alternatively it can be diverted through the reawakening of previous losses that compete for attention. Counsellors need to tolerate these disruptions and diversions without imposing a timeframe or specific focus, allowing survivors to manage the integration of losses at their own pace.

In the chaos of DA, or when ending an abusive relationship, survivors may not have the energy and resources to grieve. They may need to postpone their grieving and focus on the practical tasks of surviving. Counsellors need to accept this rather than push the survivor into grieving, and provide a holding environment in which the focus is on emotional support. This could also be a time in which to discuss the links between trauma and loss, and the importance of grieving, to prepare the client for the process. Knowing what to expect and being allowed to titrate the grieving process will restore control and self-agency to the survivor.

Grief process

Working with grief can be very painful for both survivor and counsellor. The counsellor must remain engaged and connected with the survivor and not hide behind purely procedural or cognitive techniques. The therapeutic relationship is pivotal to the grieving process as it enables the individual to restore a sense of trust in self and others. This renewed trust is crucial as the survivor begins to transform loss, restore hope, and reconnect to life.

There has been considerable research on grief (Bowlby 1980; Kübler-Ross 1969; Parkes 1986; Parkes, Relf and Couldrick 1996; Schuchter and Zisook 1993) with general agreement that it is a dynamic process, characterised by three fluid, interlinked stages that are not linear or sequential. Individuals usually vacillate between different levels of experiencing, in which they revisit aspects of the process with new knowledge and heightened awareness.

STAGE 1

The first stage is characterised by initial feelings of intense shock, numbness, unreality and disbelief. In DA this may be accompanied by a sense of relief to have escaped the abusive relationship. Survivors commonly report being in limbo, waiting for something to happen, and anticipating negative repercussions.

STAGE 2

Acute grief reactions begin to emerge in the second stage with increasing recognition of what has happened. This heralds a decrease in denial, releasing physical and psychological pain and distress. The deluge of turbulent emotions is often unexpected and uncontrollable, submerging survivors in waves of intensity. Feelings of anger, sadness, guilt, blame, remorse, regret, shame and terror coexist with ruminations around the loss. These tumultuous feelings can trigger primitive fears of abandonment which give rise to pining and the need to retrieve the loss. To restore the lost person, some survivors may identify with the traits, values or characteristics of the abuser, leading to self-denigration, while others may become vulnerable to re-entering the abuse relationship, rather than stay with these agonising sensations of loss.

Survivors may also experience periods of restlessness, aimlessness, apathy and heightened sense of unreality, in which time is suspended and meaning is lost. In combination, the anguish of the loss can evoke a sense of helplessness and hopelessness, leading to depression. Towards the end of this stage, survivors begin to notice a decrease in pain and increased ability to cope, which allows them to begin to contemplate life in the absence of the loss.

STAGE 3

The focus in the third stage is the acceptance of reality of the loss and a gradual return to physical and psychological well-being. This allows survivors to focus on the present and future, rather than the past, and begin to take pleasure and joy in life again. It is a time for reorganisation, implementing change and building a new way of life. This is crucial for the restoration of the self and hope, allowing survivors to rebuild their lives outside the shadow of abuse.

While these are seen as separate stages, they are seldom distinct and frequently overlap. Survivors of DA weave in and out of the stages depending on each individual experience of loss, before attaining emotional completion. The duration of the grieving process will vary with each individual and can be delayed, or complicated by a number of factors associated with the specific nature of loss and DA.

Factors that impact on the grieving process

There are a number of factors associated with loss and DA that can lead to complications in the grieving process. While these can impede and prolong the grief process, they need to be understood within the context of abuse, not judged as obdurate resistance. Counsellors are encouraged to assess the presence of these factors with each survivor and to sensitively work through the concomitant difficulties rather than rushing the grief process. Some of these factors may necessitate deeper therapeutic work than general grief counselling. Counsellors need to ensure that they feel competent in undertaking protracted grief work and not seek simple or rapid completion.

Grieving cannot take place until safety is established and survivors have mastered affect regulation. Some survivors of DA may benefit from explication of what to expect during the grief process. Counsellors are urged to discuss the link between trauma and loss, the importance of grieving and the stages of grief so that survivors are prepared for what is often the most painful part of the therapeutic process. As grief reactions often surface around anniversaries, birthdays and holiday periods, particular attention needs to be directed around these times.

Initially survivors of DA may experience relief rather than grief to be released from the abuse relationships. They may fear grieving as this ratifies their attachment to the abuser. They may feel that it is not legitimate to grieve what was an abusive relationship and may seek permission to do so. Many survivors feel ashamed of their dependency on the abuser, leading them to withdraw during the grief process, and retreat into social isolation.

The intense emotions evoked during grief can be overwhelming and threaten to engulf survivors. Survivors may fear disintegration, which will undermine their ability to manage the myriad practical daily tasks needed to survive. As these turbulent feelings can incite self-harm or self-medicating behaviours, counsellors need to ensure that they are appropriately contained and regulated. While survivors may seek to suppress this maelstrom of emotions, they need to be sensitively titrated to minimise prolonged grief reactions. In prolonged DA, survivors shut down all overt expressions of emotion, yet counsellors must guard against inferring that they are not felt. Such emotions may be hidden due to shame or embarrassment, or the numbing of feeling during years of abuse.

LEGITIMACY

Grieving is made more difficult in DA due to the associated taboo and stigma. As DA is generally not associated with bereavement, there are no accepted cultural mourning practices for the loss of an abusive relationship. If anything, there may be strong sanctions to view the losses in DA as blessings. This is compounded by survivors not connecting their experiences to loss or bereavement. Shame and guilt can exacerbate any difficulties that survivors have in permitting grief. The repeated denigration imposed in DA engenders deeply negative views of the self in which survivors believe that they are pathetic, crazy or evil and solely responsible for the DA. Acquiescing to culpability makes it impossible to surrender to grief, sorrow or tears. Survivors need to relinquish such negative views of self to be free to grieve and transform the loss.

There may also be guilt around survivors' own actions that have compromised personal integrity. They may feel guilty about failing to protect their children, retaliatory actions, intense feelings of revenge or wishing the abuser dead. These may be perceived as equal to or worse crimes than those committed by the abuser. Counsellors need to enable survivors to see such actions or fantasies, as normal reactions to abnormal circumstances and to grieve the loss of moral integrity.

SAFETY

Grieving cannot take place until external and internal safety has been established (Herman 2001). If the survivor is still in an abusive relationship, the counsellor needs to ensure that protective strategies are consolidated, and institute safety plans to leave the abuse relationship. Research shows that safety can be compromised even after leaving an abusive relationship, with some survivors most at risk at such a time. Safety may also be undermined through threats, harassment or contact with the abuser. Some abusers may deliberately engineer contact to sustain a level of fear which undermines and delays the healing process.

The intensity of emotions associated with DA threaten internal safety in which survivors are overwhelmed by tempestuous emotions. Uncontrollable and unpredictable waves of emotion need to be stabilised through affect regulation (see Chapter 5). In extreme cases, medication may need to be considered and discussed with the survivor to facilitate autonomous choice. The aim is to balance appropriate expression of affect without suppressing all feeling. Medication can slow the pace of grieving, making it more manageable for the survivor.

CIRCUMSTANTIAL FACTORS AROUND LOSS

The circumstantial factors around DA will vary from individual to individual, and impact in a variety of ways, some of which can complicate grieving. Factors such as how the survivor came to leave the abusive relationship, the manner of escape, level of danger, and social support will all impact on ability to enter the grieving process. Survivors who are homeless or have gone into hiding will be faced with innumerable practical tasks to ensure survival, and may not be able to grieve until these have been achieved.

RELATIONAL FACTORS

The type of attachment, nature and duration of the abuse can all complicate the grief process. Traumatic bonding, in which positive and negative aspects of the relationship become entwined, induces ambivalence which impacts on the grief process. As these are hard to disentangle, it may prevent grieving both negative and positive components. The type of abuse and level of psychological distortion around culpability will also play a significant role in terms of permission to grieve. Similarly, prolonged abuse spanning decades may impede the grief process as layers of defences and abuse symptoms have accumulated.

INTENSITY OF EMOTION

The maelstrom of emotions may be so overwhelming that they threaten to engulf the survivor leading to fear of disintegration. Many survivors describe the agony of these emotions as being more painful than the actual abuse. The tsunami-like force of feelings compels many survivors to revert to old behavioural patterns such as dissociation, self-harm or self-medicating in order to suppress seemingly unmanageable emotions. To aid containment and affect regulation careful titration is required. The intensity of emotions often comes in uncontrollable waves, which swell and surge, then slowly recede. For some survivors they do not subside and linger as dysphoric mood throughout the grieving process. Such excruciating sadness can lead to despair, resignation and hopelessness, especially when accompanied by anger and fear. Counsellors need to understand the consuming nature of these feelings, and not recoil from the felt despair, to remain sensitively attuned to the survivor's anguish.

DELAYED/POSTPONED GRIEF

Managing the practicalities of survival alongside intense emotions can lead to the postponement of grief work. Most survivors cannot afford to grieve until pressing issues such as safety, housing, financial support or legal proceedings have been resolved. In many cases this can take months if not years. The sheer struggle of managing day-to-day survival leaves no inner resources to feel. Survivors often report being on autopilot, whereby they numb all feelings so that they can navigate and get through each day.

Abusers often exploit this by instigating contact as reminders of the power and control they still have over them. One survivor depicted such experiences as uncanny in that her ex-husband sensed whenever she felt a little stronger by instigating petty demands via his solicitor to increase child access or query financial arrangements. This not only inculcated fear, but also acted as a reminder of his control. Her grieving was delayed for over a year as she felt too drained to manage the children as well as the abuser's continued control. Counsellors need to be aware that the mourning may not be safe until long after the abusive relationship has ended, and provide emotional support until the survivor is able to mobilise severely depleted energy resources.

Survivors may also suppress sadness and grief through anger. Anger is frequently seen by others, including some professionals, as a much more salient response to DA.

Anger is often experienced as more active and energising compared to sadness, which is annihilative and exhausting. However, anger is a defence against anguish, and a substitute for sorrow. It rarely dispels sadness, which tends to return during periods of intense loneliness.

MASKED GRIEF REACTIONS

Many survivors may hide their grief reactions due to shame, embarrassment or numbing feelings. When survivors do not overtly express feelings, counsellors must assume that they are. One of the long-term effects of DA is the constriction of emotional expression both somatically and verbally. Counsellors need to respect survivors' lack of overt expression and strike a balance between intrusiveness and lack of concern. Rather than questioning survivors, counsellors need to be sensitively attuned to somatic cues of sadness. Acknowledging subtle facial or vocal cues reduces intrusiveness and fosters acceptance, allowing survivors to proceed at their own pace.

A corollary to lack of overt displays of emotion is the expression of invincibility and invulnerability. This may manifest in risk-taking behaviours such as excess drinking, or engaging in unsafe sexual liaisons. This not only postpones grief but also creates the illusion of self-confidence and self-worth. Fear of dependency and lack of trust can provoke strong expressions of self-reliance and fierce independence. Counsellors need to see this as a defence against sadness and self-doubt, and testing boundaries.

MULTIPLE LOSSES

Domestic abuse invariably involves multiple losses, whether still in the relationship, or after leaving. Multiple losses resemble 'massive bereavement' (Worden 2003) in which losses meld and coalesce, with survivors never being certain precisely what is being grieved. The multiple losses experienced by survivors of DA cluster around actual loss such as loss of safety, relationship, home and familiar environment, and symbolic losses such as loss of autonomy, loss of self, loss of trust, loss of security, loss of pleasure and joy, and loss of future. Whatever the individual or multiple losses, counsellors need to encourage survivors to grieve these in order to fully recover from the trauma of DA. As these losses usually impinge simultaneously, counsellors need to be acutely aware of how painful and overwhelming the grieving process can be for many survivors. It is crucial that they understand defences to grieving as realistic concerns around disintegration and not obdurate resistance.

Before grieving can take place, survivors need to identify and acknowledge the range of losses (see Table 9.1) and process the full range of feelings. The losses experienced will vary from individual to individual and can be organised on a number of dimensions: emotional, intrapersonal, interpersonal, psychological, cognitive, physical, material and spiritual. Many survivors will have difficulty identifying their specific losses and counsellors may need to find creative ways to facilitate this. A useful technique is to invite survivors to talk about what they miss and what they do not miss about the relationship, or since leaving. What follows is an examination of commonly experienced losses to guide the counsellor's exploration of these with the client.

Emotional losses

Underlying any abusive relationship is loss of safety, in particular physical, psychological and emotional. The terror of prolonged abuse promotes a numbing of affect and results in loss of full range of feelings, especially positive ones such as pleasure, joy and happiness. In addition, the impact of trauma can result in disruptions to the stress response system, and loss of affect regulation. A further loss in DA is the capacity for love towards self, partner or children and fear of being

Table 9.1 Common losses associated with domestic abuse

Emotional

Loss of feeling safe

Loss of affect regulation

Loss of full range of feelings

Loss of positive feelings

Loss of capacity to love and be loved

Intrapersonal

Loss of self-aspects

Loss of self-esteem

Loss of connection to self

Loss of self-compassion

Loss of capacity for self-love

Loss of personal integrity

Interpersonal

Loss of relationship

Loss of intimacy

Loss of once loved partner

Loss of father for children

Loss of children

Loss of friends

Loss of family

Loss of companionship

Loss of future relationships

Loss of social support

Psychological

Loss of psychological integrity

Loss of foundation of basic trust

Loss of role

Loss of control

Loss of self-agency

Loss of being able to depend on others

Loss of security

Loss of familiarity and predictability

Loss of comfort zone

Cognitive

Loss of certainty

Loss of personal meaning

Loss of future

Loss of trust in world

Shattered assumptions

Physical

Loss of bodily integrity

Loss of health and well-being

Loss of sobriety

Loss of vitality

Loss of capacity to relax

Loss of sexual feelings and expression

Material

Loss of home

Loss of possessions and mementos

Loss of familiar environment

Loss of employment

Loss of income or partner's income

Loss of lifestyle

Loss of pets

Spiritual

Loss of engagement with life

Loss of vitality and energy

Loss of trust in world

Loss of belief in benign world

Loss of religious/spiritual beliefs

Loss of hope

Loss of belief in life

Loss of culture

loved as it is entwined with abuse. The yearning to love and be loved can be agonising and is often a recurring theme when working with survivors of DA.

Intrapersonal losses

The intrapersonal losses cluster around disruptions to aspects of self such as loss of self-esteem, self-confidence and self-efficacy. The constant and prolonged denigration by the abuser is internalised resulting in loss of self-esteem and compassion for self. Many abusers impose a distorted identity on to the survivor which results in loss of previously valued self-identity, self-worth and self-respect. In cases where the survivor has to go into hiding, there is an actual loss of identity through change of name. To this effect, survivors have to entomb their old identity, and adopt a new one with concomitant ramifications of concealment, secrecy and isolation. There may also be a loss of personal integrity, especially when the survivor is unable to protect her children, or resorts to substance misuse, or is consumed with fantasies of retaliation or wishing the abuser dead.

Interpersonal losses

Interpersonal losses cluster around the relationship with the abuser, relationships with children or family and friends, all of which can impinge simultaneously. With regard to the abuse relationship, losses include the loss of a once loved partner, loss of love and companionship, and loss of intimacy. The loss of a relationship with so much emotional investment, in which some feelings of love and concern still exist, may be difficult to grieve. Fears around surviving the loss of the relationship, how to recover from the loss, or resume life, may lead some survivors to harbour an unending hope of being reunited with the lost partner. In some instances, survivors may also fear that the abuser will carry out previous threats of suicide. The need to compensate for the loss of the relationship can make the survivor vulnerable to further abuse by seeking comfort or help from inappropriate sources. One survivor who sought help from a previous partner found herself being abused again.

If children are involved, the survivor's biggest fear may be the loss of the children through disclosing the abuse. Survivors fear that their partner's accusations of being crazy, or an unfit parent, will impact on professionals' perceptions. It is for this reason that mental health professionals must guard against pathologising survivors. Equally survivors may fear that children may be taken into care if they have not been able to protect them sufficiently. These fears are very real, and are often compounded by the abuser's threat to fight for custody of the children. If the children remain with the survivor, there may be fears of estrangement or loss of respect, resulting in deep fissures that can be hard to heal. These are poignant losses as the fear of losing the children is often a pivotal reason for not ending the abuse relationship earlier. Many survivors feel guilty that they have deprived the children of a parent and this guilt prevents them from grieving. Their guilt can prevent them from making necessary changes in family functioning. Changing family dynamics is yet a further loss that survivors may be reluctant to accept, wanting everything to remain the same, yet knowing that it is not. Some older children may identify with the abuser and become abusive to the survivor, once again undermining safety.

Losses are also incurred in other relationships such as with friends and family, who may take sides. Some abusers are incredibly charming and are able to seduce family and friends to take their side. In some instances the abuser may launch a campaign against the survivor to co-opt support from children, extended family members, friends and neighbours, as a way of isolating the survivor so impeding access to social support. Many abusers employ similar tactics with professionals by presenting themselves as perfectly affable individuals. In combination, this serves to enhance the abuser's power and control over the survivor, and reduces appropriate professional support. The loss of trust underlying social isolation obliterates hopes for future relationships or a future partner.

Psychological losses

Prolonged DA threatens psychological integrity in which survivors fear disintegration of psychological functioning and loss of sanity. When accompanied by loss of trust in self, others and future partners, fears of dependency emerge. Some survivors may experience loss of valued roles such as loving partner, father- or mother-in-law, or son- or daughter-in-law. In DA victims are coerced to submit to the dominant force and relinquish all control. Survivors need to acknowledge the loss of control especially in relation to making decisions or choices, sense of autonomy and self-agency. The chaos and unpredictability seen in abusive relationships leads to loss of predictability and certainty which also need to be explored.

Cognitive losses

The trauma of DA results in a number of cognitive disruptions and losses. These centre on loss of previously held assumptions and certainty. The betrayal of trust in intimate relationships leads to shattered assumptions about love, life and the world which are difficult to restore. Loss of trust also propels survivors to adopt a facade of self-reliance which can manifest in the counselling process. Survivors of DA need to grieve the loss of belief that they can be cherished rather than harmed in relationships, that they can be loved, and that people can be benign. DA is suffused with uncertainty leading to myriad doubts, not least whether they will survive the experience. Survivors need to mourn the loss of certainty, the loss of reassurance of a future, of growing old together, and the loss of dreams of what might have been.

Physical losses

Physical losses associated with DA include physical health, physical injury and loss of bodily integrity. The unpredictability of physical or psychological assault means that survivors have to be hypervigilant at all times thereby compromising their ability to relax. In order to protect themselves or their children, survivors need to constantly monitor the abuser's moods and anticipate what he might do next. Such hypervigilance depletes energy, impairs sleep and leads to loss of vitality. Survivors who resort to self-medication as a response to managing DA may lose their sobriety, becoming dependent on drugs or alcohol.

A major loss for many survivors is loss of sexual intimacy and expression. In the case of rape and sexual assault, the survivor is deprived of pleasurable, consensual sex. Furthermore, it is hard for many survivors to engage in loving sexual intimacy when they are being abused. The sexual intimacy integral to loving relationships is lost during DA. After the abusive relationship has ended, the survivor may miss previous sexual intimacy, or being held in a loving way. The intensity of this loss may lure some survivors back to the abuser, or to engage in inauspicious short-term, potentially destructive sexual liaisons.

Material losses

When leaving an abusive relationship, there are innumerable material losses which commonly impinge simultaneously and can seem insurmountable. In fleeing the abuse, survivors can lose their home, valued possessions, and poignant mementoes such as children's drawings or photographs. As these are usually imbued with deep personal meaning and are irreplaceable, survivors will need to grieve these highly symbolic losses. Along with the loss of home, there is a loss of familiar environment, established roots, familiar faces, lifestyle and culture. If children are involved, survivors will have to manage their losses of school and friends. Fleeing may also necessitate leaving beloved family pets behind.

There are also a number of related financial losses such as loss of income or partner's income, loss of joint social benefits, employment and general financial security. Survivors of DA may also lose financial support from their partner leading to loss of access to money or credit cards. Accompanying this may be losing the use of a car, loss of vacations and loss of private education. These losses are combined with having to manage on drastically reduced income or benefits to replace lost items such as clothes and essential possessions.

Spiritual losses

Living in or leaving an abusive relationships can be draining and survivors commonly report a loss of energy and vitality. Every day seems like a struggle with ever-depleting resources. The daily fight to survive prevents active engagement in life. The stigma, shame and loss of trust in a benign world further serves to reinforce the survivor's social isolation. This can lead to loss of hope, aching emptiness and disconnection from life. This hopelessness extends to loss of faith and spirituality. Such losses can destroy any remnants of meaning in life, making it hard to contemplate the future.

HISTORICAL FACTORS

Current losses commonly reawaken affect associated with previous losses not processed or grieved for, which demand therapeutic attention. These previous losses fuse with current loss, and redirect the focus of grief. Previous losses are highly significant and can revive past experiences of abandonment, loss or abuse. They can also prompt old patterns of behaviour to manage the loss such as self-harm or substance abuse. It is essential that counsellors are flexible when the grief focus oscillates between prior and current losses (Nord 1996) and that survivors feel supported in these detours and diversions.

PERSONALITY VARIABLES

There are a number of personality variables that can complicate the grieving process. These centre on the age of the survivor, gender and self-concept. These all have salience and are impacted by DA, and need careful consideration. In addition, assessment of attachment style, cognitive style and coping style can provide a deeper understanding of how survivors will be impacted by and manage the grief process. Most crucially, counsellors must remember to contextualise these within DA, and refrain from applying diagnostic labels pertaining to personality disturbance.

SOCIAL VARIABLES

Lack of social support can seriously impede the grieving process. The enormity of the losses and the agony of grieving can be ameliorated by being connected to others with whom survivors can weep, laugh, share and just be. In the absence of such connection survivors can retreat into further isolation. Counsellors need to assess level of social support and actively encourage survivors to establish links. This may be a time for the survivor to seek out support groups for survivors of DA as an adjunct to the therapeutic work.

Some survivors may deliberately restrict their social interactions for fear that they may be overwhelmed by uncontrollable surges of emotion. One survivor continued to be terrified of social situations two years after the abuse relationship ended as she still feared she would not be able to contain the inner maelstrom of feelings that threatened to burst through the facade of composure. Caution needs to be exercised, ensuring that the social support is satisfying to the survivor, and that quality is not sacrificed for quantity. Counsellors need to encourage the gradual rebuilding of social networks without pressurising the survivor.

Survivors living in rural areas may find it difficult to establish social support due to transport problems, while those from ethnic minority groups may face ostracism from their community. Stigmatisation may also play a role in lack of social support for male, or gay and lesbian survivors of DA. Some survivors from higher socioeconomic groups have also faced social exclusion making it difficult for them to obtain appropriate social support.

CONCURRENT FACTORS

There may be a number of current stressors that can hijack the grieving process. These include threats or harassment from the abuser, impending court dates, child access, custody, housing or financial instability. These are invariably pressing, needing immediate attention, and divert the survivor from grieving. In the case of survivors who self-medicate to the point of dependency, they should enter an addiction or rehabilitation programme before undergoing any further therapeutic work. Similarly, self-harm and suicidality need to be contained before embarking on further grief work. In such instances medication needs to be considered alongside instituting safety contracts.

COMMON DEFENCES

Common defences to grieving in survivors of DA are denial of loss, intellectualising feelings, self-harming, or adopting pretence of invulnerability or invincibility. Some survivors may also enter a period of exploring their new-found freedom by engaging in risky behaviours. Counsellors need to understand these defences within the context of the survivor's circumstances and manage them appropriately.

There are a variety of ways to transform loss, with some survivors seeking revenge while others look for forgiveness. Grief is further complicated when survivors resist grieving in order to deny victory to the abuser not realising that this denies them the potential to heal from the loss. Survivors need to grieve the full range of emotions to recover from DA. Counsellors can enable the survivor to reframe this belief by not seeing grief as 'submission but empowering evidence of indestructible inner life' (Herman 2001, p.188).

Preoccupation with revenge serves only to prolong the disavowed feelings of loss and sorrow. Counsellors need to explore these with survivors, to recognise that revenge will only recapitulate abuse dynamics and not bring the desired empowerment. In contrast, forgiveness is to deny rage and anger. Survivors need to experience the spectrum of emotions and guard against polarisation. Counsellors can help survivors become aware that both revenge and forgiveness focus on the abuser rather than the survivor, which impedes the survivor's own healing. It is when survivors focus on themselves and relinquish morbid preoccupation with the abuser that they can begin to heal.

Some survivors may become preoccupied with the desire for compensation in wanting apologies and protestations of remorse from the abuser. According to Herman (2001, p.190) this desire for compensation 'ties the patient's fate to that of the perpetrator and holds her recovery hostage to his whims'. This may manifest in resistance to healing until the abuser acknowledges the magnitude of damage inflicted. Ultimately, this serves to maintain destructive behaviours and impedes recovery. In essence, survivors need to take control and responsibility for their own healing rather than seeking compensation from the abuser, or transferring these needs onto the counsellor.

Working with grief

Working with grief can be emotionally draining for both counsellor and survivor. The counsellor must remain engaged and connected with the survivor, in a healthy relational way, to rebuild trust in relationships. The therapeutic relationship may prove to be the most powerful component in restoring trust. The mistrust of authority figures, and fear of being controlled, can result in considerable volatility, and fluctuations in engagement with the counsellor. Counsellors need to normalise and contextualise these to work with them effectively.

Grief work with survivors of DA necessitates heightened awareness of the factors that impact on and complicate grief, alongside grief counselling principles (Worden 2003). The primary goal of grief counselling is to actualise loss through emotional and intellectual acceptance of loss. It is only with emotional acceptance that survivors can identify and experience the full range of ambivalent feelings. Accompanying this is the need to find meaning in the loss. To facilitate this, counsellors need to encourage clients to make time for grieving by minimising daily commitments and channelling emotional energy towards self rather than lost object. It is essential to value that grieving is unique to each individual and to interpret manifest behaviour as normal responses to loss and grief. Counsellors also need to assess individual coping styles and common defences to grieving and if necessary refer on. Most importantly, counsellors need to be comfortable with own their sadness and grief to be attuned to the survivor's agony.

A fundamental difficulty when recovering from DA is the balance between competing demands: the practical tasks of survival and the emotional tasks of healing. Traditionally when working with survivors of DA the primary focus has been on practical support rather than emotional needs. When emotional and practical tasks run in parallel the enormity of tasks becomes overwhelming. Survivors and counsellors can overlook the impact and effect of these equally important needs.

To ensure safety and survival, survivors tend to prioritise practical tasks and shelve emotional needs until practical aspects are resolved. Counsellors may also be tempted to keep the focus on practical tasks, not just to ensure physical safety, but as indices of change. Practical tasks are more easily measured than emotional ones, and can appear easier to manage and ratify than the more nebulous emotional tasks. Indubitably the priority has to be safety, but once established, practical tasks need to be balanced with attending to emotional well-being. Counsellors need to find sensitively attuned ways in which to facilitate parity, at a manageable pace.

Addressing emotional and practical tasks individually can be difficult but when these occur in tandem it can be formidable. Along with exigent tasks such as safety, housing and financial support, survivors often have to take on other unfamiliar tasks such as being a single parent, having sole financial responsibility, and organising living arrangements. In addition, they need to adopt new roles as a separate entity from their partner, no longer being defined by him or her, make adjustments to self-concept and acquiring a new identity. This can be extremely difficult as it contrasts with the enmeshment and enforced identity ascribed by the abuser. When combined with the turbulent emotions encountered during grieving, it is hardly surprising that survivors feel overwhelmed.

Consequently survivors of DA vacillate between different support needs. Sometimes practical needs are paramount only to be replaced by emotional ones, while at times they are so intertwined that they are not separable. Counsellors need to acknowledge these changing and emerging demands, and support survivors in whatever need is most pressing rather than set a specific agenda or time frame in which to achieve goals. To provide appropriate support, counsellors need to feel comfortable in this dynamic and fluid process.

Counsellors also need to appreciate the diverse decisions that survivors of DA might make once grieving is complete. They may choose to stay in the abuse relationship, leave or return, find a new partner, or remain single. Irrespective of their choice, survivors need to feel supported by the counsellor in whatever decision is made. The only way that survivors can develop self-agency and autonomy is by taking control of their own healing and make personally meaningful choices.

The grief process cannot be bypassed or hurried, and counsellors have to be emotionally available, sensitively attuned and respectful of the survivor's process. Flexibility rather than rigidity is essential, and survivors need to know that circumvention will be understood. In some cases the grief process may need to be temporarily suspended. The counsellor needs to reassure the survivor that it can be resumed at a future point as new or unexplored aspects of the trauma or DA experience emerge.

Useful techniques

There is a range of useful techniques that can be used to aid grieving. These techniques are not designed as 'a bag of tricks' and must be implemented only within a rigorous therapeutic framework, underpinned by a thorough understanding of the impact and effects of DA. Counsellors need to ensure that the application of techniques suits the criteria of each individual client's needs. Whichever techniques are used, it is essential that counsellors identify and address the survivor's fears before implementing any grief work.

Counsellors also need to be aware of survivor compliance to engage in grief work as they may fear saying no, or challenging the counsellor. Meticulous assessment is also crucial to establish level of functionality both inside and outside the therapeutic setting. How survivors present in session is not always an accurate reflection of how they are in other environments. Counsellors act as containers and until survivors have established appropriate levels of containment, they may not be able to regulate levels of functioning. Contracting to engage with grief work may help to set appropriate boundaries of safety. If the survivor is suicidal, it will be necessary to consider medication and institute a safety contract.

Counsellors need to regulate the grief work at a manageable pace for the survivor and schedule time to process losses, initially during sessions that can be practised at home. Survivors need to know that these are best done in small, manageable chunks by setting aside regular short time periods to reflect on, write or talk about their losses. It is crucial that these exercises are under the survivor's control. Systematic desensitisation techniques can also be employed so that the survivor can tolerate exposure and master relaxation skills. Counsellors also need to time their interventions carefully to regulate the pace.

USE OF LANGUAGE

Language used in the therapeutic process is a powerful way to reality test and reframe interpretations. Counsellors can coax the mobilisation of feelings by ensuring that they use the past tense when referring to losses. It is also useful to avoid euphemisms for loss and be clear and direct in addressing the loss or losses.

TIMELINE OF RELATIONSHIP

This is a useful exercise to create a concrete record of the abuse relationship, both for client and counsellor. It is a way for the survivor to encapsulate the relationship, plot the course of DA and identify specific abuse patterns. It is also a powerful way to aid the recall of memories. One survivor was astonished at how many incidents of abuse had been 'forgotten' over a 20-year relationship, and that her partner's controlling behaviour could be traced back to the first few months of their marriage. As this can be a highly arousing and evocative exercise, some survivors may need to work on this over several weeks in session so that emerging feelings can be appropriately contained.

Survivors are encouraged to view this as a working document to which they can add, or subtract, information as they go through the therapeutic process. Traditionally such timelines instruct the client to plot significant experiences along a continuum, with positive experiences above the line, and negative below. However, survivors can be invited to be creative in how they might construct the timeline, as this fosters ownership of their experiences and engenders autonomy.

'WHAT I MISS AND WHAT I DON'T MISS'

Alongside a relationship timeline, survivors can begin to identify relationship losses by constructing a list of 'What I miss and what I don't miss'. This will provide clarification of the positive and the negative aspects of the relationship, all of which have to be grieved.

USE OF SYMBOLS

Symbols are highly evocative and bring the loss into the therapeutic setting, and therefore into the present. Survivors can bring in photographs, letters, audio-tapes, or video footage of the partner, which can then be used to trigger and explore nascent feelings. Visual images can also help the counsellor to get a clearer image and sense of the partner. Symbolic images that are salient to the survivor can be particularly powerful, as they encapsulate the depth of loss. For one survivor the image that consistently triggered sadness was one of holding hands. Whenever she encountered this image or thought about it, she would be suffused with aching sadness. Another survivor experienced the same surge of emotion whenever she saw fathers with their young children. Other symbolic objects such as special gifts or items of jewellery may also trigger grief reactions.

WRITING

Writing letters, which are not actually sent, can facilitate the expression of grief (Lattanzi and Hale 1984). Letter writing is a powerful way to express feelings to the abuser in an uncensored, safe way. They act as a vehicle to express the full range of feelings. Towards the end of the grief process, survivors can be invited to write a farewell letter to the abuser as they finally let go. Writing letters to those who have let the survivor down by taking sides may also be of benefit.

Creative writing is another way for survivors to express themselves. Writing their life story in the third person is a potent way of accessing compassion and sadness. Due to shame and guilt many survivors of DA find it hard to show self-compassion, yet when written in the third person they may be able to reframe their experiences. Writing poetry or lyrics is another way of distilling their experiences and expressing sorrow.

JOURNAL WRITING

Keeping a journal is an excellent way to record feelings and changing perceptions. While this can be painful to survivors, it is a powerful tool to record advances made. In addition, the journal acts as a reminder of what they have come through, to sustain them through their low patches. The journal is a place in which to create narrative out of chaos, record feelings and losses, log changing perceptions, and monitor growth of self-worth and self-confidence. As the journal represents survivors' triumph over trauma, they might wish to invest in a particularly appealing notebook that they can take pleasure in opening it to make entries.

DRAWING

For some survivors 'speaking the unspeakable' can be paralysing and elicit primitive defences. In contrast, drawings are a powerful way of expressing feelings, for which the person can find no words.

ROLE PLAY

Some survivors of DA respond well to role play in which new skills such as saying 'no' and setting boundaries can be practised and honed. Practising these in session until they have been mastered makes them easier to transfer to outside therapy.

COGNITIVE RESTRUCTURING

Cognitive restructuring allows survivors to identify cognitive distortions, covert thoughts and self-talk that impact on emotions. Counsellors can use cognitive techniques to enable the survivor to reality test thoughts and assumptions to prevent overgeneralisation.

MEMORY BOOK

A useful technique that can involve other family members is making a memory book, which can include narratives, photos, poems or drawings of the good aspects of the relationship. Involving children in this task can allow individuals to grieve together.

RECOVERY BOOK

Making a recovery book which contains grounding images, poetry, writing, drawings, snatches of conversation or inspirational images can sustain survivors during more difficult times. One survivor developed this further by creating a mood board on which she pasted inspirational images and objects to ground her.

SENSORY CUES

There are a number of other sensory modalities that can help mobilise feelings and memories. Music can be very evocative and trigger strong emotions. Music, songs or albums associated with the abuser can trigger memories and stir up feelings that facilitate grieving. Of all the senses smell is probably the most evocative, and can be used to good effect to elicit feelings. Survivors can bring the abuser's scent or aftershave into session to access deeply buried emotions.

USE OF METAPHOR

Metaphors that symbolise the survivor's experience can be used to grieve the loss in a more acceptable way. Personally meaningful metaphors can guide the healing process and provide meaning. Soothing imagery of a caring comforting person or relationship can be sustaining during bleaker moments.

DREAMS

Working with dreams, dream fragments or dream sequences can parallel the mourning process and reflect particular tasks of mourning. Dreams can also integrate feelings, process the trauma of DA, and identify more subtle underlying themes that need to be addressed.

EMPTY CHAIR

This technique allows the survivor to address the abuser directly in the first person and in the present time to mobilise feelings. This can be a very powerful technique that should not be employed unless the counsellor is specifically trained or experienced in its use.

OTHER MEDIATORS

While the focus has been on individual counselling, some survivors may benefit from extra emotional support. Group therapy or self-help groups can enable survivors to receive peer support from others who have experienced similar losses.

Pets and children can also be sustaining during the grief work, to develop self-compassion.

Focusing on the things that have not been destroyed can be restorative. Enabling survivors to access their innate qualities such as warmth, humour, intelligence, empathy and capacity for love can allow their pre-abuse personality to unfold. This can be facilitated through re-engagement with much valued activities such as dance, music, laughter, nature, and things that delight. Transforming loss releases energy from trauma which can be discharged to enable the survivor to reconnect to life with greater vitality and purpose.

Counsellors will be able to assess completion of the grief process when significant and consistent changes in the survivor's subjective experiencing, behaviour and symptoms are manifest (Worden 2003). Changes in self-esteem and restoration of positive self-feelings can herald adjustments in behaviour. These translate into alterations in appearance, dress and demeanour. As physical health and psychological functioning are restored, survivors experience the restoration of hope and willingness to reconnect to life.

The restoration hope

When survivors engage in the therapeutic process they are expressing hope. It takes courage and determination to go to the epicentre of sorrow, explore the devastation of continuous betrayals, and not recoil from further pain. This is precisely what the survivor is doing by reaching out, risking trust and connection to the counsellor. These inner sources of strength and hope are a direct indication that core aspects of the self are still intact and were not annihilated by DA. It is these resources that sustain survivors in the face of overwhelming adversity, which need to be cultivated through the grieving process.

Transforming loss and finding meaning in the DA experience allows for the restoration of hope. Meaning is gained as shattered assumptions about self, others and the world are explored, reconstructed and redefined (Janoff-Bulman 1985). When combined with the restoration of physical and emotional health, survivors will begin to see changes in vitality and energy. This will allow survivors to set realistic goals to rebuild their lives. The cumulative effect of setting and attaining goals rekindles hope and allows survivors to reconnect to life.

The restoration of hope allows survivors to begin to flourish rather than survive (Allen 2006a, 2006b), leading to marked changes in their quality of life. Survivors can allow more self-expression and self-reliance and begin to actively engage with life again outside the shadow of abuse. As they begin to trust, they can connect to others, risk intimacy and begin to love again.

Surviving the trauma of DA can enhance an appreciation for being alive, with greater empathy and compassion for others, a clearer self-chosen philosophy of life with deeper sense of meaning and spirituality. Solomon's (2002, p.6) view of spirituality as 'embracing love, trust, reverence, and wisdom, as well as the most terrifying aspects of life, tragedy, and death' seems all too poignant when working with survivors of DA. As spirituality is subjectively experienced involving a sense of connection with something beyond the self, survivors can make personally meaningful choices be it religion, love of nature, or passion for life.

Rebuilding life

Once survivors reconnect, they can begin to rebuild their lives, under their direction in which they are in control. As they feel more connected to others they seek new friendships, increased social support and relationships, in the knowledge that they can set healthy boundaries against further abuse or exploitation. Some survivors may seek new partners, while others choose not to. Of central importance is that survivors can identify their own needs and life goals, and take responsibility for the future direction of their lives.

While changes need to occur within the remaining family, these will be predicated on healthy boundaries and mutual respect. Family members can turn to each other or to friends for emotional nurturance without fear of abuse. Gradually survivors will refocus attention away from survival to ordinary living (Allen 2006a) with restored capacity for pleasure, laughter, joy and delight, rather than fear. Having come out of the shadow of abuse, survivors will begin to cherish life and enjoy being alive.

Summary

- Loss in DA resembles massive bereavement and demands considerable attention during the counselling process. Counsellors need to recognise that the expression of grief is a sign that healing can be an integral part of the therapeutic process when working with survivors of DA.

- Counsellors need to have a good understanding of the grief process and the stages of grief in relation to survivors of DA. To facilitate mourning, counsellors must be able to understand the factors that can complicate the grieving.

- Grieving DA is characterised by multiple losses, both past and current, that can complicate the grief process. Survivors of DA often feel relief rather than grief when leaving abusive relationships and therefore do not legitimise their grief.

- The priority in DA is to establish safety, which results in delayed or masked grief reactions. This is compounded by the intensity of emotions that threaten to engulf the survivor leading to defences to grieving. The competing demands of practical tasks and emotional needs can further prolong the grief process. Establishing safety can take months, sometimes years, with some survivors not able to grieve until years after the abuse relationship has ended.

- The multiple losses experienced in DA include physical, psychological and material losses, which all need to be grieved. Current losses can trigger previous losses, which can divert the focus of grief, with survivors vacillating between current and past losses.

- Grief can be complicated by a number of other variables such as coping style, social support and additional stressors. There are numerous stressors such as housing, financial insecurity and unavoidable contact with the abuser that can impact on the grief process.

- The therapeutic relationship is pivotal to transforming loss and reconnecting to life. Counsellors need to be comfortable around working with loss, be flexible in pacing the grief process, and be sensitively attuned to the survivor's process.

- To facilitate grieving, counsellors can employ a number of useful therapeutic techniques, although these need to be embedded within a rigorous therapeutic framework and understanding of the principles of grief counselling.

- As survivors move through the grieving process, they can start to acknowledge that healing is taking place and begin to restore hope. This will enable them to rebuild their lives with a sense of control and self-efficacy in shaping their future.

CHAPTER 10

PROFESSIONAL ISSUES WHEN WORKING WITH SURVIVORS OF DOMESTIC ABUSE

Working with survivors of domestic abuse (DA) can be rewarding and satisfying, but emotionally draining. Working with trauma has considerable impact on professionals and leads to secondary traumatic stress (STS). To manage the impact of trauma and to minimise the risk of STS, counsellors must take care of themselves and be realistic in the work that they do. This chapter looks at counsellor self-awareness, knowledge of DA, how counsellors can work with difference and issues around power and control. In particular, emphasis is placed on the impact of STS, and how to minimise this through self-care and professional support to stay connected with clients.

Counsellor's self-awareness

To avoid contaminating the therapeutic process, counsellors must mentalise their experience and responses to clients through reflection and self-monitoring. To expedite this, counsellors need to be mindful of their own experiences around power and control, domestic abuse and trauma experiences. The unique experiences and coping strategies associated with survivors of DA demands a flexible rather than dogmatic approach; survivors' individual experiences can be validated and explored. An open and engaged stance is required, in which the clinician retains respect for each client's individual way of managing the abuse. Flexibility allows counsellors to be fully in a relationship with the client rather than imposing a rigid set of techniques or procedures.

Counsellors may need to revisit their motivation and desire to work in this field, and link these to their need for power or sense of omnipotence. In addition, it is useful to look at feelings around the need for control and misuse of power. The recognition of power dynamics inherent in any therapeutic relationship despite the adoption of an egalitarian therapeutic stance is crucial, given that clients may invest power in the therapist, even in the most collaborative or co-constructive models. Particular attention also needs to be paid to the power of suggestibility in the therapeutic relationship to ensure that the counsellor does not contaminate the survivor's experience.

Counsellors who are not familiar with working with complex trauma and abuse may need to re-examine their own attachment experiences, including the role of power and control and how these impact on fears around intimacy and autonomy. It is helpful to assess preferred attachment style, and comfort around being engaged and connected. An honest assessment of what brought counsellors to this point in their professional career, and an appraisal of any nascent current personal or professional issues that may impact on their work, can ensure that personal struggles and difficulties do not become enmeshed in the therapeutic work.

Counsellors need to be aware of the degree of embodiment to develop a greater awareness of somatic resonance and somatic responses, especially when working with survivors with dissociation. This will enable counsellors to work with transference and manage their own counter-transference reactions. Close attention should be paid to issues of enmeshment and over-identification with the client, along with any evoked responses of fascination, voyeurism and preoccupation with client material. Working with survivors of DA can evoke myriad feelings, in particular uncertainty, fears, doubts and sense of inadequacy. Exploring trauma can unleash the counsellor's own unconscious defences against intimacy and primitive fears of autonomy and past experiences of victimisation. This can propel the counsellor into the role of rescuer or persecutor with concomitant counter-transference reactions (see Chapter 4).

To avoid burnout, counsellors need to recognise their own limitations and ensure a balance in the number of trauma clients in their caseload. It is imperative that counsellors manage their caseload appropriately through sensitive referrals and ask for help when necessary. Adequate training, continuous professional development, regular supervision and the establishment of a good support network are invaluable if counsellors are to work effectively. It is important that counsellors attend to their own self-care so that they can maintain a therapeutic stance that is nurturing and empathically attuned. In recognising their susceptibility to STS, counsellors can assess their own personal risk factors and calibrate a healthy balance between work, rest, play and self-nurturing. Through this, counsellors can retain a sense of meaning in their life outside the trauma work, so that they remain connected to themselves, others and their clients.

Knowledge of domestic abuse

Before counsellors embark on working with survivors of DA, or if an existing client reveals a history of DA during therapy, counsellors must ensure that they have a thorough understanding of the complex nature and impact of DA, its link to trauma and the concomitant effects. This includes knowledge of vulnerability factors such as previous history of abuse or victimisation that may make the individual more susceptible to DA. On no account should counsellors misinterpret a history of abuse or pre-morbid personality as a way of pathologising the survivor. Counsellors must have a clear understanding that while previous abuse history increases vulnerability, it is not an indicator of personality disturbance. Counsellors should avail themselves of specialist training in DA through continuous professional development. Such knowledge also allows for more accurate diagnosis, clearly specified assessment of symptoms, and the links between these and DA experiences. It also enables counsellors to evaluate their own strengths and limitations and when to refer the survivor for more specialist therapeutic intervention.

The nature of DA necessitates certain knowledge of the impact of prolonged coercive control and power, and how this impacts on the individual. Counsellors must be aware of their own attitudes and beliefs about DA so that any myths or biases are dispelled, and replaced with more accurate understanding. Counsellors will need to combine this with an examination of the socio-political, cultural and economic factors that underpin and support DA. This will help them to make links between how the use and misuse of power in the prevailing macro-system are reflected in the micro-system of personal relationships. Attention must also be paid to socially constructed meanings around gender, race, domination and submission and the hierarchical structure of families. This may become particularly prominent when working with survivors from marginalised or ethnic minority groups.

Counsellors must identify their own fears about DA and how this could impact on the therapeutic process. DA often elicits strong reactions, ranging from complete denial, through shock, to fears that threaten fundamental assumptions about safety in the world. Some of these fears may be unconscious and need to be explored so that hidden messages are not conveyed to the survivor in the therapeutic process. Beliefs around responsibility for DA need to be explored and counsellors must recognise that the responsibility of DA rests firmly with the abuser not the survivor. Counsellors need to remember that abusers have a choice whether to coerce and control their partners and that until they relinquish this desire, they are at risk of abusing. Putative allegations of provocative behaviour or psychological disturbance serve only to dilute responsibility and collude with victim blaming.

Counsellors must also explore their attitudes and feelings toward the perpetrators. If a counsellor believes that all abusers are monsters and projects this in the counselling process, then survivors may feel prevented from exploring the positive feelings of love and affection they had for the abuser between episodes of the abuse. Such projections can contaminate the client's experience and be perceived as critical, harsh and rejecting, which will undermine the survivor's trust in the counsellor. Counsellors need to guard against judging any of the participants in DA, or projecting any biases about responsibility, personal fears and conflicts on to the client. This is not to say, however, that these are invalid. Personal feelings and fears must be identified, monitored and contained in session, and subsequently explored in supervision.

COUNSELLOR'S HISTORY

Working with DA may remind counsellors of their own socialisation process with regard to different expectations and treatment of males and females, attachment, dependency, intimacy and autonomy. Counsellors may need to re-examine their own history in relation to their hopes, fears, expectations, disappointments and shame, and how these have shaped their life. Such exploration may include an examination of family dynamics, socialisation processes, and feelings of dependency, inadequacy, shame, powerlessness, victimisation and control. Counsellors may not have experienced DA but examining their subjective experiences around these dynamics may increase level of empathic understanding. Counsellors should explore their own struggle with identifying needs and asking for them to be met, and how it feels to be rejected or punished for this. Any conflicts around intimacy and autonomy must also be examined, along with child and adult attachment style. An appreciation of the difficulties entailed in striving for autonomy and control, and self-agency can be invaluable in understanding the survivor's experiences and difficulties around change. Similarly the counsellor's experience of dependency and ability to ask for help needs to be scrutinised.

THE SURVIVOR AS COUNSELLOR

Many survivors of DA are drawn to helping other survivors, and are able to bring high levels of empathy and understanding to the therapeutic relationship. This can be highly effective, provided sufficient therapeutic work has been undertaken by the counsellor to ensure that any trauma and conflicts have been processed and largely resolved. The 'wounded healer' can bestow great benefit to the therapeutic relationship, but it can also be fraught with difficulties. The abused counsellor can bring an enhanced level of understanding of DA to the therapeutic relationship, in which DA experiences are intuited, more easily crystallised and empathically understood. The abused counsellor may be more able to believe the DA experiences and be more empathically attuned to the survivor's descriptions of it.

Some counsellors who have not experienced DA may find the abuse material threatening or traumatising and disconnect from it in order to minimise its impact. Some DA experiences are so far outside their frame of reference and experience as to render them incredulous and inconceivable. Abused counsellors, in contrast, may find such experiences entirely believable because these resemble or mirror their own experiences. Thus, the survivor as counsellor can enhance crucial aspects of the therapeutic relationship by conveying more easily to clients that the DA is credible and that they are believed.

Despite these positive contributions, there are some pitfalls to the survivor as counsellor. If counsellors have not fully processed their own DA experiences, then they may project their own unresolved issues and internalised fears on to the client. This might include emoting highly subjective and personal opinions about DA and how best to recover. All clinicians, abused or not, must guard against imposing their own personal views and unresolved conflicts on to survivors. Abused counsellors must be particularly careful not to direct the survivor along the same path that they have travelled but support the survivor's individual way of coping and healing. Survivors must make their own choices about how to work through their experiences, at their own pace.

Survivors of DA who decide to offer counselling must ensure that their own conflicts have been resolved and be mindful not to project their own needs on to the client, or use the therapeutic setting as a mechanism for self-healing. They must also ensure that they will not use the therapeutic setting to reinforce their own defence mechanisms, such as dissociation, intellectualisation, sublimation, denial and displacement. It must be remembered that the impact of clients' traumatic material may restimulate previous history of abuse and cause destabilisation. In such instances, counsellors need to return to therapy. The survivor as counsellor can act as a role model to the client by providing a positive and hopeful image that it is possible to heal from DA and reconnect to the world once healing has taken place.

Some clients may feel more vulnerable and under pressure to compare themselves with the survivor as counsellor. This can leave the clients feeling less healthy or a failure in not having resolved their DA experiences yet. Some clients find themselves redirecting the focus away from their own therapeutic process on to the counsellor's experiences, thereby diluting their own experience. A further consideration is whether to disclose the abuse history. Ideally, this decision should be taken at the outset as later disclosure will impact on the therapeutic relationship. While some clinicians have reservations about self-disclosure, others believe that to deliberately withhold such information represents a betrayal of trust and re-enacts secrecy. If counsellors define themselves at the outset as survivors of DA, then clients will have some choice in making a decision about who they wish to work with. Those counsellors who prefer not to self-disclose must give open and honest therapeutic reasons, when questioned, as to why this is not in the client's interest, without appearing defensive. Such a stance has the advantage of reinforcing the primacy of the survivor's needs as the central focus of therapy.

Working with difference

To restore power and control, it is vital that survivors are given as much choice as possible in deciding on which clinician to work with. Such choices may be based on the counsellor's gender, cultural and ethnic background and sexual orientation. The gender of the counsellor is generally considered to be significant, as it can influence the therapeutic dyad both positively and destructively (Blake-White and Kline 1985; Herman 1988). Many survivors are not given a choice, however; for this reason, both male and female counsellors must be aware of how the gender dyad may impact on the survivor. It is crucial that both male and female counsellors explore their attitudes and feelings towards DA and socially constructed meanings of gender. They need to have an appreciation of differences in male and female socialisation, male hierarchical role structures, and the relationship between power and dominance. Counsellors must reinforce positive, independent and self-affirming behaviours in the survivor rather than colluding with social stereotypical behaviours such as dependency, compliance and passivity. Any underlying biases in how males and females should relate to each other also, along with erotic transference and counter-transference reactions, need to be examined so that they do not impede the therapeutic process.

FEMALE COUNSELLORS

As there are more female counsellors than males, and given the majority of survivors of DA are female, it is more likely that a female counsellor will be assigned to clients who present with DA. While a female survivor may feel more comfortable with and able to trust a female counsellor, this is not the case with male or lesbian survivors of DA. Although female counsellors are perceived to be more empathic, there are potential problems in a female/female dyad. Female counsellors need to explore their attitudes and beliefs. Some female survivors reject and devalue their gender due to the internalisation of the male abuser, while others fear being judged. Others find it hard to respect the female counsellor, seeing her as weak, pathetic, powerless and a potential victim, just as they were in the DA. By offering a safe and supportive therapeutic space, female counsellors can provide a positive role model of a strong, caring yet autonomous female, which can enable the survivor to develop a more positive view of herself.

Some female counsellors can become over-identified or enmeshed with the client, which usually reduces the survivor's autonomy and control over her life. The female counsellor also runs the risk of being overwhelmed by fears of helplessness and despair or a resurgence of her own abuse experiences. This can evoke anger at the survivor for reviving turbulent feelings and memories, leading to distancing and withdrawal. The female counsellor may misinterpret DA dynamics, which can elicit disbelief or minimisation of the severity of the experience, and leave the survivor feeling misunderstood and betrayed. The female counsellor may be frustrated and angry at the survivor's continued victim-like behaviour and the slow pace of the therapeutic work. This may represent a lack of understanding of the healing process, or represent the counsellor's sense of helplessness and powerlessness.

If the abuser was female, the survivor may have fears about working with a female counsellor, which must be acknowledged. Such work can be valuable, however, by enabling the survivor to be in a relationship with a female who is not going to abuse him or her, but is able to provide a safe therapeutic environment. Male survivors who were abused by a female generally prefer to work with a male counsellor, despite fears of being judged or ridiculed. Female survivors abused by a female may have ambivalent feelings about both male and female counsellors. Whatever the dyad, it is imperative that difference is acknowledged and explored from the outset to ensure safety.

MALE COUNSELLORS

The male counsellor often faces more difficulties than the female counsellor when working with survivors of DA. With the female survivor who was abused by a male, the male counsellor is asking his client to forget that he, the counsellor, is a man. Female survivors may have generalised fear, anger, rage and aggression towards all men, which they may project onto the male counsellor. The female survivor may see any male counsellor as a potential abuser who will abuse his power by controlling and dominating the survivor. Alternatively, the female survivor may see the male counsellor as an authority figure on whom she is dependent, evoking compliance and submissive behaviour. The male counsellor will need to reassure the female survivor that he is not an abuser and that he will not exploit or victimise her in any way.

In order to contain their anxieties and feel safe, some female survivors emasculate the male counsellor, making him feel genderless. This can evince feelings of frustration and devaluation in the male counsellor. To counteract this, the male counsellor may attempt to regain potency and power through exercising dominance and control over the survivor, thereby recreating DA dynamics. Some male counsellors may over-identify with the abuser, seeing the survivor through the abuser's eyes. Awareness of this can prompt a counsellor to overcompensate in order to show that he is a safe male, by becoming overprotective towards the survivor. If the male counsellor develops strong feelings of anger towards the abuser, he may ignore the survivor's range of feelings, including any positive feelings about the abuser.

The female survivor's fear of males may make her hesitant when narrating DA experiences for fear of arousing the counsellor. It is crucial that the male counsellor sets clear boundaries within the therapeutic relationship, in which he will not exploit the survivor in any way. He must also ensure that he does not view the survivor as an object for his own gratification, either in exerting his power, control and dominance or for erotic needs. The counsellor must make clear that he does not condone male domination or aggression and that he finds such expressions of coercive control abhorrent, dysfunctional and unacceptable. Clear firm boundaries must be kept at all times to reinforce that he will not exploit his position of trust by exploiting the survivor.

Male counsellors have the potential to provide a positive male role model to the survivor by demonstrating that not all men are like the abuser and some are capable of caring, supportive behaviours that do not lead to domination or control. This enables the female survivor to re-evaluate her perception of men and entertain the possibility of healthy relationships with males in the future. Some female survivors may benefit from working with a male counsellor, especially towards the end of recovery, in order to experience a more healthy way of relating to males.

For the male survivor abused by a male, entering therapy with a male counsellor can cause difficulties and evoke fears of further abuse. The male survivor can feel threatened and become overwhelmed. Male counsellors must set clear boundaries to provide a safe, contained environment in which the male survivor can explore his DA experiences in a non-threatening way. Some male survivors of DA prefer to work with female counsellors, in part due to cultural and traditional beliefs that women are more nurturing and less dominant, and therefore less controlling. Although male survivors abused by a female may find it easier initially to work with a male counsellor, they may fear being judged or ridiculed. Male counsellors need to reassure male survivors that this will not be the case and that their experiences will be validated and understood. As with female survivors, some male survivors may benefit from working with a female counsellor to complete the healing process.

SEXUAL ORIENTATION

The sexual orientation of the counsellor may be important for some survivors and needs to be considered when assigning clients, incorporating some degree of choice. Some counsellors do not believe that their sexual orientation is relevant, however, or wish to disclose such personal information. In such cases, rather than dismissing the importance of the client's preference, counsellors must explore with the client the significance of this and how it relates to the DA experience. Survivors in same sex relationships might prefer a lesbian or gay counsellor as they fear being judged or stigmatised by a heterosexual counsellor. In some cases, heterosexual female survivors who fear working with a male heterosexual counsellor may feel more comfortable with a gay counsellor.

CULTURAL DIFFERENCES

In the case of ethnicity, it is important to take the survivor's preferences into account. Some adult survivors of DA have strong preferences to work with a counsellor from the same race or cultural background, as they believe they will then be better understood and more able to trust, especially if they have been subjected to racism in the past. Other survivors prefer to work with a counsellor from a different cultural or ethnic origin, especially if they have experienced stigmatisation or minimisation from their community. Thus, some survivors might feel safer with a counsellor from a different cultural background who can offer an alternative perspective. Consideration also needs to be given to the ethnicity of the abuser and how the survivor feels about the counsellor and the abuser being from the same or different cultural backgrounds.

Cultural difference must be discussed in an open and honest way, to ensure that 'colour consciousness' (Berger 2001) or unintentional racism does not dominate the work. The counsellor working with survivors from a different cultural background must be aware of their different beliefs and attitudes regarding DA, seeking professional help and the expression of emotions. Some cultures have strongly enforced sanctions around the expression of emotion, and expect to be directed by the professional rather than find their own answers. The counsellor must be flexible and think about a variety of ways to help survivors from different cultural backgrounds. Counsellors need to be culture-sensitive without undermining the traditional tools of therapy of listening, empathy and support. Differences in social class may also emerge in the therapeutic setting and need to be explored in an open, non-judgemental way.

Working with trauma

Clinicians may be drawn to trauma work for a variety of reasons, not least because of their own trauma. Counsellors must be aware of any experiences that may have brought them to this line of work in order to minimise the danger of becoming trapped by the 'three most common narcissistic snares...to heal all, know all and love all' (Maltsberg and Buie 1974, p.627). In addition, working with trauma can reawaken old wounds which can impact on the clinician and impede the therapeutic work. Clinicians need to be aware that working with trauma can erode the sense of well-being, trust in the world and relationships, and faith and humanity.

When beginning to work with survivors of DA, many counsellors fear that this is specialist work with a mysterious structure and framework that requires specialist skills. The acquisition of knowledge and specialist skills can certainly assist counsellors, but they must guard against adopting a too rigid and structured approach and dismissing more traditional tools, such as being with the client rather than 'doing' or 'fixing' the client. Thus, in focusing on techniques and recovery procedures, clinicians are in danger of forgetting the importance of the therapeutic relationship. If the counsellor loses touch with the human aspects of trauma, then he or she is in danger of disconnecting from the client and thereby undermining the therapeutic process. The counsellor must remember basic skills of staying in the present, listening, noticing, intuiting and working in the here and now of the client's experience or, in the words of St Just (1999), 'showing up, shutting up, tuning in and getting what's going on'.

To become consumed with what one should do or should say can override the phenomenological aspects of the work in which two people meet and connect in the therapeutic space. Many survivors feel alien and disconnected from others as a result of DA, and to replicate this in the therapeutic setting would be counter-therapeutic. It is important to recognise and respect each client for their unique way of dealing with and surviving the trauma of DA. Survivors of DA recover in a variety of ways, and the counsellor must avoid intimating or imposing a 'right' way to heal. A more constructive approach is for counsellors to validate and respect the client's individual coping strategy and style. Ultimately, clients can heal only as much as they can, and that is not purely a reflection of counsellor skills and abilities.

EMBODIMENT

Therapist embodiment is crucial when working with survivors of DA as many survivors have had to disconnect from their body to manage physical and psychological pain. Embodied responses can be used within psychotherapy to enrich a co-constructed narrative between client and therapist, but they can also provide a deeper understanding of the embodied nature of therapeutic relationships as a good starting point to understanding the client and the counsellor. The therapeutic relationship is a space in which two bodies meet to create intersubjectivity, and that it is through this meeting of bodies that we come to understand others (Merleau-Ponty 1962). Such conceptualisation gives rise to what others have called 'body empathy' (Shaw 2003), which is a powerful way of resonating with survivors and their bodily experiences. Bodily resonance can provide much information about clients, in particular if they cannot give a verbal account of what they are feeling. To facilitate this resonance, counsellors also need to be embodied and to be open to experience their clients.

When working with dissociated clients who are not in their body, the main source of information is through embodied counter-transference (Field 1989; Samuels 1985) on a somatic or bodily level. This entails counsellors being in touch with their somatic resonance, such as when working with chaos, the counsellor writes chaotic notes, or with a client in pain, the counsellor may experience physical pain. Most commonly counsellors working with dissociated clients experience dissociation in which they space out or have lapses in consciousness. At other times, the counsellor may report an acute tingling sensation in moments of connection or when an empathic bond has been established. These physical reactions can be seen as the body's barometer to gauge unexpressed emotions within the therapy room or as a 'receiving device' sensitised to picking up cues from the client. Although these somatic reactions are invariably in response to the client's bodily experiences, counsellors must accept the somatic reactions as their own and not always an accurate reflection of the client. Some level of self-monitoring and evaluation of the origin of somatic responses is crucial in order to identify their source to minimise putative interpretations. The body is both a receiver and originator of somatic responses and counsellors need to guard against reifying subjective phenomena (Shaw 2004).

Since working with clients can evoke body resonance and cause strong bodily reactions, it is pertinent that counsellors take care of themselves physically. This can be achieved through activities that increase bodily awareness and embodiment, such as t'ai chi, mediation and physical exercise. The important factor is to balance the sometimes analytical and yet sedentary aspects of the psychotherapeutic work with interests outside the therapeutic setting that nurture physical and bodily well-being.

Impact of working with survivors of domestic abuse

The chaos and trauma inherent in DA are often replayed in the therapeutic arena, which can remind counsellors of their own socialisation processes and trigger unprocessed emotional baggage. Therefore, counsellors need to understand the professional and personal impact of working with survivors of DA in order to identify individual risk factors and personal characteristics and the social and cultural contexts in which they work. Counsellors should monitor the impact of their work and assess their coping and self-care strategies.

Working with survivors of DA is often associated with strong reactions of disbelief, anger and an erosion of the counsellor's sense of well-being manifested in feelings of helplessness, powerlessness and loss of faith in humanity (Herman 1992a). Considerable research has shown that professionals working with trauma can become affected by their work (Figley 2002; McCann and Pearlman 1989; Pearlman and Saakvitne 1995b). The impact of working with trauma is usually referred to as secondary traumatic stress (STS) (Figley and Kleber 1995). STS is characterised behaviours and emotions evoked through being exposed to or from helping a traumatised person. Commonly STS reactions are not dissimilar to the trauma responses of the survivor. The difference is that counsellors will be exposed to many accounts of trauma on a daily basis, which has a cumulative impact. Not only does this reinforce the darker side of human nature, but also it threatens the health and well-being of the therapist. Counsellors have to be containers not only of clients' material but also of the emotional impact of such material.

Secondary traumatic stress can lead to shattered assumptions: the sense of personal invulnerability, the world as a meaningful place, and a positive view of the self (Janoff-Bulman 1985) which evoke pervasive uncertainty, increased levels of anxiety and hypervigilance. The world in which counsellors thought they could make a difference by helping clients is a hostile one, which counsellors can neither control nor change. In the case of DA, although counsellors may be able to help clients to a degree, they cannot prevent the abuse of others, and as such counsellors experience a sense of being overwhelmed by the enormity of DA. Counsellors may feel helpless (just as the client does) and paralysed, such that they are unable to do anything of value. This leads to a negative view of the self in the counsellor's capacity to help survivors.

If not addressed this can lead to 'burnout' (Figley 1995), secondary traumatic stress disorder (STSD) (Pines and Aronson 1988) or compassion fatigue. Pines and Aronson (1988) describe 'burnout' as a

> state of physical, emotional and mental exhaustion caused by long-term involvement in emotionally demanding situations. It is marked by physical depletion and chronic fatigue, by feelings of hopelessness, and by the development of negative self-concept and negative attitudes toward work, life and other people. The negative self-concept is expressed in feelings of guilt, inadequacy, incompetences and failure. Such emotional exhaustion can lead to depression, sense of hopelessness, depersonalization, desensitization, habituation and normalization, in which the counsellor becomes emotionally hardened to trauma work. In turn, this can lead to mental exhaustion, a sense of disillusionment and of reduced personal accomplishment, a feeling of being deskilled and resentment of others. (Pines and Aronson 1988, p.9)

Burnout is a process rather than a fixed condition, which begins gradually and becomes progressively worse. In the initial stage of burnout, counsellors experience nascent disillusionment, in which the enthusiasm and expectations of working with traumatised clients become shattered, reduction of energy levels and unrealistic expectations of being able to work with and help all clients. To compensate for this, counsellors may overextend and over-commit themselves, over-identifying with the client, leading to inefficient expenditure of the counsellor's energy. Disillusionment is followed by stagnation, in which the counsellor no longer finds the work thrilling. As the reality of the work creeps in, the counsellor may become preoccupied with other considerations, such as the level of financial reward, career development and the amount of hours devoted to this sort of work. This can lead to frustration, in which the counsellor questions the value and effectiveness of work. The counsellor begins to see limitations of the work in relation to personal satisfaction and status, and it becomes threatening. The counsellor can become frustrated, paralysed and trapped in the work with no way to escape. If STS or burnout is not identified, the process continues, putting increasing pressure on the counsellor and leading to job strain, the erosion of idealism, and sense of failure. Counsellors must recognise the stages of burnout so that they can implement appropriate preventative strategies. To minimise erosion of self, erosion of meaning and powerlessness, counsellors need to incorporate non-traumatised clients into their caseload.

The impact of STS can be at both a professional and a personal level of functioning. In order to prevent the onset or manage the impact of STS, counsellors must be aware of the most common warning signs of STS, and regard these as alerts to potential difficulties (see Table 10.1).

Some of the symptoms of STS are due to the efforts of counsellors to contain and process their own emotional reactions and responses. Counsellors may feel that they need to constrain the therapeutic process in order to maintain their equilibrium by directing the survivor away from the trauma material or by implementing trauma techniques and procedures to contain their own emotional reactions.

IMPACT OF SECONDARY TRAUMATIC STRESS

The impact of STS is akin to that of post-traumatic stress disorder (PTSD), which can infuse the counsellor's life, both professionally and personally. Counsellors may experience PTSD-like symptoms, such as avoidance, numbing and depersonalisation. The counsellor may deliberately avoid thoughts and feelings concerning the trauma material or report being amnestic of the client's narrative. The counsellor may have a diminished interest in activities, a sense of detachment and estrangement from others, diminished affect (desensitisation) and a sense of a foreshortened future. At a physiological level, the counsellor may experience persistent arousal, including anxiety, panic and irritability, outbursts of anger, difficulty with concentrating, hypervigilance, exaggerated startle response and difficulty with sleeping. There may be shock, confusion, sadness and behavioural changes such as an increase or reduction in eating, drinking, smoking, sleeping and libido.

These reactions and behavioural changes can be seen in the therapeutic setting in which counsellors focus on the details of the survivor's story, analysing symptoms and reductions in social functioning, but are unable to conceptualise the whole picture. This may be accompanied by an inability to feel the survivor's feelings, over-identifying with clients, and a focus on doing rather than being. This can result in a loss of self-efficacy and resourcefulness and loss of autonomy, not unlike the survivor. Despite feelings of helplessness, counsellors may avoid seeking professional feedback or supervision due to shame or embarrassment. Counsellors may begin to deny their own vulnerability and ward off feelings of being burdened. In denial, counsellors may take on more and more trauma work in order to challenge themselves and test their own ability to cope. They may manifest an increasingly victim-like role, with behaviours such as blaming others,

Table 10.1 Common warning signs of secondary traumatic stress

Depression

Erosion of well-being

Dissociation

Avoidance

Alterations and lapses of consciousness

Lassitude, stupor, torpor, exhaustion

Disillusionment

Dread before session, nausea, doubts and fears around containment

Compassion fatigue

Loss of concentration, inability to think clearly or to stay focused

Forgetting a session or content of session

Confusion

Sleep disturbances, nightmares

Intrusive thoughts, imagery of client material, flashbacks

Heightened level of physiological arousal

Irritability with colleagues, partners, friends, family, children

Hypervigilance

Flat affect, not in touch with feelings

Avoiding emotion in self and others (professional and personal)

Aggression, increased displays of anger

Cynicism

Negative reactions to clients' material

Adversarial in actions and therapeutic process

Distorted beliefs about relationships, self, others and the world

Emotional distance, numbing, withdrawal

Cessation of making notes after sessions

Reduced capacity to contain or offload material

Ruminating over cases, regularly left with material and affect after sessions

Isolation, not seeking supervision, not sharing concerns, reduction in socialising

Reduced affect regulation

Narrowed, hierarchical view of severity of experiences

Shattering of assumptions about safe world

Loss of trust in relationships

Loss of faith in humanity

Self-consciousness

Deterioration in nutrition, exercise, increased use of stimulants

Cognitive impairment, difficulty making decisions, feeling distracted.

especially colleagues, peers and society, in order to retain a false illusion of invincibility.

PREVENTION OF SECONDARY TRAUMATIC STRESS

To prevent or minimise the impact of STS, the counsellor should engage in regular and adequate supervision, preferably with a counsellor who is experienced in trauma work and is thoroughly knowledgeable about the complex nature of working with survivors of DA. In addition to individual supervision, the counsellor may also consider peer and group supervision, which can reduce the counsellor's sense of isolation and provide an environment in which to give and receive support and feel a sense of belonging. In some instances the counsellor may benefit from consultation with a specialist in the field. Such support allows the counsellor to develop greater self-awareness and reflection on the work, to enhance the management of DA cases. Continuous professional development is crucial through extra training, reading current research and collaborating with others with more expertise. Making the workplace a comfortable and nurturing space in which there is mutual support and respect from others can also reduce the impact of STS on professional functioning.

Self-supervision (Casement 1990) is another important preventive strategy that allows the counsellor to live consciously and relate to and through his or her own wounds as they emerge. Through such self-reflection, trauma counselling can become a powerful channel for the growth of the therapist and the client. This is best achieved through counsellors meeting their own needs outside the therapeutic setting and outside the clients' needs. With this in place, counsellors can reduce the likelihood of disruptions to the therapeutic relationship and the premature cessation of treatment. It will also reduce the potential for acting-out behaviours, reduction of empathy and compassion fatigue.

To minimise the personal impact of STS, counsellors must be attuned to their personal needs and maintain a balance between personally meaningful life activities and work, to remain connected to the self. Yassen (1995) proposes that counsellors balance client work with involvement in other activities, including giving lectures, training others or being involved with policy-making. In addition, it is useful to establish a network for support to define and refine trauma work. Most importantly counsellors need to focus on self-support. Self-support must incorporate support for the whole person in order to facilitate the integration of trauma as part of the counsellor's whole life. Importantly, counsellors need to be compassionate with themselves and allow themselves to be fully expressive of all their emotions in their personal lives. This includes doubts and uncertainties as well as joy and happiness. They must be honest with themselves and recognise their own humanness and vulnerabilities.

Counsellors must balance the number of survivors of DA with working with more general clients perhaps on a ratio of one general client to every survivor of DA. It is also essential to take regular breaks and time off from client work. While working with survivors of DA can be extremely rewarding, counsellors need to ensure that they also pursue non-therapy-related rewards and pleasures that provide 'avocational avenues for creative and relaxing self expression in order to regenerate' (Danieli 1994), and have fun. Some clinicians argue that 'feeling free to have fun and joy is not frivolity in this field but a necessity without which one cannot fulfil one's professional obligations, one's professional contract' (Danieli 1994).

To facilitate this, counsellors should prioritise their personal life and enjoy leisure activities that incorporate physical and creative activities, relaxation and spiritual well-being. Attention should be paid to embodiment by pursuing non-verbal activities and looking after physical well-being, perhaps reconnecting with the body through regular exercise, massage, mediation, yoga or t'ai chi. Healthy sleep and dietary habits should also be practised. Self-nurture entails seeking gentleness and spontaneity in one's personal life and focusing on pleasure, play, laughter and love. Counsellors who work with survivors of DA should take regular breaks from their work to counterbalance some of the painful feelings they have to deal with on a daily basis.

Humour has a powerful restorative value in connecting the clinician with life and disconnecting from the pain inherent in trauma (Yassen 1995). Allowing humour to exist outside of session is a beneficial way to discharge powerful emotions associated with traumatic material. This often manifests as 'gallows humour' among colleagues and is a way of managing the horror of trauma and threat to mortality. If expressed appropriately, humour in session is a powerful way to establish a human connection between the client and the counsellor. Humour is a reconnection with life and can be a powerful indicator of the healing taking place. Humour in session should not always be interpreted as hostile or avoidance. If listened and attended to sensitively, humour can allow an aspect of the survivor to emerge that previously has been banished or dormant as a result of the trauma and destruction of DA.

To counterbalance loss of meaning, joy or faith in humanity, the counsellor should pursue other personally meaningful activities and passions. Time must be made for interpersonal relationships outside work. To safeguard a reasonably stress-free home environment, the counsellor must be explicit with his or her partner about the general impact of work and specify how the partner can give support. Healthy social relationships and support from friends not connected to work are important, in permitting light, everyday conversations. By pursuing and maintaining outside interests unconnected to work, the counsellor ensures a more grounded and balanced lifestyle.

The impact of working with survivors of DA is exacerbated in private practice, as clinicians may feel more isolated or disconnected from other therapists or those working in a team. Counsellors working from their own home may find it hard to contain survivors' material. The family house becomes a container for all the bad feelings of DA, which can lead to a loss of joy, freedom or hope in the home. Counsellors should consider carefully the setting in which to conduct trauma work and whether to work as part of a team or in private practice. One therapist, for example, would see a broad range of clients in her private practice at home but would undertake trauma work only as part of a team in a trauma clinic, where she had access to other colleagues. A further consideration is safety, such as the risk of abuse or violence from the abusive partner. In addition counsellors need to ensure that they have protection through membership of their professional organisations, plus adequate professional and personal insurance.

To minimise STS in private practice, counsellors need to establish good professional support networks with others working in the field and meet regularly. They should consider setting up peer supervision with other counsellors working with trauma in addition to continuous professional development and training in trauma. Counsellors must ensure that they know what other resources are available to them so that they can share their concerns. Links with other agencies such as social services, the police force and specialists in DA can be invaluable in certain situations, so that the counsellor can refer clients when appropriate. When counsellors are part of a wider network, they will be better able to contain existential fear and shame.

SYSTEMIC INDICATORS OF SECONDARY TRAUMATIC STRESS IN ORGANISATIONS

Yassen (1995) argues that STS can also impact on organisations and agencies involved in working with clients who have been traumatised, resulting in systemic indicators of STS. These cluster around the organisation's expectation that staff must be impervious to trauma in their clients and robot-like in their responses (Wastell 2005). Such systemic factors can influence the nature of the work undertaken in terms of being protocol-oriented, the well-being of the individual counsellors, and the cultural and political context of the work. This is especially true in DA, where the agency may experience limitations in the type and length of therapeutic work that is offered, inadequate safety or protection for staff, or minimal psychological support. To enhance safety and effectiveness the organisation must ensure thorough training and adequate access to other professional agencies.

Systemic indicators of STS include widespread cynicism in staff, increased illness of staff, low staff recruitment and retention, lowered motivation and productivity, and ethical or boundary violations. Some staff members may deny the personal impact of STS and project their dissatisfaction onto the organisation as a whole, which can manifest in staff being overly critical of the management structure, procedures and systems. Organisations need to be aware of this potential projection, evaluate valid constructive feedback from staff, and determine the degree to which this is an indicator of STS. Regular debriefing and open and honest communication between staff and the organisation are crucial in order to minimise the impact of STS within the organisation.

Organisations need to be aware of STS and its impact, not only on individual staff but also on the organisation, to ensure that strategies are implemented to combat and minimise the effects through appropriate management of work and staff, supervision and regular debriefing. Organisations also need to demonstrate a clear commitment to monitoring staff and providing appropriate intervention programmes that focus on identifying, detecting and dealing with STS. This should include the regular use of psychological assessment measures, including self-assessment instruments related to professionals exposed to trauma and psychological support.

To prevent and minimise the impact of STS in staff and the organisation, the organisation's management needs to consider and implement a number of crucial measures and strategies. The organisation needs to demonstrate an awareness of individual therapists' needs limits, emotional resilience and resources and to balance their work with other activities in order to ensure that they do not define themselves only as trauma counsellors. In addition, the organisation's management should actively encourage staff self-care, including activities that enable the counsellors to reconnect with their bodies and emotional reactions. This can be achieved through the promotion and provision of self-care programmes such as physical exercise, massage, meditation and martial arts. Organisations may consider forming links with gyms and leisure centres that provide such programmes at an affordable rate.

Organisations should endeavour to set appropriate limits to the work in order to help staff manage their caseloads. They should advocate the importance of nutrition, sleep and regular relaxation periods. This may be done by ensuring that members of staff have regular breaks from their work, both physically and mentally. In emphasising the importance of self-care and self-nurturing, attention needs also to be paid to maximising opportunities for pleasant feelings and positive experiences, both within and outside the organisation. This may be achieved by participating in community-building activities, regular team-building initiatives away from the workplace, or informal social activities with other members of staff.

Regular monitoring of psychological well-being is paramount and can be achieved through supervision, not only of individual cases but also of other areas of the counsellor's life. This will ensure that counsellors' current work activities are still imbued with meaning and value. Such supervision allows for the monitoring of any negative beliefs that counsellors hold about themselves, their work and their assumptions about the world. Wherever possible, organisations need to control and balance counsellors' caseloads by providing a variety of clients and work tasks. This may include encouragement to develop other skills such as training other counsellors and giving talks to the community and other professionals. Organisations need to ensure that a good professional support network is in place that they can access easily, including for peer supervision and continuous professional development. Overall, organisations need to address STS actively and openly and remain in continuous dialogue with their staff. They need to provide appropriate resources, including a pleasant working environment with sufficient personal space and mutually rewarding relationships, which incorporate reciprocal valuing and caring.

With appropriate support counsellors can minimise STS and remain empathically attuned to the client. They can focus on the therapeutic relationship as a vehicle to enable the survivor to restore trust in the self, others and the world. This allows the survivor to reconnect to the self and others and move from simply surviving to feeling alive. The counsellor who has remained connected throughout this process will have contributed to the survivor's healing but will also have been transformed in her own personal and professional growth. Thus, the counsellor not only has survived the experience but also feels alive.

Summary

- Working with survivors of DA can be highly rewarding and emotionally draining. To ensure that counsellors are able to work efficaciously with this client group it is necessary to have a thorough understanding of DA and a high level of self-awareness. Counsellors also need to be aware of how working with traumatised clients can impact on counsellors' personal and professional functioning. To manage the impact of trauma and to minimise the risk of secondary traumatic stress, counsellors must take care of themselves and be realistic in the work that they do.

- As the therapeutic relationship is pivotal when working with complex trauma, counsellors must have a high level of self-awareness, especially around their own experiences of abuse, power and control. In order to provide a safe therapeutic space, counsellors need to be aware of their motivation to work with survivors of DA to ensure that they do not become enmeshed or over-identified with them, or attempt to rescue them.

- Counsellors also require a sensitive understanding of working with difference and acknowledge any differences from the outset. Female counsellors need to be aware of the difficulties when working with male survivors of DA and how they might be perceived by female survivors. Similarly, male counsellors also need to be aware of how they may impact on female survivors and how DA dynamics may be re-enacted in the therapeutic process.

- Cultural and ethnic differences also need to be addressed. Counsellors need to be culturally sensitive when working with survivors of different cultures and social class. It is crucial that counsellors have a good understanding of differences and how to work with these in an optimal manner.

- An understanding of the impact of trauma on personal professional functioning is critical in understanding secondary traumatic stress (STS). Counsellors need to know the warning signs of STS as these symptoms serve to alert the counsellor to burnout, compassion fatigue or secondary traumatic stress disorder. Knowledge of STS is central to preventing it.

- There a number of professional and personal strategies that can minimise STS which counsellors need to implement. To avoid isolation counsellors need to build professional support networks through supervision, specialist consultations and collaboration with other agencies. Such multidisciplinary support will enhance knowledge and enable practitioners to provide a holistic approach to treatment.

- Counsellors also need to ensure self-care through balancing trauma work with more general client work, taking regular breaks, and making time to relax. To counteract working with trauma, counsellors need to stay connected to ordinary, everyday activities outside of trauma. They need to pursue valued activities and passions that allow them to take pleasure and delight in other areas of their lives. A life–work balance is crucial to avert burnout and counsellors must prioritise this so that they can be emotionally connected to their clients.

- Working with trauma can also impact on the organisation in which the professional works. There a number of systemic factors that managers need to take into consideration to minimise STS in their staff. This includes providing a conducive environment with appropriate training support, regular supervision and an understanding of the impact of trauma. It is critical that organisations specialising in working with DA provide regular supervision, psychological support and opportunities for regular breaks to ensure staff cohesion and satisfaction.

- With appropriate strategies in place, counsellors can embrace the therapeutic work without fear of being engulfed or threatened by STS. This allows them to be open to their client's experiences and remain sensitively attuned to them. With this in place they can enable survivors to move from merely surviving to being alive, and begin to rebuild their lives outside the shadow of abuse.

RESOURCES

(All websites were accessed on 3 January 2008)

UK

Domestic Violence National 24-hour Helpline
Tel: 0808 200 0247 (minicom available)
Websites: www.refuge.org.uk
www.womensaid.org.uk

Hidden Hurt
Tel: 0808 200 0247
Website: www.hiddenhurt.co.uk
A domestic abuse website with list of information and support.

Mind
Tel: 0845 766 0163
Website: www.mind.org.uk
A mental health charity that supports people in distress.

Rape Crisis
Tel: see local telephone numbers in phone directories
Website: www.rapecrisis.org.uk

Refuge: Combined Women's Aid and Refuge Helpline
Tel: 0808 200 0247
Website: www.refuge.org.uk
Email: info@refuge.org.uk

Supportline
Tel: 020 8554 9004
Email: info@supportline.org.uk
A telephone helpline providing emotional support to children, young people and adults on any issue including domestic abuse. It keeps details of other agencies, support groups and counsellors throughout the UK.

Tulip Group
Tel: 0151 637 6363
Support for parents experiencing abuse from their children.

Victim Support
Tel: 0845 303 0900
Website: www.victimsupport.org.uk
Service for the victims of crime, and those who are acting as witnesses in court.

Black Association of Women Step Out (BAWSO)
Tel: 029 2043 7390
Offers advice and support to black women who have experienced or are experiencing domestic abuse.

Chinese Information and Advice Centre (CIAC)
Tel: 020 7692 3697
Website: www.ciac.co.uk
Offers information and support on family issues, domestic abuse and immigration.

Jewish Women's Aid (JWA)
Tel: 0800 59 1203
Website: www.jwa.org.uk
Offers domestic abuse awareness raising programmes and help.

Southall Black Sisters
Tel: 020 8571 9595
Website: www.southallblacksisters.org.uk
Specialist advice and support for Asian and African Caribbean women suffering violence and abuse.

Northern Ireland Women's Aid Helpline
Tel: 0800 917 1414
Website: www.niwaf.org

Scottish Women's Aid
Tel: 0800 027 1234
Website: www.scottishwomensaid.org

Welsh Women's Aid
Tel: 0800 801 0800
Website: www.welshwomensaid.org

IRELAND

Irish Women's Aid Domestic Abuse
Tel: 1800 341 900
Website: www.womensaid.ie

WORLDWIDE

Andrew Vachss
Website: www.vachss.com
Offers information, links and international resources on domestic violence and child abuse.

Hot Peach Pages
Website: www.hotpeachpages.net
Global directory of domestic abuse agencies, hotlines, shelters, refuges, crisis centres and women's organisations searchable by country, plus index of domestic abuse resources in over 75 languages.

AUSTRALIA

National Confidential Helpline
Tel: 1800 200 526

24-hour helplines by state
ACT: (02) 6280 0900
NSW: 1800 656 463
NT: 1800 019 116
QLD: 1800 811 811
SA: 1800 800 098
TAS: 1800 608 122 or 6233 2529
VIC: 1800 015 188 or 9373 0123
WA: 1800 007 339 or 9223 1188

Domestic Violence and Incest Resource Centre
Tel: (03) 9486 9866
Website: www.dvirc.org.au
Provides information and referrals to local services for domestic violence victims, children of domestic violence throughout Australia.

Men's Line Australia
Tel: 1300 789 978 (24-hour helpline)
Website: www.menslineaus.org.au

Women's Resource Information and Support Centre
Tel: (03) 53 333 666
Website: wrisc.ballarat.net.au
Provides help and support and local referrals throughout Australia.

CANADA

Assaulted Women's Helpline
Tel: (416) 863 0511; Toll free 1 866 863 0511; TTY Toll free 1 866 863 7868
Website: www.awhl.org

Canadian National Clearinghouse for Family Violence
Tel: 613 957 2838; Toll free 1 800 267 1291; TTY Toll free 1 800 561 5643
Website: www.hc-sc.gc.ca

National Domestic Violence Hotline (Canada)
Tel: Toll free 1 800 363 9010
Covers all provinces and is bilingual (English and French).

SafeCanada
Website: www.safecanada.ca
Provides information and services on domestic violence.

Shelternet
Website: www.shelternet.ca
Connects abused women to local shelters.

USA

National Center for Victims of Crime
Tel: 1 800 394 2255
Website: www.endabuse.org
Information on domestic violence.
Tel: 1 800 621 4673
Website: www.safehorizon.org
Provides hotline, counselling centre and information on domestic violence.

National Domestic Violence Hotline
Tel: 1 800 799 7233 or 1 800 787 3224
Hotline has 24-hour access from all 52 states. There are translators available.
Website: www.ndvh.org
List of help and information on domestic violence in each state.

Services for children

UK

Childline
Tel: 0800 1111
Website: www.childline.org.uk
Confidential counselling service for children. The website has a weblink for children and young people to use.

The Hideout
Website: www.thehideout.org.uk
Link from Women's Aid for children or young people.

NSPCC Child Protection Helpline
Tel: 0808 800 5000
Website: www.nspcc.org.uk
Advice and information on parenting-related issues. The website has a weblink for children to use.

IRELAND

Childline Ireland
Tel: 1800 666 666
Website: www.childline.ie

AUSTRALIA

Australian Childhood Foundation
Tel: 1800 176 453 (national helpline)
Tel: (03) 9874 3922
Website: www.childhood.org.au
Offers information, help, support, education, counselling and advocacy.

Kidscount
Website: www.kidscount.com.au
For help in relation to child abuse and protection.

Kids Helpline
Tel: 1800 551 800

Lifeline Australia
Tel: 13 11 14
Website: www.lifeline.org.au

Stop Child Abuse
Website: www.stopchildabuse.com.au
Offers a services directory across all states.

CANADA

National Helpline
Tel: 1 866 660 0505

Child Abuse Prevention
Tel: 310 1234 (Helpline British Columbia)
Website: www.safekidsbc.ca
Provides child protection services, information, links and resources across all states.

USA

National Child Abuse Hotline
Tel: 1 877 723 2445
Website: www.childhelp.org
Provides information, links and resources on child abuse.

Services for elderly people

UK

Action on Elder Abuse
Tel: 0808 808 8141 (UK)
1800 940 010 (Republic of Ireland)
Website: www.elderabuse.org.uk
Confidential helpline providing information and emotional support to elderly people and their carers and to professionals on all aspects of elder abuse.

Help the Aged
Tel: 020 7278 1114 (England)
0131 551 6331 (Scotland)
02920 346 550 (Wales)
02890 230 666 (Northern Ireland)
Website: www.helptheaged.org.uk
Email: info@helptheaged.org.uk
Help the Aged is committed to ending elder abuse and offers advice and support to victims and their carers.

WORLDWIDE

International Network for the Prevention of Elder Abuse
Tel: 01482 465 716
Website: www.inpea.net
Aim is to increase society's ability, through international collaboration, to recognise and respond to mistreatment of older people in whatever setting. Has chapters in Europe, North America, Latin America, Asia, Africa and Australia/Oceania.

AUSTRALIA

Aged Care Crisis
Website: www.agedcarecrisis.com
Provides information on elder abuse.

Elder Abuse Prevention Line
Tel: 02 6205 3535

Elder Abuse Prevention Unit (Queensland)
Tel: 1300 651 192 or 07 3250 1955
Website: www.eapu.com.au

Seniors
Website: www.seniors.gov.au
Provides information on elder abuse.

CANADA

Ontario Network for the Prevention of Elder Abuse
Tel: (416) 978 1716 or Toll-free: 1 888 579 2888
Website: www.onpea.org

USA

National Center on Elder Abuse
Tel: 1 800 677 1116
Website: www.ncea.aoa.gov

Services for men experiencing domestic abuse

UK

ManKind Initiative
Tel: 0870 794 4121
Website: www.mankind.org.uk
Advice, information and support for male victims.

Men's Advice Line (MALE)
Tel: 0845 064 6800
Website: www.mensadviceline.org.uk
Email: info@mensadviceline.org.uk
Offers advice and support for men in abusive relationships.

Men's Aid
Tel: 0871 223 9986
Helpline available 8 a.m. to 8 p.m. seven days a week.
Website: www.mensaid.com
Free practical advice and support to men who have been abused.

Survivors
Tel: 020 7357 8299
Helpline for male victims of sexual abuse.

Victim Support
Tel: 0800 328 3623
Helpline for male victims of domestic abuse or sexual abuse.

IRELAND

Amen Ireland
Tel: (046) 902 3718
Confidential helpline, support service and information for male victims of domestic violence and their children.
Website: www.amen.ie

AUSTRALIA

Men's Domestic Violence Helpline
Tel: 08 9242 9218

Men's Health Network Helpline
Tel: 02 9743 4434

CANADA

Family of Men Support Society
Tel: 403 242 4077
Website: www.familyofmen.com
Information and help for abused males. Offers crisis support, information, links and list of resources such as shelters for abused men.

Men's Alternative Safe House: MASH Project
Website: www.mashproject.com
Information and help, including shelters for abused males.

USA

Battered Men
Website: www.batteredmen.com
List of helplines for abused males across all states.

Domestic Rights Coalition
Tel: 651 774 7010
Provides help for males who have experienced domestic abuse along with advocacy and finding shelters for abused males.

Stop Abuse For Everyone (SAFE)
Website: www.safe4all.org
List of helplines for abused males across all states. Committed to provide help and support to all males, straight or gay, as well as lesbians who have experienced domestic abuse. Also lists numerous international organisations and agencies that provide help for abused males.

Services for lesbians, gay men, bisexual and transgender people
UK

Broken Rainbow
Tel: 0845 260 4460
Website: www.broken-rainbow.org.uk
Service for lesbians, gay men, bisexual or transgender people.

London Lesbian and Gay Switchboard
Tel: 020 7837 7324
Website: www.llgs.org.uk
Offers 24-hour information and support for lesbians and gay men.

Survivors of Lesbian Partner Abuse (SOLA)
Tel: 020 7328 7389
Supports women who have experienced domestic abuse within a lesbian relationship.

Services for women with learning disabilities
UK

Beverly Lewis House
Tel: 020 8522 2000
Email: info@east-living.co.uk
A haven for women with learning disabilities who have suffered from abuse or who are at risk of abuse.

Services for female perpetrators of domestic abuse
UK

ManKind Initiative
Tel: 0870 794 4124
Website: www.mankind.org.uk

Services for male perpetrators of domestic abuse
UK

Everyman Project
Tel: 020 7263 8884
Website: www.everymanproject.co.uk
Service providing counselling and anger management services to men wishing to end abusive behaviour.

Freedom Programme
Tel: 0151 630 0651
Website: www.freedomprogramme.co.uk
Email: atcraven@aol.com
Offers a 12-week programme for any man who wishes to stop abusing women and children.

Respect
Tel: 0845 122 8609
Website: www.respect.uk.net
Helpline providing information and advice for perpetrators of domestic abuse, and domestic abuser support programme.

BIBLIOGRAPHY

Abrahams, H. (2007) *Supporting Women after Domestic Violence: Loss, Trauma and Recovery.* London: Jessica Kingsley Publishers.

Ainsworth, M.D.S., Blehar, M.C., Waters, E. and Wall, S (1978) *Patterns of Attachment: A Psychological Study of the Strange Situation.* Hillsdale, NJ: Lawrence Erlbaum.

Alexander, P.C. and Anderson, C.L. (1994) 'An attachment approach to psychotherapy with the incest survivor.' *Psychotherapy 31,* 665–673.

Allen, J.G. (1997) *Sexual Harassment from the Trauma Perspective.* Topeka, KS: Menninger Clinic and Office of Army Chief of Chaplains.

Allen, J.G. (2001) *Traumatic Relationships and Serious Mental Disorders.* Chichester, UK: Wiley.

Allen, J.G. (2006a) *Coping with Trauma: Hope through Understanding,* 2nd edition. Washington, DC: American Psychiatric Publishing.

Allen, J.G. (2006b) *Coping with Depression: From Catch 22 to Hope.* Washington, DC: American Psychiatric Publishing.

Allen, J.G. and Fonagy, P. (eds) (2006) *Handbook of Mentalization Based Treatment.* Chichester, UK: Wiley.

Allen, J.G., Bleiberg, E. and Haslam-Hopwood, T. (2003) *Mentalizing as a Compass for Treatment.* Houston, TX: Menninger Clinic.

American Psychiatric Association (2000) *Diagnostic and Statistical Manual of Mental Disorders (DSM) IV-TR.* Washington, DC: American Psychiatric Association.

Anderson, C.L. and Alexander, P.C. (1996) 'The relationships between attachment and dissociation in adult survivors of incest.' *Psychiatry 59,* 240–254.

Arnsten, A.F. (1998) 'The biology of being frazzled.' *Science 280,* 1711–1721.

Aurelius, M. (2002) *Meditations.* New York: Modern Library.

Bandura, A. (1979) 'The Social Learning Perspective: Mechanisms of Aggression.' In A. Toch (ed.) *Psychology of Crime and Criminal Justice.* New York: Holt, Rinehart & Winston.

Bartholomew, K. (1990) 'Avoidance of intimacy: An attachment perspective.' *Journal of Social and Personal Relationships 7,* 147–148.

Bashir, J. and Bashir, C. (2001) *Attempted Suicide and Self Harm: South Asian Women.* Manchester: Women's Studies Research Centre, Manchester Metropolitan University.

Batsleer, J., Burman, E., Chantler, K., McIntosh, H., et al. (2002) *Domestic Violence and Minoritisation: Supporting Women to Independence.* Manchester: Manchester Metropolitan University.

Baumeister, R.F. (1990) 'Suicide as escape from self.' *Psychological Review 97,* 90–113.

Beck, A.T. (1976) *Cognitive Therapy and Emotional Disorders.* New York: New American Library.

Berger, H. (2001) 'Trauma and the Therapist.' In T. Spiers (ed.) *Trauma: A Practitioner's Guide to Counselling.* Hove, UK: Brunner-Routledge.

Bergin, A.E. and Garfield, S.C. (eds) (1994) *Handbook of Psychotherapy and Behaviour Change,* 4th edition. Chichester, UK: Wiley.

Bifulco, A. and Moran, P. (1998) *Wednesday's Child: Research into Women's Experiences of Neglect and Abuse in Childhood and Adult Depression.* London: Routledge.

Blackman, J. (1989) *Intimate Violence: A Study in Injustice.* New York: Columbia University Press.

Blake-White, J. and Klein, C.M. (1985) 'Treating the dissociative process in adult victims of childhood incest.' *Social Casework 66,* 394–402.

Bond, S. and Bond, M.H. (2004) 'Attachment styles and violence within couples.' *Journal of Nervous and Mental Disease 192*, 12, 851–863.

Bowlby, J. (1969) *Attachment and Loss: Attachment.* London: Penguin.

Bowlby, J. (1973) *Attachment and Loss: Separation.* London: Penguin.

Bowlby, J. (1977) 'The making and breaking of affectional bonds.' *British Journal of Psychiatry 130*, 201–210.

Bowlby, J. (1980) *Attachment and Loss: Loss, Sadness and Depression*, vol. III. New York: Basic Books.

Brand, P.A. and Kidd, A.H. (1986) 'Frequency of physical aggression in heterosexual and female homosexual dyads.' *Psychological Reports 59*, 1307–1313.

Briere, J. and Scott, C. (2006) *Principles of Trauma Therapy: A Guide to Symptoms, Evaluation and Treatment.* Thousand Oaks, CA: Sage.

Briere, J. and Spinazzola, J. (2005) 'Phenomenology and psychological assessment of complex posttraumatic states.' *Journal of Traumatic Stress 18*, 401–412.

British Medical Association (BMA) (2007) *Domestic Abuse.* London: BMA.

Broken Rainbow (2005) *Annual Report 2004/2005.* Available at www.brokenrainbow.org.uk/press/annual%20reports/2004-05.pdf, accessed 10 July 2007.

Bromberg, P. (1993) 'Shadow and substance: A relational perspective on clinical process.' *Psychoanalytic Psychology 10*, 147–168.

Bromberg, P. (1998) *Standing in the Spaces: Essays on Clinical Process, Trauma and Dissociation.* Hillsdale, NJ: Analytic Press.

Brown, D. (n.d.) *PTSD* (PowerPoint® presentation). Available at www.vhjp.be/download/files/ptsd.ppt, accessed 16 May 2007.

Brown, K. (1998) *Dispatches:* 'Battered men' survey. Available at www.dewar4reserach.org/docs/bms1.pdf, accessed 29 February 2008.

Browne, A. (1987) *When Battered Women Kill.* New York: Free Press.

Buber, M. (1987) *I and Thou.* Edinburgh: T. and T. Clarke.

Calder, M.C., Harold, G.T. and Howarth, E.L. (2006) *Children Living with Domestic Violence.* Lyme Regis, UK: Russell House.

Calof, D.L. (1995) 'Dissociation: Nature's tincture of numbing and forgetting.' *Treating Abuse Today 5*, 3, 5–8.

Carlson, B.E. (1991) 'Domestic Violence.' In A. Gitterman (ed.) *Handbook of Social Work Practice with Vulnerable Populations.* New York: Columbia University Press.

Casement, P. (1990) *On Further Learning from the Patient.* London: Tavistock.

Cashdan, S. (1988) *Object Relations Therapy: Using the Relationship.* New York: Norton.

Chantler, K., Burman, E., Batsleer, J. and Bashoir, C. (2001) *Attempted Suicide and Self Harm (South Asian Women).* Manchester: Women's Studies Research Centre, Manchester Metropolitan University.

Chu, J.A. (1991) 'The repetition compulsion revisited: Reliving dissociated trauma.' *Psychotherapy 28*, 327–332.

Chu, J.A. (1998) *Rebuilding Shattered Lives: The Responsible Treatment of Complex Post-traumatic and Dissociative Disorders.* New York: Wiley.

Clarkson, P. (1993) *On Psychotherapy.* London: Whurr.

Coleman, K., Jansson, K. and Kaisa, P. (2007) *Homicides, Firearm Offences and Intimate Violence 2005/2006.* Home Office Statistical Bulletin, January. London: Home Office.

Confidential Enquiry into Maternal Child Health for England and Wales (CEMACH) (2004) *Why Mothers Die? 2000–2002.* London: RCOG (Royal College of Obstetricians and Gynaecologists) Press.

Cook, P.W. (1997) *Abused Men: The Hidden Side of Domestic Violence.* Westport, CT: Praeger.

Courtois, C.A. (1988) *Healing the Incest Wound: Adult Survivors in Therapy.* New York: Norton.

Courtois, C.A. (1999) *Recollections of Sexual Abuse: Treatment Principles and Guidelines.* New York: Norton.

Crawford, M. and Gartner, R. (1992) *Women Killing: Intimate Femicide in Ontario 1974–1980.* Toronto: Women We Honour Action Committee.

Crown Prosecution Service (n.d.) www.cps.gov.uk, accessed 29 February 2008.

Curran, D. (1996) *Tyranny of the Spirit: Domination and Submission in Adolescent Relationships.* Northvale, NJ: Jason Aronson.

Dale, P. (1999) *Adults Abused as Children: Experiences in Counselling and Psychotherapy.* London: Sage.

Dalenberg, C.J. (2000) *Counter-transference and the Treatment of Trauma.* Washington, DC: American Psychological Association.

Danieli, Y. (1994) 'Countertransference in the Treatment of PTSD.' In J.P. Wilson and J.D. Lindy (eds) *Countertransference in the Treatment of PTS.* New York: Guilford.

Davies, J.M. and Frawley, M.G. (1994) *Treating the Adult Survivor of Childhood Sexual Abuse: A Psychoanalytic Perspective.* New York: Basic Books.

Department of Health (DoH) (2005) *Interventions to Reduce Violence and Promote the Physical and Psychosocial Well-being of Women who Experience Partner Violence: A Systematic Review of Controlled Evaluations.* London: Department of Health.

Dobash, R.E. and Dobash, R.P. (1979) *Violence against Wives: A Case against the Patriarchy.* New York: Free Press.

Dobash, R.E. and Dobash, R.P. (1988) 'Research as Social Action: The Struggle for Battered Women.' In K. Yllö and M. Bogard (eds) *Feminist Perspectives on Wife Abuse.* Thousand Oaks, CA: Sage.

Dobie, D.J., Kivlahan, D.R., Maynard, C., Bush, K.R., Davis, T.M. and Bradley, K.A. (2004) 'Posttraumatic Stress Disorder in female veterans: Association with self reported health problems and functional impairment.' *Archive of International Medicine 164*, 4, 394–400.

Dozier, M. and Tyrell, C. (1998) 'The Role of Attachment in Therapeutic Relationships.' In J. Simpson and W. Rholes (eds) *Attachment Theory and Close Relationships.* New York: Guilford.

Dutton, D.G. (1985) 'An ecologically nested theory of male violence towards intimates.' *International Journal of Women's Studies 8*, 4, 404–413.

Dutton, D.G. (2007) *The Abusive Personality: Violence and Control in Intimate Relationships*, 2nd edition. New York: Guilford.

Dutton, D.G. and Painter, S.L. (1981) 'Traumatic bonding: The development of emotional attachment in battered women and other relationships of intermittent abuse.' *Victimology: An International Journal 6*, 139–155.

Dutton, D.G. and Painter, S.L. (1993) 'Emotional attachment in abusive relationships: A test of traumatic bonding theory.' *Violence and Victims 8*, 105–120.

Dutton, M.A. (1992) *Empowering and Healing the Battered Woman: A Model for Assessment and Intervention.* New York: Springer.

Ehrensaft, M.K., Moffit, T.E. and Caspi, A. (2004) 'Clinically abusive relationships in an unselected birth cohort: Men's and women's participation and developmental antecedents.' *Journal of Abnormal Psychology 113*, 2, 258–270.

Engel, G.L. and Schmale, A.H. (1972) 'Conservation-Withdrawal: A Primary Regulatory Process for Organismic Homeostasis.' In *Ciba Foundation Symposium: Physiology, Emotion and Psychosomatic Illness.* New York: Elsevier.

Ettore, E. (1997) *Women and Alcohol: A Private Pleasure or Public Problem.* London: Women's Press.

Field, N. (1989) 'Listening with the body: An exploration in the countertransference.' *British Journal of Psychotherapy 5*, 4, 512–522.

Field, T. (1985) 'Attachment as Psychobiological Attunement: Being on the Same Wavelength.' In M. Reite and T. Field (eds) *The Psychobiology of Attachment and Separation.* New York: Academic Press.

Figley, C.R. (1995) 'Compassion Fatigue as Secondary Traumatic Stress Disorder: An Overview.' In C.R. Figley (ed.) *Compassion Fatigue: Coping with Secondary Stress Disorder in Those who Treat the Traumatized.* New York: Brunner/Mazel.

Figley, C.R. (2002) *Treating Compassion Fatigue.* New York: Brunner/Mazel.

Figley, C.R. (2004) Foreword. In J.P. Wilson and R.B. Thomas (eds) *Empathy in the Treatment of Trauma and PTSD.* New York: Brunner-Routledge.

Figley, C.R. and Kleber, R.J. (1995) 'Beyond the "Victim": Secondary Traumatic Stress.' In R.J. Kleber, C.R. Figley and B.P.R. Gersons (eds) *Beyond Trauma: Cultural and Societal Dynamics.* New York: Plenum.

Foa, F.B., Zinbarg, R. and Rothbaum, B.O. (1992) 'Uncontrollability and unpredictability in posttraumatic stress disorder: An animal model.' *Psychological Bulletin 112, 218–238.*

Fonagy, P. (1999) 'Pathological Attachments and Therapeutic Action.' Paper presented at the Annual Meeting of the California Branch of the American Academy of Child and Adolescent Psychiatry, Yosemite Valley, CA, January 1999.

Fonagy, P. (2001) *Attachment Theory and Psychoanalysis.* New York: Other Press.

Fonagy, P. (2002) 'Multiple Voices versus Metacognition: An Attachment Theory Perspective.' In V. Sinason (ed.) *Trauma and Multiplicity: Working with Dissociative Identity Disorder.* London: Routledge.

Fonagy, P. and Target, M. (1997) 'Perspectives on Recovered Memories Debate.' In J. Sandler and P. Fonagy (eds) *Recovered Memories of Abuse: True or False.* Madison, CT: International Universities Press.

Fonagy, P., Steele, M., Steele, H., Leigh, T., et al. (1995) 'Attachment, the Reflective Self, and Borderline States.' In S. Goldberg, R. Muir and J. Kerr (eds) *Attachment Theory: Social, Developmental and Clinical Perspectives.* Hillsdale, NJ: Analytic Press.

Fonagy, P., Gergely, G., Jurist, E.L. and Target, M. (2002) *Affect Regulation, Mentalization and the Development of the Self.* New York: Other Press.

Fonagy, P., Target, M. and Gergely, G. (2003) 'Attachment and borderline personality disorder.' *Psychiatric Clinics of North America 23,* 91, 103–123.

Ford, J.D. and Kidd, P. (1998) 'Early childhood trauma and disorders of extreme stress to predictors of treatment outcome with chronic PTSD.' *Journal of Traumatic Stress 11,* 743–761.

Ford, J.D., Courtois, C.A., Steele, K., Van der Hart, O. and Nijenhuis, E.R.S. (2005) 'Treatment of complex posttraumatic self regulation.' *Journal of Traumatic Stress 18,* 437–447.

Frankl, V. (1946) *Man's Search for Meaning.* London: Hodder & Stoughton.

Frayne, S.M., Seaver, M.R., Loveland, S., Christiansen, C.L., Spiro, A. and Parker, V.A. (2004) 'Burden of medical illness in women with depression and post traumatic stress.' *Archive of International Medicine 164,* 1306–1312.

Freud, A. (1936) *The Ego and the Mechanism of Defence.* New York: International Universities Press.

Freud, S. (1914/1958) 'Remembering, Repeating, and Working Through.' In *Standard Edition of the Complete Psychological Works of Sigmund Freud,* vol. 12. London: Hogarth Press.

Fromm, E. (1973) *The Anatomy of Human Destructiveness.* New York: Holt Paperbacks.

Gabbard, G. and Wilkinson, S. (1994) *Management of Counter-transference with Borderline Patients.* Washington, DC: American Psychiatric Press.

Gerbode, F. (1989) *Beyond Psychology: An Introduction to Meta Psychology,* 2nd edition. Palo Alto, CA: IRM Press.

Goldberg, H. (1982) 'Dynamics of Rage between the Sexes in a Bonded Relationship.' In L.R. Barnhill (ed.) *Clinical Approach to Family Violence.* Rockville, MD: Aspen Systems.

Golding, J.M. (1999) 'Intimate partner violence as a risk factor for mental disorders: A meta-analysis.' *Journal of Family Violence 14,* 2, 19–132.

Goodwin, J. (1993) *Rediscovering Childhood Trauma: Historical Casebook and Clinical Applications.* Washington, DC: American Psychiatric Press.

Gunderson, J.G. (1984) *Borderline Personality Disorder.* Washington, DC: American Psychiatric Press.

Halperin, D.A. (1983) 'Group Processes in Cult Affiliation and Recruitment.' In D.A. Halperin (ed.) *Psychodynamic Perspectives on Religion, Sect and Cult.* Boston, MA: John Wright.

Harlow, H.F. and Harlow, M. (1971) 'Psychopathology in Monkeys.' In H.D. Kinnel (ed.) *Experimental Psychopathology.* New York: Academic Press.

Harter, S. (1999) *The Construction of the Self: A Developmental Perspective.* New York: Guilford.

Henderson, A.J.Z., Bartholomew, K. and Dutton, D.G. (1997) 'He loves me; he loves me not: Attachment and separation resolution of abused women.' *Journal of Family Violence 12,* 169–191.

Henderson, L. (2003) *Prevalence of Domestic Violence among Lesbians and Gay Men.* London: Sigma.

Henwood, M. (2000) *Domestic Violence: A Resource Manual for Health Care Professionals.* London: Department of Health.

Herman, J.L. (1988) 'Father–Daughter Incest.' In F.M. Ochberg (ed.) *Post Traumatic Therapy and Victims of Violence.* New York: Brunner/Mazel.

Herman, J.L. (1992a) *Trauma and Recovery.* New York: Basic Books.

Herman, J.L. (1992b) 'Complex PTSD: A syndrome in survivors of prolonged and repeated trauma.' *Journal of Traumatic Stress 5,* 377–392.

Herman, J.L. (2001) *Trauma and Recovery,* 2nd edition. London: Pandora.

Herman, J.L. (2002) 'Evolution of Trauma Therapy.' Paper presented at Trauma Conference. Psychological Trauma: Maturational Processes and Therapeutic Interventions. Boston University School of Medicine and Trauma Center, Boston, MA, 31 May–1 June 2002.

Herman, J.L. (2005) 'Justice from the victim's perspective.' *Violence Against Women 11,* 571–602.

Herman, J.L. (2006) 'My Life and Work.' In C.R. Figley (ed.) *Mapping Trauma and its Wake: Autobiographical Essays by Pioneer Trauma Scholars.* New York: Routledge.

Herman, J.L. (2007) 'Shattered States and their Repair: An Exploration of Trauma and Shame.' The John Bowlby Memorial Lecture presented at the Centenary John Bowlby Memorial Conference 1907–2007, Shattered States: Disorganised Attachment and its Repair, London, 9–10 March 2007.

Herve, H.F.M. (2002) 'The Masks of Sanity and Psychopathy: A Cluster Analytical Investigation of Subtypes of Criminal Psychopathy.' Doctoral dissertation, Department of Psychology, University of British Columbia.

Hester, M., Pearson, C. and Harwin, N. (2007) *Making an Impact: Children and Domestic Violence – A Reader*, 2nd edition. London: Jessica Kingsley Publishers.

Hirigoyen, M-F. (2004) *Stalking the Soul: Emotional Abuse and the Erosion of Identity.* New York: Helen Marx Books.

Horley, S. (1988) *Love and Pain: A Survival Handbook for Women.* London: Bedford Square Press.

Humphreys, C. and Thiara, R. (2002) *Routes to Safety: Protection Issues Facing Abused Women and Children and the Role of Outreach Services.* Bristol: Women's Aid Federation of England.

Humphreys, C. and Thiara, R. (2003) 'Mental health and domestic violence: "I call it symptoms of abuse".' *British Journal of Social Work 33*, 2, 209–226.

Island, D. and Letellier, P. (1991) *Men who Beat the Men who Love Them.* Binghamton, NY: Harrington Park Press.

Jacobson, N. and Gottman, J. (1998) *Breaking the Cycle: New Insights into Violent Relationships.* London: Bloomsbury.

James, K. (1999) 'Truth or fiction: Men as victims of domestic violence.' In J. Breckenridge and L. Laing (eds) *Challenging Silence: Innovative Responses to Sexual and Domestic Violence.* Sydney: Allen & Unwin.

Janoff-Bulman, R. (1985) 'The Aftermath of Victimisation: Rebuilding Shattered Assumptions.' In C.R. Figley (ed.) *Trauma and its Wake: The Study and Treatment of Post Traumatic Stress Disorder.* New York: Brunner/Mazel.

Janoff-Bulman, R. (1992) *Shattered Assumptions: Towards a New Psychology of Trauma.* New York: Free Press.

Jones, L., Hughes, M. and Unterstaller, U. (2001) 'Post-traumatic stress disorder (PTSD) in victims of domestic violence.' *Trauma Violence Abuse 2*, 99–119.

Jukes, A. (1993) *Why Men Hate Women.* London: Free Association Books.

Jukes, A. (1999) *Men Who Batter Women.* London: Routledge.

Kahn, M. (2000) 'Domestic violence against women and girls.' *Innocenti Digest 6*, 1–22.

Kahn, M.E., Ubaidur, R. and Hossain, S.M.I. (2001) 'Violence against women and the impact on women's lives: Some observations from Bangladesh.' *Journal of Family Welfare 46*, 2, 12–24.

Kaschak, E. (ed.) (2001) *Intimate Betrayal: Domestic Violence in Same Sex Relationships.* Binghamton, NY: Haworth Press.

Klein, M. (1946) 'Notes on Some Schizoid Mechanisms.' In M. Klein (ed.) (1980) *Envy and Gratitude and Other Works 1946–1963.* London: Hogarth Press.

Kohut, H. (1971) *The Analysis of the Self.* New York: International Universities Press.

Kohut, H. (1972) 'Thoughts on Narcissism and Narcissistic Rage.' In P. Ornstein (ed.) *The Search for Self: Selected Writings of Heinz Kohut*, vol. 2. New York: International Universities Press.

Kohut, H. (1977) *The Restoration of the Self.* New York: International Universities Press.

Krause, E.D., Kaltman, S., Goodman, L.A. and Dutton, M.A. (2006) 'Role of distinct post traumatic stress disorder symptoms in intimate partner violence re-abuse: A prospective study.' *Journal of Traumatic Stress 19*, 4, 507–516.

Kritsberg, W. (1988) *The Adult Children of Alcoholics Syndrome: From Discovery to Recovery.* Toronto: Bantam.

Krystal, J.H. (1988) *Integration and Self Healing: Affect, Trauma and Alexithymia.* Hillsdale, NJ: Analytic Press.

Kübler-Ross, E. (1969) *On Death and Dying.* New York: Macmillan.

Lachkar, J. (2004) *The Narcissistic/Borderline Couple: A Psychoanalytic Perspective on Marital Treatment*, 2nd edition. Hove, UK: Brunner-Routledge.

Laing, R.D. (1967) *The Politics of Experience and the Bird of Paradise.* Harmondsworth: Penguin.

Lattanzi, M. and Hale, M.E. (1984) 'Giving grief words: Writing during bereavement.' *Omega 15*, 45–52.

Levine, P.A. (1997) *Waking the Tiger.* Berkeley, CA: North Atlantic Books.

Lewinsohn, P.M. (1975) 'The Behavioural Study and Treatment of Depression.' In M. Hersen, R. Eisler and P. Miller (eds) *Progress in Behaviour Modification.* New York: Academic Press.

Lewis, D.O. (1998) *Guilty by Reason of Insanity.* New York: Ballantine.

Lichtenberg, J.D. (1989) *Psychoanalysis and Motivation.* Hillsdale, NJ: Analytic Press.

Liotti, G. (1992) 'Disorganised/disoriented attachment in the etiology of the dissociative disorders.' *Dissociation 5*, 196–204.

Lockley, P. (1999) *Counselling Women in Violent Relationships.* London: Free Association Books.

Lomas, P. (1987) *The Limits of Interpretation: What's Wrong with Psychoanalysis.* London: Penguin.

Lomas, P. (1994) *Cultivating Intuition: An Introduction to Psychotherapy.* London: Penguin.

McCann, I.L. and Pearlman, L.A. (1989) 'Vicarious traumatisation: A framework for understanding the psychological effects of working with victims.' *Traumatic Stress 3*, 131–149.

McCann, I.L. and Pearlman, L.A. (1990) *Psychological Trauma and the Adult Survivor: Theory, Therapy and Transformation.* New York: Brunner/Mazel.

McCann, I.L., Sakheim, D.K. and Abrahamson, D.J. (1988) 'Trauma and victimisation: A model of psychological adaptation.' *Counselling Psychologist 16*, 4, 531–594.

MacLean, P.D. (1990) *The Triune Brain in Evolution: Role in Paleocerebral Functions.* New York: Plenum.

Magdol, L., Moffit, T.E., Caspi, A., Newman, D.L., Fagan, J. and Silva, P.A. (1997) 'Gender differences in partner violence in a birth cohort of 21 year olds: Bridging the gap between clinical and epidemiological approaches.' *Journal of Counselling and Clinical Psychology 65*, 1, 68–78.

Magnavita, J.J. (1999) *Relational Therapy for Personality Disorders.* New York: Wiley.

Main, M. (1999) 'Attachment Theory: Eighteen Points with Suggestions for Future Studies.' In J. Cassidy and P.R. Shaver (eds) *Handbook of Attachment: Theory, Research and Clinical Applications.* New York: Guilford.

Mair, M. (1989) *Between Psychology and Psychotherapy: A Poetics of Experience.* London: Routledge.

Maltsberg, J.T. and Buie, O.H. (1974) 'Countertransference: Hate in the treatment of suicidal patients.' *Archives of General Psychiatry 30*, 625–633.

Meins, E. (1997) *Security of Attachment and the Social Development of Cognition.* Hove, UK: Psychology Press.

Meloy, J.R. (1992) *Violent Attachments.* Northvale, NJ: Jason Aronson.

Melzack, R. (1990) 'The tragedy of needless pain.' *Science 362*, 27–88.

Merleau-Ponty, M. (1962) *The Phenomenology of Perception.* London: Routledge & Kegan Paul.

Merrill, G. (1996) 'Ruling the Exceptions: Same-sex Battering and Domestic Violence Theory.' In C.M. Renzetti and C.H. Miley (eds) *Violence in Gay and Lesbian Domestic Partnerships.* Binghamton, NY: Haworth Press.

Miller, B.D. (1992) 'Wife Beating in India: Variations on a Theme.' In D.A. Counts, J.K. Brown and J.C. Campbell (eds) *Sanctions and Sanctuary: Cultural Perspectives on the Beatings of Wives.* Boulder, CO: Westview.

Miller, D.T. and Porter, C.A. (1993) 'Self-blame in victims of violence.' *Journal of Social Issues 39*, 2, 139–152.

Millon, T. (1977) *Millon Clinical Multiaxial Inventory Manual.* Minneapolis, MN: National Computer Inventory and Computer Systems.

Millon, T. (1996) *Disorders of Personality: DSM IV and Beyond*, 2nd edition. New York: Wiley.

Millon, T. and Grossman, S. (2007) *Moderating Severe Personality Disorders: A Personalised Psychotherapy Approach.* New York: Wiley.

Mitchell, E. and Gilchrist, E. (2004) 'Can Knowledge of Panic Attack Help to Explain some Domestic Violence Offending?' Paper presented at the British Psychological Society Division of Forensic Psychology, Leicester, UK, 22–24 March 2004.

Moffit, T.E., Caspi, R., Rutter, M. and Silva, P.A. (2001) *Sex Differences in Antisocial Behaviour.* Cambridge: Cambridge University Press.

Mollica, R.F. (1988) 'The Trauma Story: The Psychiatric Care of Refugee Survivors of Violence and Torture.' In F.M. Ochberg (ed.) *Post Traumatic Therapy and the Victims of Violence.* New York: Brunner/Mazel.

Mollon, P. (2000) 'Is Human Nature Intrinsically Evil?' In U. McCluskey and C. Hooper (eds) *Psychodynamic Perspectives on Abuse: The Cost of Fear.* London: Jessica Kingsley Publishers.

Mollon, P. (2002a) 'Dark Dimensions of Multiple Personality.' In V. Sinason (ed.) *Attachment, Trauma and Multiplicity: Working with Dissociative Identity Disorder.* London: Brunner-Routledge.

Mollon, P. (2002b) *Remembering Trauma: A Psychotherapist's Guide to Memory and Illusion*, 2nd edition. London: Whurr.

Morgan, D.R. (1998) *Domestic Violence: A Health Care Issue.* London: British Medical Association.

Motz, A.P. (2000) *The Psychology of Female Violence: Crimes against the Body.* New York: Brunner-Routledge.

National Center on Elder Abuse (1997) *Trends in Elder Abuse in Domestic Settings.* Washington, DC: National Center on Elderly Abuse.

Newham Asian Women's Project (1998) *Young Asian Women and Self Harm: A Mental Health Needs Assessment of Young Asian Women in East London.* London: Newham Inner City Multifund and Newham Asian Women's Project.

Nord, D. (1996) 'Issues and implications in the counselling services of multiple AIDS-related loss.' *Death Studies 20*, 389–413.

Ochberg, F.M. (1988) *Post Traumatic Therapy with Victims of Violence.* New York: Brunner/Mazel.

Ogg, J. and Bennet, G. (1992) 'Elder abuse in Britain.' *British Medical Journal 305*, 998–999.

Olio, K. and Cornell, W. (1993) 'The therapeutic relationship as the foundation for treatment with adult survivors of sexual abuse.' *Psychotherapy 30*, 512–523.

Orwell, G. (1990) *Nineteen Eighty-Four.* London: Penguin.

Parkes, C.M. (1986) 'Orienteering the care giver's grief.' *Journal of Palliative Care 1*, 5–7.

Parkes, C.M. (2001) *Bereavement: Studies of Grief in Adult Life*, 3rd edition. Philadelphia, PA: Taylor & Francis.

Parkes, C.M., Relf, M. and Couldrick, A. (1996) *Counselling in Terminal Care and Bereavement.* Baltimore, MD: BPS Books.

Pearlman, L.A. (1998) 'Trauma and the self: A theoretical and clinical perspective.' *Journal of Emotional Abuse 1*, 7–25.

Pearlman, L.A. (2001) 'The Treatment of Persons with Complex PTSD and other Trauma-related Disruptions to the Self.' In M.F. Friedman, J.P. Wilson and J.D. Lindy (eds) *Treating Psychological Trauma and PTSD.* New York: Guilford.

Pearlman, L.A. (2003) *Trauma Attachment Belief Scale (TABS) Manual.* Los Angeles, CA: Western Psychological Services.

Pearlman, L.A. and Courtois, C.A. (2005) 'Clinical applications of the attachment framework: Relational treatment of complex trauma.' *Journal of Traumatic Stress 18*, 449–459.

Pearlman, L.A. and Saakvitne, K.W. (1995a) *Trauma and the Therapist: Counter-transference and Vicarious Traumatization in Psychotherapy with Incest Survivors.* New York: Norton.

Pearlman, L.A. and Saakvitne, K.W. (1995b) 'Treating Therapists with Vicarious Traumatization and Secondary Traumatic Stress Disorders.' In C.R. Figley (ed.) *Compassion Fatigue: Coping with Secondary Traumatic Stress Disorder in Those who Treat the Traumatized.* New York: Brunner/Mazel.

Perry, B.D. (2000) *Violence in Childhood: How Persisting Fear can Alter the Developing Child's Brain.* Available at www.childtrauma.org/ctamaterials/vio_child.asp, accessed 29 February 2008.

Pines, M. and Aronson, E. (1988) *Career Burnout: Causes and Cures.* New York: Free Press.

Pistole, C.M. and Tarrant, N. (1993) 'Attachment style and aggression in male batterers.' *Family Therapy 20*, 3, 165–174.

Porter, S. (1996) 'Without conscience or without active conscience? The etiology of psychopathy revisited.' *Aggression and Violent Behaviour 1*, 2, 179–189.

Powell, G.F. and Bette, B.A. (1992) 'Infantile depression, non-organic failure to thrive and DSM-III-R: A different perspective.' *Child Psychiatry and Human Development 22*, 3, 185–198.

Pryke, J. and Thomas, M. (1998) *Domestic Violence and Social Work.* Ashgate, UK: Arena.

Putnam, F.W. (1989) *Diagnosis and Treatment of Multiple Personality Disorder.* New York: Guilford.

Renzetti, C. (1992) *Violent Betrayal Partner Abuse in Lesbian Relationships.* Newbury Park, CA: Sage.

Respect (2004) *Statement of Principles and Minimum Standards of Practice for Domestic Violence Perpetrator Programmes and Associated Women's Services.* London: Respect.

Revitch, E. and Schlesinger, L.B. (1981) *Psychopathology of Homicide.* Springfield, IL: Charles C. Thomas.

Ross, C.A. (1997) *Dissociative Identity Disorder: Diagnosis, Clinical Features and Treatment of Multiple Personality.* New York: Wiley.

Rothschild, B. (2000) *The Body Remembers.* New York: Norton.

Rothschild, L. (2003) 'A taxometric study of personality disorder.' *Journal of Abnormal Psychology 112*, 4, 657–666.

Roy, M. (1988) *Children in the Crossfire: Violence in the Home – How Does it Affect our Children?* Deerfield Beach, FL: Health Communications.

Saakvitne, K.W. and Pearlman, L.A. (1996) *Transforming the Pain: A Workbook on Vicarious Traumatization.* New York: Norton.

Saakvitne, K.W., Gamble, S.G., Pearlman, L.A. and Lev, B. (2000) *Risking Connection: A Training Curriculum for Working with Survivors of Childhood Abuse.* Lutherville, MD: Sidran Foundation Press.

Sale, A.U. (2001) 'Nowhere to go.' *Community Care* 19–25 July, 22–23.

Salter, A.C. (1995) *Transforming Trauma: A Guide to Understanding and Treating Adult Survivors of Child Sexual Abuse.* Thousand Oaks, CA: Sage.

Samuels, A. (1985) 'Countertransference: The "mundus imaginalis" and a research project.' *Journal of Analytical Psychology 30*, 47–71.

Sanderson, C. (2006) *Counselling Adult Survivors of Child Sexual Abuse*, 3rd edition. London: Jessica Kingsley Publishers.

Scarf, M. (2005) *Secrets, Lies, Betrayals.* New York: Ballantine.

Schore, A.N. (2001) 'The effects of early relational trauma on right brain development, affect regulation and infant mental health.' *Infant Mental Health Journal 22,* 201–269.

Schore, A.N. (2003a) *Affect Dysregulation and Disorders of the Self.* New York: Norton.

Schore, A.N. (2003b) *Affect Dysregulation and the Repair of the Self.* New York: Norton.

Schuchter, S.R. and Zisook, S. (1993) 'The Course of Normal Grief.' In M.S. Stroebe, W. Stroebe and R.O. Hansson (eds) *Handbook of Bereavement: Theory, Research and Intervention.* New York: Cambridge University Press.

Schwartz, H.L. (2000) *Dialogues with Forgotten Voices: Relational Perspectives on Child Abuse Trauma and Treatment of Dissociative Disorders.* New York: Basic Books.

Scott, J.P. (1987) 'The Emotional Basis of Attachment and Separation.' In J.L. Sacksteder, D.P. Schwartz and Y. Akabane (eds) *Attachment and the Therapeutic Process: Essays in Honor of Otto Allen Will Jr., MD.* Madison, CT: International Universities Press.

Secretary of State for the Home Department (2003) *Safety and Justice: The Government's Proposals on Domestic Violence.* London: The Stationery Office.

Seligman, M.E.P. (1975) *Helplessness: On Depression, Development and Death.* San Francisco, CA: W.H. Freeman.

Shapiro, F. (1995) *Eye Movement Desensitisation and Reprocessing: Principles, Protocols and Procedures.* New York: Guilford.

Shaver, P., Hazan, C. and Bradshaw, D. (1988) 'Love as Attachment: The Integration of Three Behavioural Systems.' In R.J. Sternberg and M. Barnes (eds) *The Psychology of Love.* New Haven, CT: Yale University Press.

Shaw, R. (2003) *The Embodied Therapist: The Therapist's Body Story.* Hove, UK: Brunner-Routledge.

Shaw, R. (2004) 'The embodied psychotherapist: An exploration of the therapist's somatic phenomena within the therapeutic encounter.' *Psychotherapy Research 14,* 3, 271–288.

Shepherd, J. (1990) 'Victims of personal violence: The relevance of Symond's model of psychological response and loss theory.' *British Journal of Social Work 20,* 309–332.

Siddiqui, H. (2003) 'Asian and Ethnic Minority Women's Groups.' In S. Amiel and J. Heath (eds) *Family Violence in Primary Care.* Oxford: Oxford University Press.

Siegel, D. (1999) *The Developing Mind.* New York: Guilford.

Solomon, R.C. (2002) *Spirituality for the Skeptic: The Thoughtful Love of Life.* New York: Oxford University Press.

Spinelli, E. (1994) *Demystifying Therapy.* London: Constable.

St Just, A. (1999) 'Lecture Notes for a Workshop on Trauma.' Guildford, UK: University of Surrey.

Stark, E. and Flitcraft, A.H. (1988) 'Women and children at risk: A feminist perspective on child abuse.' *International Journal of Health Studies 18,* 1, 97–119.

Stark, E. and Flitcraft, A.H. (1996) *Women at Risk: Domestic Violence and Women's Health.* London: Sage.

Stein, H., Allen, J.G. and Hill, J. (2003) 'Roles and relationships: A psychoeducational approach to reviewing strengths and difficulties in adulthood functioning.' *Bulletin of the Menninger Clinic 67,* 281–313.

Stern, D.N. (1985) *The Interpersonal World of the Infant: A View from Psychoanalysis and Developmental Psychology.* New York: Basic Books.

Stien, P.T. and Kendall, J. (2004) *Psychological Trauma and the Developing Brain: Neurologically Based Interventions for Troubled Children.* New York: Haworth Maltreatment and Trauma Press.

Stosny, S. (1995) *Treating Attachment Abuse: A Compassionate Approach.* New York: Springer.

Stroebe, W. and Stroebe, M.S. (1987) *The Psychological and Physical Consequences of Partner Loss.* Cambridge: Cambridge University Press.

Szinovacz, M.E. (1983) 'Using couple data as a methodological tool: The case of marital violence.' *Journal of Marriage and the Family 45,* 633–644.

Tedeschi, R.G. (1999) 'Violence transformed: Posttraumatic growth in survivors and their societies.' *Aggression and Violent Behaviour 4,* 319–341.

Terr, L.C. (1991) 'Childhood traumas: An outline and overview.' *American Journal of Psychiatry 148,* 1, 10–20.

Thornhill, R. and Palmer, C.T. (2000) *A Natural History of Rape: Biological Basis of Sexual Coercion.* Cambridge, MA: MIT Press.

Van der Kolk, B.A. (1987) *Psychological Trauma.* Washington, DC: American Psychiatric Press.

Van der Kolk, B.A. (1989) 'The compulsion to repeat the trauma: Re-enactment, revictimisation, and masochism.' *Psychiatric Clinics of North America 12,* 2, 389–411.

Van der Kolk, B.A. (1994) 'The body keeps the score: Memory and evolving psychobiology of posttraumatic stress.' *Harvard Review of Psychiatry 1*, 253–265.

Van der Kolk, B.A. (1997) 'Trauma, Memory and Self Regulation: Clinical Applications of Current Research.' Paper presented at Harvard Medical School Summer Seminars, Nantucket, MA, September 1997.

Van der Kolk, B.A., Roth, S., Pelcovitz, D., Sunday, S. and Spinazzola, J. (2005) 'Disorders of extreme stress: The empirical foundation of complex adaptation to trauma.' *Journal of Traumatic Stress 18*, 389–399.

Van Deurzen-Smith, E. (1988) *Existential Counselling in Action*. London: Sage.

Vaughan, G. (2000) 'Violence, Sexuality and Gay Male Domestic Violence.' In K. Buckley and P. Head (eds) *Myths, Risks and Sexuality*. Lyme Regis, UK: Russell House.

Walby, S. (2004) *The Cost of Domestic Violence*. London: Women and Equality Unit.

Walby, S. and Allen, J. (2004) *Domestic Violence, Sexual Assault and Stalking: Findings from the British Crime Survey*. Home Office Research Study no. 276. London: Home Office.

Walker, L.E. (1979) *The Battered Woman*. New York: Harper & Row.

Walker, L.E. (1984) *The Battered Woman Syndrome*. New York: Springer.

Walker, R., Logan, T.K. and Jordan, C.E. (2004) 'An integrative review of separation in the context of victimisation: Consequences and implications for women.' *Trauma Violence Abuse 5*, 2, 143–193.

Wastell, C. (2005) *Understanding Trauma and Emotion: Dealing with Trauma – An Emotion Focussed Approach*. Maidenhead: Open University Press.

Wellard, S. (2003) 'Victims on the margins.' *Community Care* 6–12 March, 32.

Welldon, E.V. (2004) *Mother, Madonna, Whore: The Idealisation and Denigration of Motherhood*. London: Karnac.

Williamson, E. (2006) *Women's Aid Federation of England 2005 Survey of Domestic Violence Services Findings*. London: Women's Aid Federation.

Wilson, J.P. (2002) 'The Abyss Experience and Catastrophic Stress.' Paper presented at St Joseph's University, Philadelphia, PA, 11 October 2002.

Wilson, J.P. (2003) *Empathic Strain and Posttraumatic Therapy*. New York: Guilford.

Wilson, J.P. (2004) 'Broken Spirits.' In J.P. Wilson and B. Drozdek (eds) *Broken Spirits: The Treatment of Traumatized Asylum Seekers, Refugees, and War and Torture Victims*. New York: Brunner-Routledge.

Wilson, J.P. (2006) 'The Posttraumatic Self.' In J.P. Wilson (ed.) *The Posttraumatic Self: Restoring Meaning and Wholeness to Personality*. New York: Routledge.

Wilson, J.P. and Lindy, J.D. (eds) (1994) *Countertransference in the Treatment of PTSD*. New York: Guilford.

Wilson, J.P., Friedman, M.J. and Lindy, J.D. (2001) *Treating Psychological Trauma and PTSD*. New York: Guilford.

Winchester, R. (2002) 'Common assault.' *Community Care* 14–20 November, 24–26.

Winnicott, D.W. (1958) *Collected Papers: Through Paediatrics to Psychoanalysis*. London: Tavistock.

Winnicott, D.W. (1965) *The Maturational Process and the Facilitating Environment: Studies in the Theory of Emotional Development*. New York: International Universities Press.

Women's Aid (2007) www.womensaid.org.uk, accessed 29 February 2008.

Women's Aid Federation (2005) *The Survivor's Handbook*. Bristol: Women's Aid Federation.

Worden, J.W. (2003) *Grief Counselling and Grief Therapy: A Handbook for the Mental Health Practitioner*, 3rd edition. London: Brunner-Routledge.

World Health Organisation (2000) Factsheet no. 239. Quoted in Women's Aid Federation (2005) *Domestic Violence: Frequently Asked Questions Factsheet 2004/2005*. London: Women's Aid Federation.

World Health Organisation (2002) *Abuse of the Elderly – Facts*. Geneva: WHO.

World Health Organisation (2006) *Intimate Partner Violence and Alcohol*. Geneva: WHO.

Wortman, C.B., Battle, E. and Lemkau, J.P. (1997) 'Coming to Terms with the Sudden Death of a Spouse or Child.' In A.J. Lurigio, W.G. Skogan and R.C. Davis (eds) *Victims of Crime: Problems, Policies and Programs*, 2nd edition. Newbury Park, CA: Sage.

Yassen, J. (1995) 'Preventing Secondary Traumatic Stress Disorder.' In C.R. Figley (ed.) *Compassion Fatigue: Coping with Secondary Stress Disorder in Those who Treat the Traumatized*. New York: Brunner/Mazel.

Zimbardo, P. (1969) *The Human Choice: Individuation, Reason and Order versus Deindividuation, Impulse and Chaos*. Lincoln, NE: University of Nebraska.

SUBJECT INDEX

AUTHOR INDEX

CPSIA information can be obtained at www.ICGtesting.com
Printed in the USA
BVOW050036120112

280111BV00008B/1/P